JORDAN AND THE ARAB UPRISINGS

Columbia Studies in Middle East Politics

COLUMBIA STUDIES IN MIDDLE EAST POLITICS
Marc Lynch, Series Editor

Columbia Studies in Middle East Politics presents academically rigorous, well-written, relevant, and accessible books on the rapidly transforming politics of the Middle East for an interested academic and policy audience.

Jordan and the Arab Uprisings

REGIME SURVIVAL AND POLITICS
BEYOND THE STATE

Curtis R. Ryan

Columbia University Press
New York

Columbia University Press
Publishers Since 1893
New York   Chichester, West Sussex
cup.columbia.edu
Copyright © 2018 Columbia University Press
All rights reserved

Library of Congress Cataloging-in-Publication Data
Names: Ryan, Curtis R., author.
Title: Jordan and the Arab uprisings : regime survival and politics beyond the state / Curtis Ryan.
Other titles: Columbia studies in Middle East politics.
Description: New York : Columbia University Press, 2018. | Series: Columbia studies in Middle East politics | Includes bibliographical references and index.
Identifiers: LCCN 2017049197| ISBN 9780231186261 (cloth) | ISBN 9780231186278 (pbk.) | ISBN 9780231546560 (ebook)
Subjects: LCSH: Jordan—Politics and government—1999– | Arab Spring, 2010–
Classification: LCC JQ1833.A58 R93 2018 | DDC 956.9504/5—dc23
LC record available at https://lccn.loc.gov/2017049197

Contents

Preface and Acknowledgments

This book explains how Jordan weathered the Arab uprisings, but it also provides an analytical understanding of Jordanian politics that is meant to last far beyond the era of the "Arab Spring" and the regional instability that followed. Each chapter tackles a different dynamic in the kingdom's politics, tracking each theme before, during, and after the regional Arab Spring but also indicating how it is key to understanding Jordanian politics overall.

While domestic political dynamics are the main focus, the framework also emphasizes that Jordan's domestic politics takes place within a broader regional setting. Regional context and external constraints deeply affect internal politics for both regime and opposition in Jordan. My analysis therefore takes the international setting seriously and shows its impact on domestic politics in the kingdom. As a small state, weaker than its neighbors by almost every conceivable measure, Jordan remains militarily, economically, and politically vulnerable. While this is a constant feature of Jordanian politics, it is also a change in terms of the scale of externally generated challenges (such as the massive influx of Syrian refugees) and explicit security threats (from regional wars to the rise of ISIS) in the era of the Arab uprisings. Domestic-international linkages affect Jordanian domestic politics to such an extent that it would be impossible to understand Jordan's internal politics without also examining its regional setting.

The research for the book included considerable field work and interviews with countless Jordanians, in places that ranged from street protests to palaces. My analysis of Jordanian politics draws on almost thirty years of study of the country, including my first arrival in Jordan in the summer of 1989. But most of the interviews, meetings, and discussions for this project came from repeated trips to the kingdom during and after the Arab Spring period—specifically, in ten research visits between December 2010 and August 2016. In every research visit to Jordan, my emphasis has been to talk to as many people as possible, from different walks of life, ideological perspectives, and levels of economic or political power. While the interpretations and analyses in this book are entirely my own, I draw on insights from leftists, liberals, conservatives, Islamists, pan-Arab nationalists, royalists, revolutionaries, reformers, and even Jordanians who see themselves as nonpolitical.

I have met at length with activists, opposition party officials, former prime ministers, government officials, cabinet ministers, members of parliament, journalists, business people, and even King Abdullah II and Queen Rania. I have tried through multiple visits to the country to get to know Jordan from left to right, secular to religious, and—in terms of power—top to bottom. Throughout the book I have tried to include, via direct quotes, as many and as diverse a selection of Jordanian voices as I can, to give a comprehensive picture of the country's politics. I therefore owe thanks to many—seemingly countless—Jordanians. While I cannot thank everyone, I will single out those who were especially generous with their time and their thoughts on various aspects of Jordanian politics. I will also include many with whom I met but discussed matters other than politics.

First, thanks go to King Abdullah II and Queen Rania for agreeing to meet and for being very gracious with their time. I met several times with King Abdullah and once with Queen Rania. While my meetings with the king always focused on various topics in Jordanian politics and policy, my meeting with Queen Rania was not about Jordanian politics at all but instead about her educational outreach efforts. Similarly, when I met with Prince Talal bin Muhammad, we spoke mainly of Jordanian history and society. In my meeting with Prince Ali bin al-Hussein, we did not discuss Jordanian politics but instead focused entirely on efforts of the Asian Football Development Project (AFDP) to bring soccer to children in Syrian refugee camps and Jordanian host communities. I thank Prince Talal and Prince Ali for their insights and time. And I thank Merissa Khurma for making my meeting with Prince Ali possible, for helping me visit Za'atari refugee camp, and for her friendship. Regarding research on the refugee issue in Jordan, I thank UNHCR and especially Andrew Harper for his many insights.

The palace meetings with King Abdullah and Queen Rania would not have been possible without the efforts and support of many people at the Royal Hashemite Court (RHC). Some have since shifted to other jobs and positions but at the time worked for the RHC. I especially thank Imad Fakhoury, Khalid Dalal, Sharif Abdullah, Muin Khoury, Fares Braizat, Francesca Sawalha, Christina Hawatmeh, and Rusul Arabiyyat.

In the course of many trips to Jordan, I have met with many current and former government officials. But I want to acknowledge several who have been particularly generous with their time and thoughts: former senators and prime ministers 'Awn Khasawneh, Taher al-Masri, and Fayez Tarawneh, and former cabinet ministers Kamel Abu Jaber, 'Abd al-Ilah al-Khatib, Omar al-Razzaz, Ayman Safadi, Ibrahim Saif, and Malek Twal.

At the Center for Strategic Studies (CSS) at the University of Jordan, I thank its director, Musa Shteiwi, and former director, Mustafa Hamarneh, not only for their insights but also for working together on multiple workshops over the years. Peter Seeberg kindly included me in several CSS workshops via the Danish Jordanian University Cooperation (DJUCO). I thank the entire staff at al-Quds Center for Political Studies and especially its director, Oraib Rantawi. And I thank Marwan Muasher, former minister and diplomat and vice president for studies at the Carnegie Endowment.

I have long been impressed with the superb citizen media platform and online magazine *7iber*, and I am grateful to everyone there. Special thanks go to its current editors and also many of its founders, some of whom have since moved on to other, equally important projects. Thank you Lina Ejeilat, Ramsey George Tesdell, Reem al-Masri, and Naseem Tarawneh. I am grateful to Abdullah Shami and everyone at Café Politique and Maqha Amman for having me as a guest in the first place and for many conversations afterward. Thanks also to Mohanned al-Arabiat, Faris Ghawi, Sandra Hiari, Hadeel Maaitah, and Sami Samawi.

I have been fortunate enough to have had countless conversations over the years with Jordanians who are fellow writers, including journalists, scholars, and other analysts. I thank here especially Sara Ababneh, Muhammad Abu Rumman, Lamis Andoni, Hassan Barari, Hisham Bustani,

Randa Habib, George Hawatmeh, Adnan Hayajneh, Abdul-Wahab Kayyali, Suleiman al-Khalidi, Sa'eda Kilani, Daoud Kuttab, Suha Ma'ayeh, Muhammad al-Masri, Sufian Obeidat, Basil Okoor, Thoraya el-Rayyes, Osama al-Sharif, Rana Sweis, Jamal Shalabi, Nawaf Tell, Hazem Zureiqat, and Tareq Zureiqat.

In the course of my research, I have met with numerous diplomats from both Jordan and other countries. Special thanks go to Adi Khair, Walid Hadid, and Bishr Khasawneh at the Jordanian Foreign Ministry; to Dana Zureiqat, director of the Jordan Information Office at the Jordanian Embassy in the United States; to former Jordanian ambassadors to the United States Alia Bouran and Prince Zayd bin Ra'ad; to U.S. ambassadors to Jordan Robert S. Beecroft, Edward Gnehm, and Stuart Jones; and to Seif Usher, formerly of the British Embassy in Jordan.

At Appalachian State University, Phillip Ardoin, Tony Calamai, Brian Ellison, Jesse Lutabingwa, Neva Specht, and Sheri Everts contributed to the travel funding that made this research possible. The Project on Middle East Political Science (POMEPS) funded one of my many research trips to Jordan. The National Democratic Institute included me as part of their election observation team in 2013. I am also grateful to Chatham House for including me in their research efforts on the impact of Syrian refugees in Jordan. I especially thank Neil Quilliam, Tim Eaton, and Doris Carrion.

Caelyn Cobb, Miriam Grossman, Marisa Lastres, and Anita O'Brien of Columbia University Press offered their support and guidance and helped bring this project to fruition. Thanks to John Bebber for helping me rework the bibliography, to Carly Wilson for help in copyediting, and to Michael Taber for the index. Thanks also go to the two anonymous reviewers of the manuscript, who helped improve the project, and to Marc Lynch and Anne Routon, who first believed in this book and helped make it a reality.

I am grateful to Jillian Schwedler, Marc Lynch, Pete Moore, Laurie Brand, Morten Valbjorn, Janine Clark, Andre Bank, Ellen Lust, Yoav Allon, Sean Yom, and Ziad Abu Rish for various comments and insights on Jordanian politics.

For various acts of generosity and kindness, I thank Rula Awwad, Mary Nazzal-Batayneh, Aysar Batayneh, Mazhar al-Jazirah, Madian al-Jazerah, Maram al-Jazireh, Rama Kayyali Jardaneh, Bana Toukan, and Nadine Toukan.

I have tried to be thorough in these acknowledgments, but the individuals I have noted above are actually only a small portion of the people

I have met with, interviewed, or discussed Jordanian politics with. I therefore thank every grassroots activist, opposition party official, government minister, parliamentarian, and journalist who contributed much to this volume but requested anonymity. I have been careful, in line with the strictest practices of social science research, to maintain that anonymity.

Finally, after all my many years of travels to Jordan, I thank the many Jordanians who engaged in typically Jordanian acts of kindness and hospitality. Shukran. This book is especially for you.

Abbreviations

AFDP	Asian Football Development Project
CNF	Conference on National Reform
CSS	Center for Strategic Studies, University of Jordan
GCC	Gulf Cooperation Council
GID	General Intelligence Directorate
HCCNOP	Higher Committee for the Coordination of National Opposition Parties
IAF	Islamic Action Front
IEC	Independent Electoral Commission
IMF	International Monetary Fund
IRGC	Islamic Revolutionary Guard Corps
IRI	International Republican Institute
ISIS	Islamic State in Iraq and Syria
JAF	Jordanian Armed Forces
JCP	Jordanian Communist Party
JIPTC	Jordan International Police Training Center
JNCW	Jordanian National Commission for Women
KASOTC	King Abdullah Special Operations Training Centre
MB	Muslim Brotherhood
MP	member of parliament
NCHR	National Center for Human Rights
NCR	National Coalition for Reform

NCRS	National Committee for Retired Servicemen
NDI	National Democratic Institute
NEPCO	National Electric Power Company
NGO	nongovernmental organization
PDP	People's Democratic Party
PLO	Palestine Liberation Organization
PR	proportional representation
PSD	Public Security Directorate
PUP	Popular Unity Party
RHC	Royal Hashemite Court
SEZ	Special Economic Zone
SMDP	Single Member District Plurality
SNTV	single non-transferable vote
UNHCR	United Nations High Commissioner for Refugees
UNICEF	United Nations Children's Fund
WEF	World Economic Forum
WFP	World Food Program

CHAPTER I

Continuity and Change Amid the Arab Uprisings

M ark Twain once allegedly said that "reports of my death have been greatly exaggerated." In many ways, this quip summarizes expectations regarding Jordan and its many challenges, not just since the Arab uprisings of 2011 but even since independence in 1946. Jordan is described as "on the brink" so often over the years that it seems to be a chronic condition.[1] Living on the brink but also surviving against the odds are essentially the norms of Jordanian politics throughout the history of the kingdom. But with the onset of the regional "Arab Spring" in 2011, the constraints were intense even by Jordan's fairly rugged standards. Jordan was under severe strain regionally, economically, and even in terms of its internal politics, with protests in the streets, economic crises, war across multiple borders, refugees flowing in, and struggles between government and opposition over the future of the country.

Indeed, the old joke about Jordan's political geography—that it lies "between Iraq and a hard place"—was never particularly funny, but it was also never more true than in the years of the regional Arab Spring (roughly 2011–2013) and in the many years of regional instability that followed the Arab uprisings more generally (roughly 2011 onward). Given Jordan's sometimes tumultuous history in Middle East regional politics, that is really saying something. Yet during those years, Jordan remained more stable than any of its neighbors, despite rising tensions and conflicts across its northern, eastern, and western borders. Violent conflict seemed to be growing in all three directions: with Syria aflame amid a horrific civil war, renewed violence and internal conflict in Iraq, intermittent wars between Hamas and Israel, and the rise of a Salafi jihadist "Islamic State"—better known as ISIS—in Iraq and Syria, challenging not only those states but also Jordan and the entire region. Jordan's myriad security concerns were, in short, not at all hypothetical and indeed all too real.

Yet the Arab Spring had started in a very different way—not in external border threats, civil wars, terrorism, and seemingly endemic violence but rather in democratically minded and youth-driven protest movements across the region. Activists had rallied for reform and change, railed against corruption and social injustice, and called for democracy, pluralism, and responsive governance across the region. Authoritarian regimes confronted mass mobilizations of their own societies, from Morocco to Bahrain, and from Syria to Sudan. Jordan's former foreign minister, Marwan Muasher, referred to this as a "second Arab awakening" that ultimately—despite all its twists and turns—amounted to a long-term struggle for pluralism across the region.[2] The era seemed to herald the onset of tremendous changes and challenges to the regional order. Some regimes fell, while others persisted and even doubled down on their own authoritarianism. The Arab uprisings, in short, marked a period of both profound changes and significant continuities in Arab and Middle East regional politics.

This book provides an analysis of Jordan's experience in the years during and beyond the regional Arab uprisings. In doing so, it examines the events in a broader domestic, regional, and even temporal context. In some respects, Jordan has been here before. Protests, demonstrations, and extensive struggles over reform and reaction are not at all new to Jordanian politics. Nor is regional insecurity or, for that matter, endemic economic crisis. Similarly, Jordan's cautious foreign policy during the Arab Spring pursued mostly familiar courses, including attempts to maneuver between relatively more powerful but also unstable neighbors, all while also attempting to alienate no one.

Yet there were many differences in the otherwise familiar script. Perhaps the single most pressing question emerging from these various angles remains whether Jordan's time-honored approaches to domestic political change, economic challenges, and foreign policy would be enough to carry the kingdom through the continuing challenges of domestic and regional politics during and after the Arab uprisings. The question, put another way, is not just to what extent Jordan survived, reformed, or regressed during the Arab Spring, but also whether the Jordanian path is ultimately sustainable. This book, then, is about Jordan's past and present, and also about its prospects for the future.

The Regional Arab Spring

The Arab uprisings began late in 2010 and shook the entire Middle East to its foundations.[3] Protests were not new to Middle East politics, but the seemingly sudden outbreak on such a large scale and across the entire region was indeed unprecedented. Protesters marched, chanted, and demanded change in Tunisia, Egypt, Libya, Syria, and Yemen—the most dramatic and tumultuous sites in the Arab Spring. But mass demonstrations also broke out in Algeria, Bahrain, Jordan, Morocco, Saudi Arabia, and Sudan. These were not just separate mobilizations but part of a truly pan-Arab and region-wide phenomenon in which protesters demanded political change as well as economic and social justice.[4]

Most accounts see the Arab Spring starting in December 2010 with mass protests in Tunisia, historically not the main trendsetter in Arab politics. The roots of the revolts, of course, were longer term and ran far deeper than the specific events usually cited as triggers to regional uprisings. Public and media attention tended to focus on events such as the self-immolation of Muhammad Boazizi in Tunisia, who set himself on fire in protest against state abuse, leading many to protest in outrage over the sheer despair that marked this act. Similarly, in Egypt, the death of Khalid Sa'id in detention and at the hands of police turned into the Egyptian Arab Spring rallying cry, "We are all Khalid Sa'id." These events were important, and they galvanized opposition to authoritarian regimes in Tunisia and Egypt, but they were not themselves causal. Rather, the uprisings had deeper roots in political grievances against authoritarian rule and economic and social injustice. Still, the Arab Spring did represent a kind of social and political explosion across the region.[5]

Activists and government officials alike from across the Arab world followed the events in Tunisia and Egypt with great interest, with social media and satellite television broadcasting almost every new development. If Tunisia created a political wave that would cross its borders, affecting the entire region, then Egypt's revolution of January 2011 amounted to a political tsunami. Arab satellite television stations soon had to shift to split screens to show the many simultaneous demonstrations and protests across multiple Arab capitals and other cities and towns throughout the region. This wasn't just any wave of protests, however. This time, regimes fell.

Tunisia's President Zine al-'Abedin Ben 'Ali fled the country. Egypt's President Husni Mubarak was overthrown in part by a massive popular revolution but also in part by a military seeking to save itself. Following the Tunisian and Egyptian revolutions, uprisings emerged in Libya and Yemen as well. Libya's longtime dictator Muamar al-Qadhafi was overthrown and brutally executed after the Libyan revolution turned into a civil war, with NATO military intervention backing the rebel side. In Yemen, President Ali Abdullah Saleh, after many delays, finally acquiesced to a regime transition negotiated by the Gulf Cooperation Council (GCC), and yet another dictator left office. But Saleh would later return, helping fuel a Houthi rebellion against his successor, igniting a new Yemeni civil war. The GCC had intervened in a different way in Bahrain, a GCC member state, with an armed force rolling into the country to back the regime against democratic protesters. GCC military forces crushed the nascent democratic movement at Pearl Roundabout in the capital, Manama, setting the stage for a reactionary counterrevolution as the monarchy held on to power with Saudi and GCC backing.

In Syria, the Ba'thist police state of Bishar al-Asad responded to peaceful demonstrations with extreme violence. Eventually, antiregime demonstrations too turned to the use of force, to defend themselves against state repression. Syria's revolution turned out to be the most violent chapter of the regional Arab Spring—a far cry from its initial peaceful and democratic impulses. The Syrian revolution turned into a seemingly endemic civil war, dragging in regional and global powers and even transnational jihadi and terrorist movements, all with extensive implications for neighboring Jordan. The Syrian war had profound effects on Jordan in terms of domestic and regional security, the economy, and extensive refugee flows into the country.

Like their counterparts across the region, Jordanians too had participated in the political demonstrations, rallies, and protests that marked the early years of the regional Arab Spring. But the Jordanian version looked markedly different from that of its more volatile neighbors since it involved mostly peaceful struggles between regime and opposition via protests, demonstrations, and sometimes even elections. Unlike Tunisia, Egypt, Syria, Libya, or Yemen, Jordan had not, thus far, succumbed to revolution, civil war, or violent insurrection. Jordan's Arab Spring and post–Arab Spring experience was not marked by such extremes, but politics within the kingdom during the years of the Arab uprisings were anything but docile or silent.

Was Jordan an exception to the Arab Spring? Jordan's King Abdullah II argued that the country was indeed exceptional, that it could forge a third way between revolution and authoritarian reaction. Might it in fact forge its own unique path, navigating the Arab Spring through its own reform program and hence avoiding the violent revolutionary (or worse) turmoil that had engulfed so much of the region? Or was it simply a matter of time before Jordan too experienced revolutionary change? Alternatively, and perhaps despite internal reform efforts, would Jordan succumb to external pressures and implode like several of its neighbors? In short, would Jordan rise above the dark turn to the Arab Spring in terms of reactionary dictatorship or chronic violence and instability and instead not only survive but perhaps even prosper amid some of the most intense challenges in its entire history? These are the questions that gave rise to this book, which explores these concerns and provides an analysis of key elements in the past, present, and future of politics in the Hashemite Kingdom.

Transitions to Democracy, Persistent Authoritarianism, or Liberalizing Autocracy?

The events of the Arab Spring shook not only the region but also the field of Middle East political science, challenging understandings of Middle East politics.[6] Political scientists and scholars from other disciplines have examined regional politics seemingly from every direction, but the dramatic turns of events from 2011 onward included cases of revolution, counter-revolution, outside intervention, civil war, and, just as important, states where none of these outcomes transpired. All required explanation, including the "why not here?" cases. Understandably, even scholars tended to be caught up in the moment, at least in initial responses to the Arab Spring, especially when it seemed overwhelmingly positive, as youth-led popular movements and unarmed civilian prodemocracy movements appeared to signal a new age, toppling dictatorships in a region long known for persistent authoritarianism.

Indeed, the very term *Arab Spring* was clearly originally meant in a fundamentally positive way, referring to a flowering of democratic possibilities in what had been an overwhelmingly authoritarian context. But those optimistic moments, which were very real, were in many parts of the region overtaken by regimes striking back.[7] This also led to many rhetorical abuses of the seasonal analogy—the Arab Spring, it seemed, had turned to the Arab Autumn (skipping summer entirely) and soon arrived at the Arab Winter.

Overused analogies aside, the Arab uprisings had shifted from moments when societies seemed to have the upper hand over states to the reverse, with states and regimes doubling down on their own repression and authoritarianism, shifting tactics and strategies, perhaps, but demonstrating in a brutal and bloody way the very idea of persistent authoritarianism. Years before the Arab uprisings even began, the political science literature on authoritarian persistence had emerged to explain "why not?"—why not the Middle East, even as other literatures had hailed waves of democratization elsewhere?[8] To be clear, most writers were not making culturally deterministic arguments but were instead investigating empirically the remarkable durability of authoritarian regimes in the Middle East.[9]

Despite myriad claims that the field of political science or Middle East studies had somehow missed the Arab Spring, political scientists working on the region had spent the previous several decades examining everything from civil society activism and social movements to persistent authoritarianism—all topics of direct relevance to the era of the Arab uprisings and beyond. Yet in the broader field of political science, the Middle East often seemed to be regarded in both comparative politics and international relations as the outlier field, the one that had its own unique qualities, and that too often seemed to be the exception to theories and perspectives across the discipline. Political scientists who are regional specialists, of course, have long pushed back against these notions. Yet given the persistence and seeming durability of authoritarian political systems across much of the region, many questioned whether this would ever change.

Vast literatures in political science have studied the waves of democratization that have swept the modern world, but often with scant reference to the Middle East.[10] The transitions literature, for example, examined the wave of democratization in the 1970s and 1980s across Latin America and southern Europe, with particular emphasis on pacts emerging between regime and opposition elites to achieve a successful transition from dictatorship to democracy.[11] In 1989–1991, another wave of democratization appeared to be under way, as regimes fell like dominos (indeed, the only time the domino theory ever worked was in reverse), as communist systems collapsed across Eastern Europe and eventually also the Soviet Union. Other moments of authoritarian collapse and successful democratization would follow elsewhere, but questions remained about the Middle East, and especially about Arab politics. Would there ever be a democratic wave in the Arab world? The Arab Spring of 2011 was the closest the region has, so far, come to anything like it. But in many ways the events themselves instead served to reinforce the literature on robust or durable authoritarianism in the Middle East.[12]

Still, the fact that most regimes in the region survived, and that authoritarian rule for the most part persisted, should not obscure the reality that regional politics had nonetheless changed dramatically. The seeds had been planted much earlier, but the Arab Spring did see a dramatic rise in the level of popular mobilization and activism across the region. In its early days, many political scientists studying the Middle East therefore reexamined literatures that had previously seemed inapplicable to the Middle East. This included the literature on transitions from authoritarianism to democracy.[13] Yet the transitions literature (sometimes known as "transitology") seemed to have limited applicability to Arab regional politics certainly before 2011 but even at the height of the Arab Spring as well—just when it seemed it might apply. There was much tumult, mobilization, and protest across the region, indeed to astounding levels, but regime change really occurred only in Tunisia and Libya, and to a lesser extent (in the sense of partial regime change) in Egypt and Yemen. For all the movement and turmoil, there were few actual transitions. And among these, only Tunisia seemed to be going through even a partial democratic transition. The transitions literature had its own limitations in any case, but now it seemed to be a decidedly optimistic enterprise in the face of the volatility characterizing so much of regional politics, including but not limited to multiple regional wars and the world's largest refugee crisis.

This led some political scientists to look in the opposite direction: not for what has been criticized as "democracy spotting" or being "democrazy" but rather toward explaining persistent and even resurgent authoritarianism in the Middle East, and especially in Arab politics.[14] In this literature, political scientists examined how regimes survive, even in the face of massive popular mobilization. The literature on the persistence of authoritarianism focused on states themselves and the many lives of regimes driven to ensure their own security, durability, and survival above all other goals.

Regimes have strategies. They make tactical and strategic adjustments. In short, they adapt. Arab regimes in particular resisted the "third wave" of democratization via "upgrading authoritarianism," as Steven Heydemann put it.[15] Similarly, Joshua Stacher argued that "adaptable autocrats" have myriad strategies to adjust to new challenges to their rule, not just through coercion or brute force (although in these cases that applied too) but also through cooptation, inclusion, and—at times—selective exclusion. Even state-led reform, Stacher asserts, should best be seen as "autocratic adaptation." This very adaptability of authoritarian regimes (even in many different forms) "explains why this form of governance continues to be relevant even in the age of popular mobilizations, uprisings, and potential revolutions."[16] Perhaps ironically, regimes change in order to stay the same.

In my own earlier work on regime survival strategies, focusing then on Egypt, I argued that the set of survival strategies at hand for many ruling regimes includes coercion, containment or cooptation, and even diversion—that is, the use of foreign policy and the regional or international stage to put off domestic pressures.[17] In his work on authoritarian persistence, also focusing on Egypt, Jason Brownlee argues that regime maintenance is also predicated in large part on institutions and coalitions of ruling elites.[18] Institutions of the state and elite coalitions are both rearranged and reorganized by the regime to prevent greater change, to thwart reform, and to achieve what is, after all, job one for any regime: maintaining its own survival. Regimes have arsenals of options to work with, cynical though that sounds. And we can assume that regimes do in fact want to survive, and that they will therefore make adjustments and use whatever means they deem necessary to ensure their own security and longevity.[19] The literature on the durability of authoritarianism in the region suggests that these arsenals, while certainly including coercion and repression, also include shifting patronage, coopting opponents, instigating minimal reforms to forestall greater change, managing elections, and even liberalizing (minimally) not to replace autocracy but to preserve it.

Studying why dictatorship persists, despite efforts against it, is naturally a depressing enterprise. But alternative approaches had turned in a different direction, away from the cynical and self-serving strategies of states and regimes, toward politics within society itself. These more optimistic literatures examined signs of democratization or at least liberalization, not just in the form of state institutional change but also by examining the emergence of civil society organizations and social movements and other forms of public activism and engagement.[20]

Having overly optimistic expectations regarding where this is all going, however, has been criticized as "democracy spotting." Lisa Anderson, in a cogent critique, noted the biases especially within American political science toward normative expectations about democracy and democratization, and hence the danger of seeing signs of these and missing much of what was really going on in the region. Scholars, she argued, were too likely to engage in "searching where the light shines" rather than engaging in perhaps a more thorough examination of the political landscape.[21] But Anderson was critical of the authoritarianism literature too. Each of these literatures, even when studying seemingly opposite phenomena, had a tendency to err on the side of being overly deterministic in their expectations. In this book I have tried to be mindful of Anderson's critique, as I draw on all the above literatures but without any expectation of democratic or authoritarian inevitability. As we shall see, literatures from civil society to the persistence of authoritarianism have useful things to say in understanding the politics of Jordan and many other countries.

Yet it would be pointless for advocates of one or another of these perspectives—ranging from democratic transitions to persistent authoritarianism—to have declared victory in the wake of the Arab Spring. The region did see a resurgence of authoritarianism, to be sure, but there was no reason to believe that this was some kind of final stage. Similarly, while democracy was not, in fact, breaking out across the region, that didn't nullify the emergence of civil society, grassroots levels of organization, social movements, or prodemocracy activism. As Lynch has noted, "authoritarianism is rarely as stable as it appears during the days of normal politics, but equally rarely as ephemeral as it might seem during revolutionary moments."[22] These various literatures, in short, tell us about different aspects of political life and are not really in some kind of contest.

Some scholars were focusing on states and regimes and some on political mobilization from within society, either alongside or even against the state. There were valuable studies exploring political activism and mobilization *despite* authoritarianism. The point is that to fully understand the dynamics of authoritarianism and the prospects for liberalization or democracy or simply for change of any kind (without any particular normative expectations), one must examine both state and society. These literatures are equally important and give insights into different questions. The more socially oriented literatures moved away from a state-centric focus toward politics as practiced through civil society and social movements. Scholars examined organizations, nonstate institutions, and grassroots movements challenging the dominance of states not only within a prevailing regime but also across society. These literatures were often especially interested in prospects for real change. The surge in studies of civil society from the 1990s onward, for example, examined different forms of citizen organization outside the direct control or purview of the state. These did not turn into building blocks for a steady march toward democracy, but in 2011 and after, such efforts did provide the groundwork for organization and even institutional bases for greater grassroots mobilization efforts.

Lina Khatib and Ellen Lust have demonstrated, however, that understanding the real depths of social and political activism requires moving beyond formal civil society organizations to include informal forms of political engagement and mobilization.[23] Asef Bayat, in his influential work, pushed much further in the direction of a grassroots focus, beyond civil society institutions or indeed institutions of any kind, to focus on the importance of individuals and everyday forms of politics.[24] Lisa Wedeen, again in groundbreaking work, examined how individuals challenge regimes in other ways, acting as if they are complying when in fact they are not—and acting as if they have acquiesced when instead they are pursuing their own paths while carefully navigating the controls of the state.[25] Finally, scholars such as Marc Lynch pointed to the changed politics of new media, new technologies, and the transformative effect of creating truly transnational opportunities for communication and mobilization in the Arab public sphere.[26] It is important to note that all these studies were written before the Arab uprisings but showed avenues for mobilization for both individuals and society, regardless of the efforts of states.

For these reasons, this book, while concerned with the question of regime adaptability and survival, also examines Jordanian politics beyond the state, including efforts at individual and collective mobilization and activism for change. It is about both state and society in Jordan, about government and opposition, and about regime elites and grassroots activism alike. Unlike Egypt and Syria, Jordan has tended not to pursue high levels of violent repression. Coercion is there, to be sure, but not comparable to that of the more brutal regimes. The Jordanian state has instead prided itself on its use of "soft security"—that is, minimal coercion—with a larger reliance on cooptation, minimal and cautious reform efforts directed from above, as well as extensive economic and military support from regional and global allies.

Even years after the Arab Spring protests, neither side of the government-opposition spectrum in Jordan could afford to be too comfortable. Many regime elites felt certain that they had survived the Arab uprisings, while many reform activists were increasingly disillusioned. Years had passed. Many challenges were met, and many opportunities missed. Yet politics in the Arab states did not begin or end with the Arab Spring. Much remains unresolved and will depend not just on state and society within Jordan or other countries in the region but also on the regional setting.

The Importance of the International Setting

Part of Jordan's story is about domestic politics. But for Jordan, and indeed any other country, domestic politics does not take place in a vacuum. The regional and international setting matters significantly and shapes much of what is possible within the domestic sphere. To understand domestic outcomes, therefore, it is essential to look not only at the case itself but also at its international setting. It is important, in short, to link comparative politics and individual country cases to international relations. Especially for smaller states, outside support is often vital to regime and also state survival. There is an entire literature for this, too—small states conceived not just as geographically small but also in terms of relative weakness or vulnerability in the international or regional system.[27] "Small states," such as Jordan, are often especially vulnerable to regional turmoil like that of the Arab uprisings and the wars that followed. Jordan remains economically, politically, and militarily weaker than its neighbors and hence dependent on economic support, foreign economic and military aid, and strong regional or global allies for its survival.[28]

But alliances, of course, do not come without strings attached. They may indeed bolster the state, as intended, but there remains the important question of political costs. If the key foreign ally has its own preferences, does it seek to impose these on its weaker allied state? This has strong implications for linking international relations and alliance politics to internal politics and struggles for domestic change. Wealthy and influential global allies, like many of the states in the European Union, for example, are likely to press for greater domestic openness and change, while more reactionary states, like regional power Saudi Arabia, are just as likely to push in the opposite direction. U.S. policy, not known for its consistency, can appear at either end of that spectrum, with strong implications for or against domestic change. Jordan, as this book shows, has found itself subject to all the above pressures. In a recent study, Sean Yom argues that the interference of powerful Western states in the Middle East has more often than not had negative effects on prospects for democratic change. Drawing on the cases of Jordan, Kuwait, and Iran, Yom argues that Western interventionism provides an enabling effect for enduring authoritarianism.[29]

And here the question of security dilemmas, traditionally a concept in international relations, is especially important even in a domestic politics setting. International relations scholars note that states in the international system often find themselves arming and improving their defenses in an effort to ensure their own security, yet in doing so they may unintentionally trigger alarm and worse among their neighbors. The "dilemma" in the security dilemma refers to the tendency of defensive efforts—that is, efforts to enhance security—to backfire and actually undermine a state's own security, and even to create a spiral of insecurity. As I have argued elsewhere, there is a domestic corollary to the traditional external security dilemma.[30] Jordan and other states in the region and beyond also have an internal security dilemma. Efforts to ensure external security (and Jordan does not have a shortage of potential threats) can militate against domestic efforts at greater openness and reform, ensuring perhaps more secure borders but also undermining the credibility, legitimacy, and ultimately security of a ruling regime.

As the Arab uprisings wore on and revolutions turned into civil wars, with terrorist organizations like al-Qa'ida and the Islamic State taking root in territories of neighboring states, Jordan's concerns with regional Arab wars and with ensuring its external security seemed to outweigh or derail its domestic Arab Spring efforts at reform and change. Few countries reside geographically in such difficult circumstances. And from 2011 onward, those circumstances only got more difficult, with conflict across almost every border. Indeed, the country was battered by negative regional trends as the region and even Jordan's immediate neighbors were mired in revolution, counterrevolution, civil war, insurgency, occupation and resistance to occupation, repression, terrorism, state-led counterterrorism that often seemed to be still more terrorism, foreign intervention, militant Salafi jihadist movements, and rising regional sectarianism. Yet the kingdom, while vulnerable to these more negative winds of change, so far has succumbed to none of them. Would it instead be affected by more positive winds of change? By the more idealistic goals of youth and other movements for greater openness, reform, and change? The grassroots movements themselves, the rise in activism, and the increase in the use of new technologies and social media all suggested that meaningful change was finally a real possibility.

The Jordanian Case and the Approach of This Book

Many of the political science literatures cited above give cause for pessimism and seem to suggest, together, that Jordan—like most cases—is likely to see greater grassroots activism, civil society, and attempts at liberalization but to have these be met by even stronger forces arrayed against change. Even as social pressures mount, ruling regimes are likely to adjust their arsenals as needed in order to simply hold on, perhaps while allowing some surface-level changes to co-opt, divide, and defuse opposition. These types of measures may be meant cynically, as "pseudo-democratic" reforms. But even changes from above might sometimes be taken beyond the limited parameters intended by a regime. This nexus of domestic and regional pressures and insecurities can also trigger, even in different time periods, remarkably similar moments of struggles over reform and change, almost as though government and opposition are following a familiar script but with different terms and slogans. As struggles for and against reform and change continued in Jordan, many government officials and opposition activists alike could certainly feel a sense of déjà vu—of having gone through much of this before. *Plus ça change, plus c'est la même chose*—the more things change, the more they stay the same.

But in Jordan and across the region, politics was characterized by both continuity and change, and even some of the familiar and seemingly repetitive aspects often featured subtle changes—changes worth noticing and investigating, as this book intends to do. Ultimately, the Jordanian case underscores not just the salience of many of the above theories but also why it is essential to examine national politics (for any case) from both state and society angles—as a struggle between regimes attempting to secure their own survival and more diverse elements mobilizing across society for change. As this book will show, authoritarian resilience remains a key feature of Jordanian politics, but so too does social and political mobilization across a wide range of opposition forces.

Jordan exists in one of the world's most difficult neighborhoods, surrounded by more powerful neighbors whose problems seem continually to spill over their borders into the Hashemite Kingdom. While these regional and security dynamics have been key features of Jordanian politics and policy ever since independence in 1946, they seemed especially urgent and intense during and after the regional Arab uprisings. As a small state that is weaker by almost any measure than its various neighbors in an often volatile region, Jordan has tended to put great emphasis on recurring rounds of domestic reform, coupled with active international diplomacy and even savvy foreign policy to ensure that its economic and security needs are met, both domestically and regionally.

The kingdom was not blessed with significant resource endowments and has neither sufficient oil nor water supplies. Indeed, Jordan was struggling to maintain energy supplies, including electricity and natural gas, for its own citizens even before the regional uprisings and wars. The economy has no significant resource endowments, aside from limited amounts of phosphates and potash. The kingdom has therefore attempted to pursue alternative energy sources, such as developing solar and wind power, but these are also long-term efforts. In the short term, the country remains energy and aid dependent.

Even before the Arab Spring began, the kingdom was struggling economically, and its geographic location has always made the country especially vulnerable to the trials and tribulations of its neighbors. Jordan has a massive unemployment rate, especially for youth, with an unusually high cost of living (already a dangerous combination), and depends on foreign aid to meet more than half of its annual state budget. The kingdom therefore operates with a persistent budget deficit and hence prioritizes positive foreign relations with external allies and benefactors, including the United States, the European Union, and the wealthy Arab Gulf states. Jordan has used its geopolitical importance and regional setting as leverage to retain the support and good will of affluent Western powers and sometimes also Gulf allies. But this also means that the kingdom operates in a chronic fiscal crisis that has grown worse over the years.

During the Arab Spring era, Jordanian activism seemed to be at an all-time high, not only in the streets but also through other forms of protest, including petitions and various manifestos issued as challenges to the regime. Activists gathered in public debates as well as in online forums, openly discussing almost every issue in Jordanian politics. Jordan's internet lit up with social media and other online portals as activists and other citizens connected with one another, debated, discussed, and organized. Unlike many other states in the region, however, Jordan has not (so far) seen revolution, civil war, or regime change. So what exactly is it a case of? Supporters of the regime and the state—and there are many Jordanians in this category—often emphasize that Jordan is a case simply of survival, against great odds when one considers both the economic situation and the regional turmoil. Even supporters differ, however, on whether this survival is due to deft and far-sighted policy or simply to more reactive attempts to "muddle through" and survive the latest internal and external challenges.

In terms of the political science literature, Jordan often matches almost whatever middle case is offered. When scholars speak of "hybrid regimes" or "liberalizing autocracies," these terms fit the Jordanian case.[31] If there is a middle path, Jordan is likely to take it. It is a small state dependent on the good will of key allies to support its economic and security efforts, and it shifts domestic political coalitions and regional alliances in a never-ending effort to maintain its own regime security, while trying to maintain consistent, long-term relations with more powerful global allies. Jordan has sustained itself through countless challenges, even when it appears to be, once again, "on the brink."

Describing Jordan as a middle case means, among other things, that it is neither fully authoritarian nor fully democratic, although it is more the former than the latter. It is a hybrid regime, not just a liberalizing autocracy but a *perpetually* liberalizing autocracy. And this is a key part of the case and a key argument of this book: there is considerable movement and seemingly constant change, yet much remains the same. This is a state strategy. In many ways, Jordan shows how a state can be in continual movement without moving from essentially the same spot. Jordan's regime survival, despite the many pressures unleashed by the Arab uprisings, I argue, is based on a combination of state strategies (including recurrent reform efforts), divided opposition movements, and extensive international support related to its geopolitical importance to other, more powerful international actors.

It is also important to note, however, what this book does *not* do. It makes no argument about cultural, ethnic, or religious determinism or exceptionalism. Nor do I subscribe to the notion that monarchies themselves are so exceptional as to be immune from the dramatic changes of Middle East regional politics. Political scientists have debated the issue of "monarchical exceptionalism" precisely because the eight Arab monarchies survived the Arab Spring while many of the authoritarian republics did not.[32] But like Gregory Gause, I argue that each monarchy has a different story to tell and has survived largely owing to its own strategies, domestic support coalitions, and external supporters (and, in the case of the "oil monarchies," its own resources).[33] It is not monarchy itself as a regime type that is the key variable but actions, strategies, tactics, and allies—all of which are explored in this book.

Jordan itself has thus far mastered the fine art of muddling through, of just managing to survive and continue, despite a neighborhood awash in unrest, instability, and violence. Yet short of revolution, civil war, or regime collapse, a great deal happened in Jordan in the era of the Arab uprisings, as state, society, and old and new forms of opposition mobilized across Jordanian politics. Political struggles raged over reform, opposition, elections, identity politics, social and economic justice, foreign policy, and national security. Mindful of the various literatures noted above, this book therefore looks closely at both state and society, at elite and grassroots politics, at internal and external politics and policies, for a more complete picture of Jordan during—and long after—the Arab uprisings. With these concerns in mind, the book does not focus on *either* an elite-level regime analysis or a grassroots-level analysis of opposition forces but rather examines *both*. Political outcomes emerge from the intersection of government and opposition efforts, even when they are pushing in opposite directions. This book examines precisely how these dynamics work and provides inside looks at both the government and the opposition, and at their strategies, tactics, goals, and interpretations of key events in the era of the Arab uprisings and well beyond.

This book examines how Jordan managed to weather the Arab uprisings, even as the region around it seemed to be in flames in every direction. The kingdom did not emerge unscathed. So how did both state and society manage to maneuver through these challenges? And is this a sustainable model for Jordan's future, or, indeed, for other countries to perhaps learn from? For both government and opposition, what changed and what did not? These are important questions, in no small part because the forces that led to the Arab uprisings have not disappeared in Jordan or anywhere else in the region.

Most political science research on the Arab uprisings has, of course, noted how dramatic and important they have been for the entire region. Yet there has also been a corresponding tendency to overdramatize regional choices as stark sets of binaries—revolution or counterrevolution, stability or instability, democratization or authoritarian retrenchment. But sometimes regime survival is not about dramatic changes or radical challenges but about smaller levels of change. Jordan represents this kind of case—it is not situated at the polar endpoint of any of these binaries but rather somewhere in the middle. Throughout this book, I try to move beyond these binaries to investigate more subtle levels of change across Jordanian politics.

Road Map for the Book

Jordanian politics from the Arab Spring onward has shown notable changes and continuities, and these are discussed and analyzed in detail in the chapters that follow. In most cases these changes amount to more than the regime wanted to give in on, and also considerably less than opposition forces were hoping for. But they are often enough to allow the regime, the opposition, and the country to muddle through, with some continuities but also with some notable changes. The chapters each examine, in turn, a key dynamic in Jordanian politics—deep-rooted and even "traditional" forms of opposition, newer forms of opposition and activism, struggles over identity politics, struggles over elections, struggles over reform, and the importance of regional and external constraints—each of which is vital to understanding Jordan overall. The chapters examine how these topics matter to the whole, and precisely what aspects remain the same and what aspects have changed in the era of the uprisings. For every chapter, and hence for every topic, the focus is on changes and continuities before, during, and beyond the Arab Spring: What amounts to politics as usual? What represents more of a rupture from past patterns?

Chapter 2 sets the stage for the rest of the book by examining what happened in Jordan's version of the regional Arab Spring, with emphasis on opposition mobilization in the form of mass protests and how the state responded. The chapter examines the extent to which these waves of protests represented a rupture from Jordanian politics as usual.

Chapters 3 and 4 turn to the nature of political opposition in the kingdom. Chapter 3 examines the dynamics of unity and disunity in Jordan's traditional political opposition, while chapter 4 looks at some of the newer forms of opposition and activism that emerged in Jordanian politics during the Arab Spring era, including the Hirak popular movements and other forms of opposition activism. Successful opposition movements often draw from across the social spectrum and manage to mobilize despite state efforts to divide or demobilize them. For this reason, chapter 5 examines the contentious issue of identity politics within the kingdom, since unity or division along these lines can make or break prospects for opposition coalitions and for reform and change.

Chapters 6 and 7 look at the specific political struggles in Jordanian politics over various reform efforts. Chapter 6 examines the long-standing struggle between government and opposition over elections, electoral laws, and questions of representation. Chapter 7 focuses on Jordan's recurrent reform struggles, from earlier "reformist" periods to the modern politics of the Arab Spring and post–Arab Spring eras. For all the struggles and all the politics, what, if anything has changed? These chapters provide specific answers.

Chapter 8 places Jordanian politics in its regional context, examining how Jordan's international relations and external constraints affect its internal politics. The chapter analyzes specifically the impact of three major issues—the Syrian civil war, the rise of ISIS and other jihadist challenges, and the massive influx of Syrian refugees—on politics in the Hashemite Kingdom.

Finally, chapter 9 ties the preceding chapters together, looking at where Jordan has been as well as where it seems to be going. Overall, the book provides an analysis of Jordan's domestic and regional politics, government and opposition dynamics, and changes and continuities in Jordanian political life with a view to understanding and explaining Jordanian politics before, during, and long after the era of the Arab uprisings.

CHAPTER II

The Arab Spring Protests in Jordan

As the Arab uprisings spread across the Middle East in 2011 and 2012, many wondered if Jordan would be next. Popular revolutions ousted dictators in Tunisia, Egypt, and Libya and soon challenged longtime rulers in Bahrain, Yemen, and Syria. Yet even among these regional upheavals, Jordan appeared to be a virtual oasis of calm. Given the volatility of its immediate neighbors and neighborhood, that seemed nothing short of remarkable. But was Jordan an oasis of stability? Or was that merely a mirage? Neither characterization seemed really accurate.[1]

As noted in the previous chapter, Jordan has, since independence in 1946, forged a middle path whenever one is available. During the Arab Spring period, roughly 2011 to 2013, and in the years of regional unrest that followed, it tried to do so once again. And in many ways this was true not only of the regime itself but also of many in the opposition who called most often for reform, not revolution. As this book makes clear, however, some of the general imagery regarding the Arab Spring is not entirely accurate. Media and other accounts often saw the uprisings as unprecedented, spontaneous, and rooted mainly among young, tech-savvy activists. While this is part of the story, it is only a part. Jordan actually has a long history of protests, and while there was a significant upsurge in youth activism and street protests, such activities ranged widely across different parts of Jordanian society, including in labor movements.[2] And whether oasis or mirage or neither, in Jordan, as elsewhere across the region, protesters hit the streets to demand real change.[3] This chapter examines Jordan's unique experience with the Arab Spring, from protests and street demonstrations to the revolving door of numerous changing governments, as social forces and the state each attempted to harness the moment. While it is clear that Jordan experienced some version of the Arab Spring, it is also clear that Jordanians themselves had very different images of just what exactly "Arab Spring" meant when applied to the Hashemite Kingdom.

The Arab Spring in Jordan

"So," said a prodemocracy activist, "are you like Jordanians, disillusioned that there will be any real change?" It was the summer of 2013, and we had just sat down to discuss the state of affairs in Jordan. Much had changed even since the protests of 2011 and 2012, and for many, after initial optimism, pessimism was once again setting in. "Do you think Jordan will ever *have* an Arab Spring?" asked another activist. This conversation was in stark contrast to another one, a few days later, in which a conservative Jordanian and self-proclaimed "loyalist" stated proudly that there was no Arab Spring in Jordan, nor should there be.[4] For conservatives, the Arab Spring was not something that Jordanians should wistfully pine for but rather something they should be proud to have avoided or survived. Jordan was a stable and peaceful oasis in an otherwise volatile region, they argued. It had not succumbed, and it would not. But these two rather polarized views are not just in disagreement over the desirability of a Jordanian Arab Spring, they also reflect completely different senses of what that phrase even means.[5]

For the more liberal activist, *Arab Spring* meant a largely secular, prodemocracy movement that led to a genuine political opening in the kingdom, with meaningful and lasting reform, and a real shift toward Jordanian democracy, even in the context of a constitutional monarchy. For her conservative counterpart, however, it meant social unrest, revolution, and civil war. It meant disorder, instability, and violence. With these polarized visions, some Jordanians pondered whether Jordan could ever arrive at an Arab Spring—meant as a noble and democratic goal to be achieved—while others were thankful that Jordan had survived what they saw as a regional onslaught of mayhem and instability. All viewed Jordan as the key exception to an increasingly pervasive norm in Arab politics, in which change (for better or worse) rocked the region.

Jordan's Hashemite monarchy had its own take on these questions, presenting the Arab Spring as both a constraint and an opportunity. The negative version, the one associated with disorder and violence, was an Arab Spring that Jordan had survived, through careful security arrangements and its own reform process. The more positive version, the one associated with liberalization and change, in contrast, was not something that Jordan had survived or avoided. Rather, Jordan was modeling an alternative and decidedly Jordanian and homegrown version of the Arab Spring, one based on reform without revolution, change without chaos or instability. Along those lines, King Abdullah II argued that the Arab Spring was therefore a needed stimulus to reinvigorate earlier reform efforts, allowing these efforts to overcome institutional and ideological resistance even within the state itself. In one of my discussions with King Abdullah, he put it this way: "Quite honestly, at one point towards the end of the first ten years, I got frustrated of fighting against the system. I think we were about to become complacent. But what saved us all was the Arab Spring. I think that was the root shock that I particularly needed again to move the process forward. So, in Jordan we saw that in the Arab Spring there was an opportunity to move the political process forward."[6]

Jordan, the king argued, would indeed be an exception to the instability that had ensued elsewhere in the region during and after the Arab Spring, because Jordan was unique as a monarchy and a regime that was reforming itself. He continued: "This is also why Jordan's political process, what we are trying to do in Jordan, is much bigger than Jordan. Because if we can show that a monarchy can go to political reform, consensually, do evolution instead of revolution, then where is the other story? So the way I look at it is if people say, 'well is the King sincere or not?' It is bigger than me, and it is bigger than Jordan."[7]

Many Jordanians strongly support the king and share this viewpoint. These more conservative and royalist Jordanians generally describe themselves as loyalists, and some organized counterdemonstrations in response to those of reform and democracy activists. Their presence in social media is extensive and at times marked by key government slogans turned into Twitter hashtags, such as #God #Country #King.

But not all Jordanians share this optimistic view. Many, in fact, feel that their hopes were raised in 2011 and dashed soon thereafter. Regime critics see in the events of the Arab Spring echoes of earlier promising reform efforts that ultimately ran aground on the shoals of the Jordanian status quo. Yet at the very outset, at least, some saw Jordan as among the most likely states to follow in the path of Tunisia or Egypt. One analysis noted that "Jordan's young and well-educated population seems ripe for the message of the Arab Spring. The country has serious economic troubles, endemic corruption, and a clear lack of political freedom. Thus it is not surprising that uprisings in Egypt and Tunisia quickly spread to Jordan." Demonstrations and protests had indeed spread, but not an uprising. The same analysis concluded that the Jordanian version, while including protests and demonstrations across the country, nonetheless did not lead to actual revolution but rather to little more than "Arab Spring Lite."[8]

In three separate analyses, each approximately a year apart over the first three years of the Arab Spring, the *Economist* magazine continually shifted its assessment of Jordan's prospects amid regional change. Even the headlines tell the tale of a regime that went from a defensive and embattled posture to one that seemed more comfortable and secure. But the emphasis in the previous sentence should, perhaps, be on the word "seemed," not on the word "secure." In 2011 the *Economist* wrote that Jordan and its king were "caught in the middle as usual." In 2012 the title changed to "Jordan and Its King: As Beleaguered as Ever," while in 2013 the editors changed their assessment once again to "Jordan: Surprisingly Stable for the Moment."[9] By 2013, in short, the magazine's assessment had changed dramatically and sounded much more optimistic about the regime's prognosis. "With aplomb," the editors noted, "the king is weathering storms at home and abroad." Yet the *Economist* analysis was still careful to note that this was likely "not a turning point but merely a reprieve."[10]

In some respects, the Jordanian regime had actually benefited, albeit paradoxically, from the tenacity of regional unrest, from the West Bank and Gaza to Syria and Iraq. Inside Jordan, many activists backed off in their demands on the state, especially after the first two years of protests, fearing that Jordan too could tip toward the kind of violence and instability that so mired many of its neighbors. Activists had not dropped their demands, but many had toned them down, at least temporarily, while warily watching the violence across Jordan's borders. Regional unrest hadn't extinguished domestic Jordanian activism, but it had at least temporarily dampened the fires. Regime and opposition alike tread warily and with unease, fearing the potential spillover of other conflicts into Jordan itself. And regional turmoil had, in fact, done just that.

The Syrian war in particular may have bought the regime some time in its relations with its opponents, but it also brought additional stresses on the kingdom, including the influx of hundreds of thousands of Syrian refugees. But even here, amid regional violence and a massive refugee crisis, Jordan suffered considerable strain in attempting to deal with the crisis, but it was also able to gain large increases in foreign aid to the kingdom, as Jordan's allies attempted to shore up the kingdom against domestic and regional threats, both economic and political. Jordan's many regional and global allies—from Saudi Arabia to the United States and the European Union—increased their aid contributions in an effort to stabilize the kingdom and help it avoid joining the regional instability.

So was Jordan the Arab exception? And if so, in which sense of "Arab Spring"? Across countless topics and issues in regional politics, Jordan often seems to lie between various extremes. In the context of the Arab Spring, that chronic sense of muddling through seemed to apply, so far. Yet from 2011 to 2017 Jordan was not at all silent. The protests had rocked Jordan too, but they hadn't descended into civil war or exploded in a full-scale uprising against the regime. Regarding the state itself, Jordan had taken neither a fully democratic nor a fully authoritarian path as it maneuvered its way through domestic and regional pressures. But Jordan's path and its general stability changed several times during the years of the regional Arab uprisings. The protests of 2011–2012 in many ways echoed an earlier period of unrest and social protest in Jordan—in April 1989—which remains a pivotal moment for government, opposition, and protest in Jordanian politics. Even many protesters themselves were particularly cognizant of the comparisons to the events of 1989, as these continue to serve as a benchmark against which both protest and reform are sometimes measured in Jordanian politics.

Precursors to the Arab Spring: Echoes of 1989

Some Jordanian activists still refer to the dramatic events of April 1989 as a Jordanian "Intifada"—pointedly using the term usually used to describe Palestinian uprisings against Israeli rule in the West Bank and Gaza. But

Jordan's unrest in 1989 had very different origins and objectives. The demonstrations had been triggered in large part by austerity measures implemented for an International Monetary Fund (IMF) economic stabilization program. The demonstrations soon turned to riots. Activists are often quick to note that protests in both eras began with demonstrations in the south of the country. The demonstrations of 1989, like those of 2011, expanded quickly to include protests not only against austerity measures and difficult economic circumstances but also against widespread government corruption, while calling for greater and more genuine democratization.

What alarmed the Hashemite regime in both 1989 and 2011 was the large presence and even predominance of ethnic East Jordanian or Transjordanian citizens in the demonstrations. Overall, the largest ethnic division within Jordanian politics is actually within its own majority Arab community—that is, between Palestinian Jordanians (those whose roots are west of the Jordan River, many of whom came to Jordan as refugees of the Arab-Israeli wars of 1948 and 1967) and East Jordanians, also known as Transjordanians or East Bankers, since they trace their roots to east of the Jordan River. In general, the Hashemite state, army, security services, and public sector have been dominated largely by East Jordanians, while Palestinian Jordanians have come to play a very large role in the private sector. Some activists, especially in the South, argued that the regime's own neoliberal economic reforms had shifted Jordan's economy from the public to the private sector, resulting in a dramatic change in the social and political balance of power within domestic politics. For some, at least, this also takes on ethnic dimensions.

This topic is complicated enough that is warrants its own chapter and hence is discussed in more detail in chapter 5. But for the moment it is important to note that the demonstrators in 2011 themselves could not be dismissed as the "usual suspects" of opposition in Jordan: leftist parties, Islamists, and/or Palestinian-Jordanian activists. Rather, the demonstrations ranged across the ideological spectrum and at times spanned ethnic, religious, and class divides as well. Yet most protesters seemed to come from tribal and East Jordanian backgrounds. In short, both the traditional sources of opposition and the bedrock constituencies of regime support seemed to be out on the streets facing that very regime. More important, and more alarming for the regime in both the 1989 and 2011 cases, the latter group seemed to outnumber the former.

In 1989 King Hussein responded to the riots and protests by dismissing the extremely unpopular government of Prime Minister Zaid al-Rifa'i (whose government had lasted from 1985 to 1989). Hussein sacked the government and initiated a broad program of political and economic liberalization. The 2011 demonstrations seemed to constitute a similar shock to Jordanian politics and society. In this instance, King Abdullah II also dismissed the government of an unpopular Prime Minister Rifa'i (in this case Samir al-Rifa'i, the son of Zaid al-Rifa'i). Like his father before him, King Abdullah pledged to restore the kingdom to the path of more genuine political and economic reform.

King Abdullah II had ascended the throne in 1999, following the death of his father, King Hussein. Hussein may have started the economic liberalization process, in 1989, but his son pursued it even more vigorously, charting a neoliberal course for Jordanian development that would involve extensive privatization measures and emphasis on trade, investment, and development of communications and other infrastructure. By "neoliberalism" in this context I am referring to policies aimed at economic rather than social or political liberalism—that is, policies emphasizing free market capitalism, privatization, and fiscal austerity. The Jordanian regime's commitment to these policy goals, and indeed to this development model, endeared it to many key Western powers such as the United States, and also to key global financial institutions such as the World Bank and the IMF. But the economic policies of neoliberalism, in Jordan and everywhere else, have real social and political implications and predictably trigger resistance, particularly when free markets and privatization seem to come at the expense of social safety nets, welfare provisions, and subsistence-level incomes. As we shall see throughout the book, protests and opposition in Jordan have often demanded more political liberalization and less economic liberalization, at least in the sense of restoring social welfare and bolstering incomes and access to basic services.

At the level of the state itself, however, economic development agendas had more often than not outweighed political reform efforts, with various political reform initiatives rising and falling, but not necessarily moving forward. While many regime opponents blamed the regime for this lack of progress, many in the regime blamed an old-guard bureaucracy, entrenched conservative elites, and hardline institutions such as the General Intelligence Directorate (GID), or Mukhabarat. While the precise direction of blame varied, the eruption of protests in 2010 and 2011 made clear that Jordanian patience had worn thin, as protesters took to the streets, demanding real change.

Hitting the Streets: Jordan's Arab Spring Protests

Jordan's Arab Spring demonstrations actually predated—by a few weeks— the larger mass movements that emerged in both Tunisia and Egypt. And even these were predated by an upsurge in labor activism and workers' rights protests.[11] So technically protests were actually under way in November and December 2010, but most of the drama, in Jordan and especially across the region, occurred in and after 2011. In the Jordanian case, however, demonstrations numbered in the hundreds and sometimes thousands (in a country of approximately seven million people). They thus never echoed the massive gatherings of millions in Egypt's Tahrir Square and elsewhere across Egypt. And unlike their counterparts in Tunisia and Egypt, most Jordanian protesters were more likely to call for reform, not revolution.[12]

In November and December 2010, before the regional Arab Spring emerged, Jordan's main Islamist party—the Islamic Action Front—along with the al-Wahda (Unity) Party, staged protests against the latest electoral law. They had boycotted the November 2010 elections over this issue, and while they were not calling for the fall of the regime, they were demanding substantive change in the form of new and more inclusive electoral laws, and also the restoration of a more constitutional monarchy. But even these demonstrations were soon outpaced by regional events, as Tunisian and Egyptian demonstrators poured into the streets in their countries demanding far more radical change, including the overthrow of their regimes.

Within Jordan, the year 2011 therefore began with street demonstrations in Amman and other cities across Jordan, inspired by the Tunisian and Egyptian revolutions and calling for reform but not necessarily regime change in the Hashemite Kingdom. The demonstrations actually began outside the capital, largely in East Bank and to some extent tribal Jordanian communities that had previously been thought of as bedrock supporters of the regime. Protests began in places like Dhiban, Tafilah, Ma'an, and Kerak. The anger and resentment that led to these demonstrations was palpable and had been growing for a very long time. They called for the ouster of the prime minister and his government but not for the toppling of the king. Yet there was an intensity to the demonstrations, and the calls for reform and change were quite serious.[13] Many even hoped that the king would lead the reform effort, and that their own grassroots efforts would "liberate" the king from an otherwise conservative old guard elite, giving him the space to lead efforts at genuine reform. Yet many conservative and antireform elites in the regime had similar, if opposite, hopes: that the king would thwart this latest round of reform efforts and grassroots activism. But the protests themselves were aimed as much against particular policies as they were against individuals. The vitriol against Prime Minister Samir al-Rifa'i was directed in large part against the overall neoliberal economic reform agenda. Demonstrators saw the prime minister as the latest in a line of neoliberal technocrats and identified him with unpopular programs for privatization that had undercut the social safety net in the kingdom, changing economic, social, and political dynamics.

Other protesters decried perceived corruption in state-led business transactions. This they blamed on the neoliberal economic reform process but also, at times, on specific individuals. Here protesters tread on a very thin and even dangerous line. Insulting the dignity of the king or a member of the royal family is a crime in Jordan under lèse-majesté laws. Most protests, and most protesters, steered clear of personal attacks on the king or queen for that reason. But those who did not had already crossed a long-established red line in Jordanian politics. Having crossed the line, these more virulent protesters sometimes saw no reason for additional restraint. Reporting on the first year of protests, veteran journalist Nicolas Pelham noted that "by regional standards, the turnout of protesters has been puny. Few rallies attract more than five thousand demonstrators; many are attended by only a few score. It is possible to visit the capital and not hear their cries. East as well as West Bankers appear reluctant to join a movement whose slogans are openly seditious. But what they lack in numbers, they compensate for in tenacity and depth."[14]

Most protests remained focused on reform within the prevailing system, but others would push the limits and red lines further. In the words of Marwan Muasher, one of Jordan's leading reform advocates: "Jordan has not seen large-scale demonstrations since the Arab uprisings began. But there are constant small ones. The occasions for protest have ranged from calls for a redistribution of power among the three branches of government to demands for social equality, more attention for rural areas outside the capital, and combatting corruption. Protests have focused on changes within the regime rather than on regime change."[15]

Most protests followed a fairly well-established script, as Jillian Schwedler has noted.[16] They remained relatively small in number; protesters gathered and marched in predictable routes, chanted for a matter of hours, and then dispersed, often to return the following week, after Friday prayers, to resume the protests. But in other parts of the Arab world, massive unrest in capitals had been predicated on longer-term protests, occupying central squares and encamping in the very center of busy capital cities. From Tahrir Square in Cairo to Pearl Roundabout in Manama, Bahrain, youth-led protest movements seemed intent on staying until change was secured. Such overnight occupy-style tactics have been rare in Jordan. But one exception to this began as perhaps the most promising prodemocracy demonstration of Jordan's Arab Spring era: the March 24 protest movement.

Jordan's March 24 (#Mar24) movement established itself in a central area of Amman: Gamal 'Abd al-Nasser Square, better known in Jordan as Dawar al-Dakhiliyya, or Interior Circle, since it was near the Ministry of the Interior. As an intersection of multiple Amman neighborhoods, streets, and major overpasses, the site was chosen because it was located in an area central to daily life in Amman. Protesters were decidedly patriotic. Their chants were prodemocracy, proreform, and also pro-Jordan. The traditional red-and-white-checked keffiyahs (head scarves often worn by men), often seen as a symbol of Transjordanian identity, were ubiquitous in the crowd, as were patriotic songs. Even today, many democracy advocates, especially youth activists, see that as a high point in Jordan's Arab Spring, soon to be followed by one of its lowest points.

The protesters were ultimately pelted with stones and then charged by pipe-wielding thugs, or *baltajiyya*, who, along with the police, dispersed the demonstrators. More than a hundred people were injured, and one protester died, apparently of heart failure. But the broader effect was chilling. For demonstrators who saw Jordan as the Arab exception, this seemed more like Egypt's infamous "Battle of the Camel" (in February 2011) in which plainclothes secret police and thugs astride donkeys and camels charged youth demonstrators in Tahrir Square. For many young activists, the March 25 attack on the March 24 movement was deeply demoralizing.[17] And since most assumed the thugs had been sent deliberately by the state, many felt it was a turning point suggesting that the monarchy was not with the reformers after all but had perhaps thrown its weight behind the more reactionary forces of the status quo.

Other demonstrations nonetheless followed. But many secular and liberal protesters began to withdraw, leaving much of the protest field to largely tribal East Bank youth activists known as Hirak, who often crossed previously untested red lines. Other protests featured mainly Islamist demonstrators affiliated with the Muslim Brotherhood. These two types of groups at times attempted to coordinate in particular locations but also in ensuring that a particular day's protests would take place not just in the capital but throughout the country. At other times they seemed to be at odds, in a complicated and delicate maneuvering of Jordan's resurgent issues with identity politics. It was more often the Hirak who could or simply would test red lines and regime patience.

The Hirak activists associated with Amman's Haya al-Tafilah neighborhood (which in turn is associated with the sometimes restive and economically marginalized town of Tafilah), were known in particular for their daring and perhaps recklessness in confronting the regime. Some activists from this group decried the king and his entourage as "Ali Baba and the forty thieves," with assorted chants to that effect. They also posted online their displeasure with the regime, accusing it of being the main source of corruption in Jordan.[18] Their challenges were at times direct and personal, crossing all previous red lines in more traditional government-opposition relations. Any activists suggesting that the king abdicate, calling for a republic, or who were deemed to have insulted the king or queen or royal family were arrested. In the town of Tafilah itself, protests were often similarly direct and confrontational. It was in Tafilah, for example, that protesters were rumored to have pelted the king's motorcade with rocks and bottles, although accounts of this alleged incident vary widely. Some suggest that there was a clash between young activists and the Jordanian gendarmerie (known in Jordan as the Darak) but that the king was miles away from the scene. Either way, this didn't fit the previous narrative of "bedrock support for the Hashemite regime."

When Hirak youth protests crossed these various red lines, they were in some ways echoing older generations that had themselves only recently done so. Even before the Arab uprisings, the National Committee for Retired Servicemen (NCRS) had issued a hard-hitting manifesto (*bayan rasmi*) to the regime that they had served, claiming it was antidemocratic, myopic, corrupt, and in danger of turning Jordan into the de facto Pales-tinian state or alternative homeland (*al-watan al-badil*). Similarly, a group of thirty-six tribal leaders issued their own manifesto (The *Bayan* of the 36), making almost identical charges. Both groups crossed previous red lines by attacking the regime directly and even charging that Queen Rania and her relatives were a major part of the problem.[19]

But the manifesto of the retired military officers was perhaps the big-gest rupture in terms of being the first major challenge to traditional red lines in protest against the state and its agenda. The officers called for change while condemning the regime's policy priorities, while tribal leaders railed against the allegedly intrusive role of the queen, even going so far as to compare her to deposed first ladies Leila Tarabulsi of Tunisia and Suzanne Mubarak of Egypt.[20] This was a particularly brazen challenge, and one that the king did not take lightly. But a key point is that public questioning, in this case in 2010, had begun before the Arab Spring protests, and many of these challenges would have been unthinkable in the era of King Hus-sein. For King Abdullah II, as one Jordanian analyst noted, "all his choices are contested; his choice of prime minister, his choice of crown prince, his choice of wife. All are contested."[21] While the two monarchs and their respective eras are indeed different, there is also the notable social and political difference of politics in the era of the internet and social media.

Still, the challenges from heretofore loyal bastions of regime support were striking. The retired military officers, in effect, opened the door for other challenges, for other manifestos, and indeed for the rise of the Hirak—often activists of similar backgrounds in terms of families, clans, and tribes but from different generations. Yet that, of course, is precisely why the retired officers' challenge represented such a startling and dramatic rup-ture from previous political norms in Jordanian politics: these challengers had spent their lives serving the state. They came from the most influential and historically loyal families and tribes. And their brazen critique of the regime was searing.[22] No other group could have gotten away with such a blatant challenge to the regime. But the retired officers were then, and are now, one of the most influential pressure groups in Jordanian politics. At a time when Jordanians complained of increasingly localized politics and even of inter- and intratribal conflicts, the retired officers represented mili-tary veterans and former security officials in a truly national sense, span-ning the major tribes and the various regions of the country and, of course, with roots in Jordan's powerful defense and security establishment. In a sense, then, this challenge came from within the key pillars of regime strength—the military and the tribes—developed and nurtured by King Abdullah I (1946–1951) and by King Hussein (1952–1999).

In each of these cases of opposition to the regime or its policies—that is, the military veterans, the group of thirty-six sheikhs, and the Hirak—the roots were in communities that felt increasingly betrayed by their own regime. Their previously unquestioned attachment to the regime was now clearly an open question. Each of these movements was rooted largely in Jordan's East Bank tribal communities. They were secular and nationalistic and generally distrustful of Islamist movements. But they also tended to see themselves as the builders of the Jordanian state. The bargain, for many of these activists, was that they, their families, and their communities all engaged in state service. They all served, and they expected the state to serve them as well, and at minimum to provide services and include them in decision making about those services. Some, especially among the older generations, couched their opposition in terms of identity politics, including their criticisms of the queen and her family.

There is a fairly ugly nativist version of this narrative, in which ultranationalists see themselves as having built Jordan, whereas Palestinians, no matter how long they have been in the kingdom, are still from Palestine, not Jordan. These elements have been described as everything from Jordanian Likud to a Jordanian "Tea Party movement" (comparing them to the ultraconservative U.S. movement of the same name). Jordan's identity politics are discussed in some detail in chapter 5. But these more chauvinistic and right-wing elements did not represent most Hirak activism, as most Hirak groups seemed to avoid this level of rhetoric, saving their vitriol not for Palestinians but for the regime itself, or at least for its policies.

Among the many Hirak movements across Jordan, the number of participants varied greatly. The Hirak were, after all, new to the Jordanian political scene. They did not amount to a single movement but rather involved a host of different organizations, varying in size, level of organization, and even agenda. In contrast, when Jordan's oldest opposition movement, the Muslim Brotherhood and its affiliated Islamist organizations, decided to display its numbers in protests, these could reach into the thousands rather than dozens or hundreds. In October 2012 the Islamist movement did just that, attempting to field the largest protest in modern Jordanian political history. Loyalists responded in kind, vowing to counter and even dwarf the Islamists in terms of turnout, on the same day and in the same location.

The demonstrations, led by the Muslim Brotherhood on the one hand and loyalists on the other, were to be competing shows of strength. Jordan's Public Security Directorate (PSD), the main national police force, had feared violent clashes between the two. So PSD representatives met repeatedly with organizers of the loyalist counterprotest, eventually persuading them to postpone their demonstration.

The PSD had, for the most part, maintained its policy of "soft security" toward Arab Spring demonstrations. Unlike their counterparts in other Arab states, Jordanian protesters were not met with volleys of gunfire or cut down by rooftop snipers. The PSD was proud of its record on the whole. But it expected demonstrators, in turn, to stick to agreed upon scripts regarding what was acceptable. One of the key exceptions to the PSD's record occurred on July 15, 2011, when police began beating protesters and activists and then turned on many of the journalists who were covering the event. While this was an exception to the more pervasive soft security approach preferred by the PSD, proreform activists routinely complained that every demonstration included a contingent of loyalists and sometimes *bultajiyya*. To make matters worse, they argued, these figures were often seen at demonstration after demonstration, conversing with police and security officials. Prodemocracy activists, in short, saw the two groups as working together and thus viewed the counterdemonstrations not as a mirror image of their own grassroots activism but rather as a carefully orchestrated part of the security state's approach to public protest. One prodemocracy activist who attended scores of protests noted:

> Some who go to counterprotest go as independent loyal Jordanians. But there is always a small loyalist group, marching ahead of the actual protest, and it is always the same people. They look like they are on parole. . . . They then discuss and chat on the ground with the police. They always coordinate with each other. There was even a counter-demonstration that chanted for *raising* gas prices. Some have also been seen carrying guns to the counterprotests, and the police don't stop them at all. Again, they are linked to the police.[23]

Proreform activists sometimes gave credit to the PSD for exercising restraint, but they also complained about geographically uneven approaches to policing. An activist who attended protests in multiple cities across the country, for example, argued that "the policing issue is disturbing, and it seems to reflect past regime development priorities: favoring Amman over other areas. So there is this over the top police presence in Amman. But in places like Kerak there is virtually none, because the police themselves are from the same families, clans, and tribes."[24] Jordanian security officials, for their part, reject this argument. Different levels of policing, they argue, are rooted in different-size populations. Hence Jordan's largest city and capital sees the largest policy presence while provincial cities and towns see considerably less.[25]

Still, protesters continued to gather, like clockwork, in proreform and anticorruption demonstrations every Friday in 2011 and 2012. But after months of smaller protests, usually numbering in the hundreds, Jordanians returned to the streets in much larger numbers for the Islamist-led rally to "Save the Nation" by turning to genuine reform before it was too late. The Muslim Brotherhood insisted that it would turn out fifty thousand people in the largest protest in Jordanian history, and that these would be drawn not just from the Islamist movement but from a variety of groups across the political spectrum. Before postponing their counterprotest, loyalist organizers had promised to field 200,000 people, in a competitive display of strength between the two movements. With the protest field to themselves, however, the Islamist-led demonstration produced perhaps fifteen thousand people. Loyalists jeered what they saw as a paltry turnout. But Islamists noted, correctly, that this was still a massive demonstration by Jordanian standards. It probably would have been seen as such if the Islamists themselves had not fixated on the specific number of fifty thousand. This also made the numbers and turnout, rather than the substance of the events, the main focus of media coverage.

Many in Jordan's state-linked media had also spent more than a week decrying the looming event as exclusively an Islamist affair, even though other groups and organizations participated. Still, the media onslaught, by reframing the event as Islamist-only, with a subtext that it was also perhaps a Palestinian demonstration, had created the usual pervasive worry that participation would be read as disloyalty and as opposition to national unity. In this context, many activist groups dropped out at the last minute, including labor unions, many Hirak popular movements, and the National Front for Reform, led by former prime minister Ahmad 'Ubaydat.[26] Nonetheless, the gathering of perhaps fifteen thousand people led Zaki Bani Irshayd, deputy secretary general of the Muslim Brotherhood, to declare that "the Jordanian spring has begun." Despite multiple attempts to thwart the protests or dilute their numbers, Bani Irshayd wrote, "the demonstration went ahead—the largest in the country's history—putting Jordan on the path of true reform. . . . Many in Jordan now speak of this demonstration as the beginning of the Jordanian spring."[27]

Irshayd, and the Islamist movement more broadly, rejected the regime's reform efforts as little more than posturing. They vowed to boycott the elections in 2013 and promised instead to stay in the streets until real reform was achieved. Irshayd himself, seen as something of a firebrand among the Islamist leadership, was arrested by the regime two years later, in 2015, not for street activism but for online comments in a Facebook post. The Islamist leader had criticized not the Jordanian regime per se but rather a key Jordanian ally—the United Arab Emirates. For an aid-dependent Jordan in the midst of a severe economic crisis, criticism of the UAE was deemed more subversive than direct physical protests within Jordan itself.

Street activism and other protests did continue, especially on Fridays, not only in Amman but across the country. The most jarring of these, however, took place in November 2012. If the October 2012 protests were the largest in the country's modern history, the November riots were the most direct challenge to the regime in the Arab Spring era. The trigger event, as in previous mass riots, such as those of 1989 and 1996, was economic austerity associated with an IMF economic adjustment and austerity program. This time, acting in accordance with IMF expectations, the government cut fuel subsidies, leading to an immediate hike in fuel prices. This included gas for home furnaces and even for cooking, and the price hikes came just as temperatures were dropping with the onset of winter. Riots spread to many cities and towns across the country, with clashes between rioters and police.

One protester was killed in an exchange of fire with police, and dozens of people—police and protesters alike—were injured across the country. Economic austerity may have triggered the riots, but they were also decidedly political. Some turned extreme, calling for the ouster of the king and blaming the monarchy for Jordan's chronically disastrous economic conditions.[28] Many Jordanians watched news reports on television, shocked at the level of rioting, with stones and Molotov cocktails flying in the air. Some were convinced that this was finally "it"—the Jordanian revolution had actually begun. Yet after several days of unrest, the protests dissipated, joining the legacy of the kingdom's most intense economic and political riots in modern times but ultimately producing no Jordanian revolution.

Many regime officials stress the economic aspects of unrest and anger in the country, but they often miss that Jordanians assign political blame as well. It is vital to get the depth of economic stress and insecurity that the great majority of Jordanians feel, but it would be a mistake to then see this as "just" about the economy. Every Jordanian protest decries corruption. Anticorruption was and is the single most pervasive and even unifying aspect of opposition in the kingdom, even more than antiausterity or prore-form or prodemocracy sentiments. So the political question is whom the public associates with corruption. Whom do people blame for these condi-tions, and for yet another round of belt-tightening and austerity? Almost all point to government officials. Some, more radically perhaps, blame the monarch and the monarchy. Some turn the issue into an identity politics matter, blaming neoliberal Palestinian-Jordanian technocrats. But some also come close to reversing that, insisting that the age-old East Jordanian tribal-based elite, including the vast intelligence and security services, are at the heart of the matter, by maintaining an outdated entitlement state for themselves.

The bottom line here is that ordinary Jordanians resent having to make severe economic sacrifices that they simply can't afford, especially if they are convinced that the rich and powerful who dominate the state are making no such concessions themselves. As one Jordanian analyst put it, "Ramadan is coming. Some will fast for God. Some will fast with no choice and are just going hungry." He continued: "We are going backward. The status quo is untenable. If we don't introduce changes we will pay a price. They came to the conclusion that the Arab Spring stopped in Syria. They think the Arab Spring is through, and they think the reform movement here is small. . . . So what to do? Reform. Concede some power. Don't rig elec-tions. People can handle even rough economic times, but not if they think it is the fault of the state."[29]

Countless Jordanians would agree with that assessment. This is why, even with deep economic roots, Jordan's crisis would ultimately postdate the Arab Spring and would continue to be marked by a lack of faith in the system itself and a fairly pervasive belief that inequality (not just in an eco-nomic sense) as well as injustice and unfairness are unacceptable yet rou-tine aspects of Jordanian public life. It takes just a small spark to set off that kind of depth of feeling and of despair regarding prospects for change. It is also for that reason that genuine reform is essential.

Yet as the Arab Spring wore on, even with the violent uprising of November 2012, regime officials and regime loyalists seemed noticeably more comfortable, noticeably more certain that they had survived the unrest after all. Opposition groups too began to pull back. Even Jordan's Muslim Brotherhood distanced itself from the November riots. They made clear repeatedly that they were for reform and a constitutional monarchy but not for the calls heard in some of these riots for regime change. Other opposition groups also seemed jolted by the vehemence on display in many of the riots, and they too backed off and tempered their use of language. Reform, not revolution, would be the watchword.

To the relief of many in the regime, after days of riots, the protests subsided almost as quickly as they had started. Yet for many in Jordan's opposition, and indeed many Jordanians across the political spectrum, including even many regime supporters, the fragility embodied in moments like the November 2012 riots suggested that the status quo had thus far survived but was not ultimately sustainable. To do more than just survive the next crisis, Jordan would have to engage in meaningful reform. To survive and even to prosper, in short, Jordan would have to change. Opposition forces called for large-scale changes in governance, representation, and policy, but many state responses were more short term and reactive to the dramatic events of the Arab Spring protests. Most noticeable among these state reactions was the tumultuous turnover in governments, as prime ministers and cabinets rose and fell rapidly in the early years of the Arab Spring.

State Responses and a Revolving Door of Governments

Part of the "story" of Jordan and the Arab Spring is about grassroots activism and protest movements, to be sure. But it is also a story of top-down attempts at perhaps minimal reform, with sometimes profound differences even at the top echelons of the ruling elite regarding the depth of necessary concessions. Should the regime resist pressures, including those from street demonstrators, for greater change, inclusion, and government accountability? Or should it heed King Abdullah's own comments and grasp the Arab Spring as an opportunity finally to push through changes that had stalled or languished since the earlier round of reformism in the 1989–1993 period? There are genuinely reform-minded people in Jordan's government, palace, and bureaucracy, but there is also no shortage of conservatives resisting reform, nor of absolute reactionaries. While reform elements looked to the king for signs that this time they could indeed proceed, reactionary elements argued for battening the hatches and girding Jordan for a political storm of hurricane-like proportions. As protests spread across Jordan in December 2010 and early 2011, many Jordanian officials assumed that minimal concessions would follow, but only after the protests had settled down. Yet the protests showed no sign of respite, and in February the king surprised even some in the ruling elite by moving quickly to dismiss the Rifa'i government that he had only recently appointed.

What followed was a succession of short-lived governments under a series of new prime ministers (see table 2.1). In repeatedly sacking prime ministers and governments, the monarchy was in many ways following a long-standing tradition in Jordanian politics, and one that many Jordanians find decidedly unconvincing in terms of degrees of change. In a fairly scathing assessment of this practice, the *Economist* quoted a Western diplomat, saying, "In Jordan prime ministers are there to be sacked." Prime ministers, it notes, are often "'a buffer, a shock absorber,' between the people and the king. In the past half-century they have lasted barely a year."[30] Similarly, the International Crisis Group has suggested that "heads of government are a valuable buffer between the monarch and the public at times of discontent."[31] During the first nineteen months of the Arab Spring, Jordan saw five different governments and five different prime ministers. The Rifa'i government had just begun its second term in office when the Arab Spring arrived, and it barely lasted another two months. Its replacement, the government of Prime Minister Ma'rouf al-Bakhit, lasted only from February to October 2011.

TABLE 2.1
Jordanian Prime Ministers and Governments During the Arab Spring

Prime Minister	Term
Samir al-Rifa'i	October 2010–February 2011
Ma'rouf al-Bakhit	February 2011–October 2011
'Awn al-Khasawneh	October 2011–May 2012
Fayez Tarawneh	May 2012–October 2012
Abdullah an-Nsour	October 2012–June 2016

Jordanian protestors had been calling for serious anticorruption efforts and for deeper levels of democratic reform. What they got, in Prime Minister Bakhit, was a politician who was more of a throwback to an earlier Jordan. Bakhit was a conservative, East Jordanian political veteran—in more ways than one. He was a former army general and a member of the very influential Abbadi tribe. He had also been prime minister before, presiding over one of the most disparaged elections in modern Jordanian history in 2007. From a corruption-laced casino deal to the embarrassingly failed elections of 2007, the earlier Bakhit government was almost the antithesis of what protesters were actually asking for. But he may also have been the exact kind of reassuring figure that more conservative East Jordanians were looking for.

Bakhit's occasional reemergence at the top of the Jordanian political scene has tended to coincide with moments of extreme insecurity for the regime. His earlier tenure, for example, had come in the wake of the worst terrorist attack in Jordanian history. On November 9, 2005, terrorists affiliated with al-Qa'ida in Iraq carried out suicide bombings at three luxury hotels in the Jordanian capital. The Amman bombings killed almost sixty people, injured hundreds, and traumatized the entire country. Enter Bakhit, from a strong tribal background and a long career in the military and intelligence services. When he took office after the bombings, many understood the signal of a military officer taking charge of government at a time of severe insecurity. But in 2011 the signal seemed almost tone deaf. From the military and intelligence background to the previous record in terms of corruption and hostility toward reform, the new prime minister certainly did not represent the reform and change that so many Jordanians were hoping for.

But as instability and varying degrees of unrest continued, so too did the revolving door of governments and prime ministers. In October 2011 the king dismissed Bakhit and appointed a new prime minister—'Awn al-Khasawneh. Khasawneh came from a very different mold indeed. He was not actually a politician at all but rather a highly regarded and internationally known judge on the International Court of Justice. A strong proponent of democratic reform and the rule of law, Khasawneh seemed to be committed to wiping out corruption—which was, of course, one of the chief demands of all protesters, of all backgrounds and ideologies. In his letter of designation to the prime minister, the king charged him with the critical role of revising the kingdom's problematic electoral laws and overseeing a series of amendments to the constitution. Khasawneh's government would also oversee the establishment, for the first time in Jordan, of an independent electoral commission charged with modernizing and cleaning up the registration and voting process in the country.

Khasawneh took his role very seriously, but he almost immediately riled many antireform hard-liners in the regime and soon found himself at odds with the king himself. He took his role so seriously, in fact, that he acted as a prime minister in the more traditional sense of a constitutional monarchy. That is, he acted independently of the monarch and pursued policy as if sovereign authority lay with the government. He had been appointed; the letter of designation was clear. Now he expected the palace to let him do his job without interference. More important, he expected to govern without the seemingly constant interference of the intelligence services. The enormous and intrusive role of the Mukhabarat was, in fact, something that most Jordanians opposed—from street demonstrators, to reformers both within the regime and without, to the prime minister himself.[32]

Khasawneh emphasized that his government would be "reform-oriented," and that "I will reform it myself with no interference from any party whatsoever."[33] Nonetheless, the struggle between state institutions began immediately. Khasawneh argued that the palace and GID were interfering with daily governance and making his job nearly impossible. The king, for his part, argued that Khasawneh was dragging his feet on completing the reform process. Matters came to a head quickly. A mere six months after taking office, Khasawneh took the unprecedented move of resigning—in May 2012—while abroad on a state visit to Turkey. The abrupt fall of the Khasawneh government was deeply demoralizing for many democracy activists. One, still stung by the unexpected turn of events, felt it marked the end of Jordan's Arab Spring. "We are lost," he said, "Everyone here is lost. The opposition. The regime. Everyone."[34]

Khasawneh's short and tumultuous tenure had clearly inspired many democracy and reform activists by suggesting that they were being heard and that the state was finally responding to their concerns. Many of those who had been appalled at the appointment of Bakhit were genuinely excited at the prospect for the Khasawneh government. His appointment suggested that the palace had indeed heard the calls for reform and for a genuine departure from business as usual in Jordan. Yet the honeymoon period lasted barely six months. Like many of his predecessors, Khasawneh's tenure therefore proved short lived. The pendulum of Jordanian politics, in fact, seemed to swing back in the opposite direction, as Prime Minister Khasawneh was immediately replaced by a conservative, veteran politician and former prime minister, Fayez Tarawneh.

Like Bakhit, Tarawneh had served as prime minister before and had also assumed key posts at critical times of transition in Jordanian politics. Specifically, Tarawneh had previously served as prime minister during another critical moment—the 1999 transition in the monarchy from King Hussein to King Abdullah. He was a longtime member of the Jordanian Senate and had held a host of key positions in the Jordanian government and foreign service. He had, for example, served as foreign minister, as Jordan's ambassador to the United States, and as chief of the Royal Hashemite Court. Tarawneh came from a powerful and influential family and tribe in Kerak and was regarded as a stalwart conservative. Just as many read the Khasawneh appointment as a proreform signal from the monarchy, many accordingly read the Tarawneh appointment as precisely the opposite and a sign that the veteran or old-guard elite remained very much in power in the kingdom.

Yet Tarawneh's second stint as prime minister also turned out to be brief, as the revolving door of government continued to spin. Tarawneh was dismissed as prime minister after five months but in many ways was elevated in power by becoming once again chief of the Royal Court. The Tarawneh government was replaced by a new one led by former minister and member of parliament Abdullah an-Nsour. Nsour was therefore the fifth prime minister of Jordan since the start of the regional Arab Spring. He was a veteran politician who had previously been elected twice to parliament, appointed twice to the Senate, and served in numerous cabinet posts including holding, at different times, the ministerial portfolios for foreign affairs, planning, media, trade, and investment.

As much of a veteran politician as he was, Nsour nonetheless also had a reputation as an independent thinker, with some significant credibility as an advocate for at least some level of democratic reform and as an outspoken critic of corruption in government. He was generally viewed as neither as liberal as Khasawneh nor as conservative as Tarawneh or Bakhit. Nsour's appointment was greeted with cautious optimism in reform circles and even with some surprise, since many media outlets had reported for weeks that another regime veteran, the more conservative Faisal Fayez, would be the appointee. Nsour was one of the few reformist voices in the recently dissolved parliament, and he had opposed the controversial electoral law that he was now charged with implementing.[35]

Continuity and Change

For Jordan, the early years of the Arab Spring seemed to suggest—at least initially—that profound levels of change might be on the way. Protesters' demands had been extensive but mostly reformist rather than revolutionary. But they were also real, and at times they crossed previously established red lines and demanded radical changes in Jordanian politics and governance. The winds of change had not, therefore, swept past Jordan. Jordan hadn't "missed" the Arab Spring. Rather, the Arab Spring had simply taken, at least for the moment, a more reformist turn. While protests certainly pre-dated the Arab Spring, the level, intensity, and even diversity of protest movements across Jordan was significant and suggested the largest level of social and political mobilization that Jordan had seen since the days of the April 1989 "Jordanian Intifada."

Jordan's Arab Spring had from 2011 to 2013 featured routine levels of protest and demonstrations across the country, with the state responding with various reform initiatives (discussed in later chapters) and with a seeming revolving door of governments. Prime ministers and governments rose and fell rapidly. Even by Jordanian standards, five prime ministers and five governments in two years was a rapid rate of turnover and served as an indication of the level of instability generated by widespread social mobilization and political protest, as governments and the regime cast about for appropriate responses to public demands.

On the other hand, the overall pattern of relatively peaceful protests and government responses fit with the broader trajectory of Jordanian political history. By 2013 that pattern seemed to have settled down, as Prime Minister Nsour stopped the revolving door and managed to serve a full four years in office. Nsour steered Jordan through another round of controversial new electoral laws, constitutional amendments, and elections. But his government also seemed to mark the end of the earlier, more tumultuous era of the regional Arab Spring. By as early as 2013, in fact, the pace of change had slowed to a crawl, and many Jordanians, both for and against reform, were deeply concerned with the instability and violence of their neighbors, and with the fear that these dynamics might spill over into Jordan.

Yet even years after the Arab Spring, Jordan continued to face the same questions that had led to the 2011 demonstrations in the first place. These included demands that the state engage in a more meaningful reform process, dealing seriously with corruption, and increasing pluralism, inclusion, and civil liberties in the kingdom, while also addressing a more equitable and inclusive distribution of resources and economic opportunities. Even years after the protests of the Arab Spring, Jordan's economy was, if anything, in even worse condition and essentially in a state of continuous fiscal crisis.

Protests continued, albeit not at the same pace or scale that had characterized 2011–2012. The list of reform demands was long, and at times even opposition forces seemed to pull in opposite directions, while state officials ranged from reformists to reactionaries. Like its politics of protests, Jordan's struggles over reform were not brand new, but the stakes seemed to be particularly high in the era of the Arab uprisings, especially with regions ablaze all around the kingdom.

From the perspective of opposition forces, the key was not just influencing the regime to adopt more significant change but also mobilizing grassroots support and creating a meaningful and effective opposition coalition, one characterized by unity and not succumbing to its own fissures and divisions. The next two chapters examine these key opposition dynamics.

CHAPTER III

Political Parties and the "Traditional" Opposition

The Arab uprisings underscored the varying levels of political opposition in every Arab country, as activists mobilized in protests and
demonstrations. The Arab Spring gave rise to new forms of activism and political mobilization, but it also energized older and more "traditional" forms of opposition. Within Jordanian politics, opposition forces
have historically organized as political parties, even when these were illegal.
Some of these movements are almost as old as the Hashemite regime itself,
dating to the early postindependence period or what many see as the heyday
of opposition party politics in the 1950s. This chapter examines the traditional party-based opposition before, during, and after the Arab uprisings,
and in particular the potential for opposition unity in efforts to press the
regime for greater levels of reform and change.

The topics of political opposition and activism in Jordan are sufficiently
large in scope, however, to warrant two chapters. In this one I will examine Jordan's traditional opposition forces, especially in the form of the
Islamist movement and leftist and Pan-Arab nationalist political parties,
and in chapter 4 I will expand this analysis beyond the traditional opposition toward newer forms of grassroots opposition activism in Jordanian
politics. In both cases, the emphasis is on continuity and change as a result
of the Arab uprisings.

Opposition politics, activism, and protests in Jordan can in many respects
be divided between those before and after 1989. From independence in 1946

to 1989, protest within the kingdom tended to be rooted in Palestinian nationalist movements, leftist and Pan-Arab nationalist parties (especially the communist, Nasserist, and Ba'thist movements), and the Muslim Brotherhood. While the leftist and Pan-Arab nationalist groups dominated opposition discourse in the 1950s and 1960s, the end of the Arab Cold War and the beginnings of an Islamist revival across the region affected Jordan too, leading to a relative decline of the left and the corresponding steady rise of the Muslim Brotherhood as a force in Jordanian politics.[1]

Each of these groups remains active today, and together they constitute the traditional opposition in the kingdom. While the leftist and nationalist forces have dwindled to ever smaller numbers, based in tiny and largely ineffective political parties, Jordan's vast Islamist movement remains a force in the form of not one but two Muslim Brotherhoods, with enormous influence in the kingdom's professional associations as well as in its own political party, the Islamic Action Front (IAF). These leftist and Islamist groups are often rivals, but Jordan's earlier round of unrest and reform (1989–1993) saw moments of unity and alliance across ideological lines, so that Jordan's opposition at such moments suddenly seemed to be a formidable and diverse force rather than a diffuse and divided set of rival opposition movements. In addition, Jordan has seen a steady rise in membership and activism by even more hardline Islamists in the form of the growing Salafi movement in the kingdom.[2] This chapter will concentrate on reformist and democratic activism in Jordanian politics, but it is noteworthy that militant and jihadi forms of Salafi activism have also been on the rise, especially in the shadow of the Syrian civil war and the emergence in Syria and Iraq of the militant "Islamic State."[3]

Jordanian politics has, in fact, seen decades of proreform and prodemocracy political activism, but with little effective change on the Jordanian political system itself. As documented here and in chapter 2, there is no shortage of antireform resistance on the part of many elites within the regime and across society. Even reformers within the regime and across state institutions complain routinely about the reactionary politics of "old-guard" forces or institutions such as the Mukhabarat. But lack of success in implementing reform and achieving progressive change cannot entirely be the fault of a government or regime. It is also a question of unified and effective opposition.

The ingredients for a broad-ranging and even unified reform coalition exist in Jordanian politics, and since 1989 we have seen numerous attempts at creating such coalitions against authoritarian policies. Yet despite their efforts at unity and activism, opposition forces and proreform activists have had little success in achieving meaningful political change. The regime has long used structural and institutional means (especially through the ever-changing laws regarding elections, parties, and parliamentary participation) to check and contain the power of opposition forces. It has also tended to use a divide-and-rule strategy, splitting opposition forces along the lines of the many fissures in Jordanian society—between Palestinians and Jordanians, leftists and Islamists, and even different tendencies within the Islamist movement itself—and thus rendering difficult, if not impossible, any effective opposition coordination. The opposition has also managed quite often to splinter and divide itself, even without state prodding.

In the sections below, I first examine the traditional opposition in the form of opposition political parties and consider the successes and failures of these forces in gaining political power and influence over the decision-making process through the ballot box.[4] It is in this context also that efforts by the country's traditional opposition at forging cross-ideological/cross-party cooperation will be explored. The chapter then turns to opposition in Jordan in the context of the Arab uprisings, and finally to what post–Arab Spring political opposition looks like in Jordan, and what this may suggest for the emergence of new forms of democratic opposition and potentially a new reform coalition in Jordanian politics.

Opposition Parties and Electoral Politics

Much of the traditional locus of opposition in Jordan has been the country's legal political parties. Yet Jordan's party system, aside from the Islamist movement, is notoriously weak. Political parties were illegal in the kingdom for more than thirty years, until the Jordanian regime reestablished elections for parliament in 1989 after a long hiatus and legalized political parties in 1991.[5] Many in the opposition welcomed the return of parties, elections, and more active parliamentary life as a return to the more vibrant politics of the 1950s.[6] Many party activists also complain of the chronic weakness of Jordan's modern political parties and party system, which they see as being in marked contrast to that earlier era. Yet as Ellen Lust has demonstrated, this historical image may not actually be true.[7] Parties and party systems are indeed weak in Jordan, yet that was also the case in the

1950s. In short, parties and the party system were weak then, and they are even weaker now.

What has changed, however, is the reversal in fortunes across the ideological spectrum. Even if the parties themselves did not command large segments of voters, the earlier liberalization period saw weak Islamist parties competing with then-ascendant leftist parties in the heyday of Pan-Arabism, with Pan-Arab nationalist, Ba'thist, socialist, and communist parties all competing for votes. In the 1950s the secular left and Pan-Arabist parties competed not only with the then-small Islamist movement but also mostly with each other. In short, cross-ideological alliances between parties were rare. In the post-1989 period, the reverse is true. The Islamist movement—in the form of the Jordanian Muslim Brotherhood (MB) and its legal party the Islamic Action Front—has been the most popular and best organized of the opposition forces, while the parties of the left remain to some extent in the shadow of the Islamists, competing for far smaller segments of the electorate.

This shift in hegemony within the Jordanian party system—from the secular left to religious right—reflects broader trends across the Middle East from the 1950s to the present. As Jillian Schwedler and Janine Clark have noted, the entire region (especially from the 1970s onward) saw an ideological transformation featuring the rise not only of Islamist movements but also of moderation and accommodation between the secular left and religious right, in which parties and movements that once seemed diametrically opposed found some elements of common ground, leading to previously unthinkable alliances and coalitions in Arab politics.[8] Michaelle Browers has reached similar conclusions, arguing that "the relationship among competing ideologies of opposition in the contemporary Arab region is best characterized as accommodationist, with strategic alliances forming among more pragmatic and moderate wings of otherwise opposed ideological factions of marginalized groups."[9]

In the Jordanian case, this transformation led leftist parties to work more often with, rather than against, the Islamist movement, and, just as important, it led them to abandon many intraleft rivalries to work with one another. Some of the longest-standing leftist parties in Jordanian politics include the Jordanian Communist Party (JCP), the People's Democratic Party (PDP, better known as Hashed and linked to the Democratic Front for the Liberation of Palestine), the Popular Unity Party (PUP, linked to the Popular Front for the Liberation of Palestine), and two Jordanian Arab

Socialist Ba'ath parties (one historically with links to Syria and one to Iraq). Yet in the post-1989 era, perhaps because of their small size, these parties were far more likely to try to cooperate and ally with one another than was the case in the 1950s and 1960s, when domestic political parties often rivaled one another, in effect reproducing domestically the external ideological conflicts of inter-Arab regional politics and the "Arab Cold War."[10] After the restoration of parliamentary elections in Jordan in 1989, however, these leftist and Pan-Arab nationalist parties—even combined— tended to garner far less popular support (in terms of either membership or voters) than a Muslim Brotherhood–affiliated political party like the IAF.[11]

Jordan's Muslim Brotherhood is actually as old as the Hashemite monarchy itself. Unlike its counterparts in Syria or Egypt (before the Arab uprisings of 2011), the Jordanian Muslim Brotherhood enjoyed a more cooperative relationship with the state as a loyal opposition organization that accepted the legitimacy of its Hashemite rulers. And unlike Hamas, the Jordanian MB has no militant wing and instead focuses on democratic activism, and on organizing through a civilian party (the IAF), membership in professional associations, and extensive charity work.[12] For most of its history, the Jordanian MB was a fairly broad movement that included different wings, usually seen as "hawkish" or "dovish" in their approaches to elections, participation, and cooperation with the regime itself. More militant Qutbist Islamists or ultraconservative (but historically avoiding participation entirely) Salafi strains of Islamism have, however, generally appeared outside the framework of the Jordanian Muslim Brotherhood.[13]

Given their long history of organization and activism, Jordan's Islamists were well placed for electoral success once the liberalization process began in 1989. Since then, Jordan has held multiple rounds of national parliamentary elections, with changes to the electoral law and hence to the rules of the game every time. In the first of these elections, in 1989, an assortment of leftist party candidates secured together a mere thirteen of the eighty seats in parliament, while the Muslim Brotherhood and independent Islamists garnered thirty-four seats.[14] Together, however, these opposition parliamentarians constituted a majority and used their numbers to elect an Islamist leader, Dr. 'Abd al-Latif al-'Arabiyyat, speaker of parliament.

Surprised and dismayed at the success of the Islamists in particular, the regime quickly moved to change the parliamentary electoral rules from the "bloc vote" system, whereby voters have as many votes as there are seats in a given district, to a "one-person, one-vote" system, hoping this would forestall similar opposition inroads in future elections. Indeed, it was assumed that, left with only one vote to cast, voters would place family and kinship ties above ideological considerations in their choice of candidates, thus diminishing the electoral prospects of Islamist contestants.[15] As intended by the regime, the revised electoral system produced a marked reversal of fortunes for Islamist and leftist parties in the 1993 election, reducing their representation, respectively, to twenty-two and seven out of eighty parliamentary seats.[16] Following the electoral debacle in 1993, and in what would become a recurring theme, opposition parties decided to boycott the elections of 1997 entirely, demanding a change in the electoral law.[17] The resultant 1997–2001 legislature was thus made up almost entirely of loyalist and conservative tribal elites, while opposition forces remained effectively unrepresented in parliament until the next elections in 2003.

Following the royal succession from King Hussein to King Abdullah II in 1999, parliament was dissolved, but new elections—expected in 2001— were delayed for two full years to 2003, due mainly to the regime's security concerns amid regional turmoil. These regional conflicts included the Palestinian uprising against Israeli rule in the West Bank and Gaza in 2000 and the U.S. invasions of Afghanistan in 2001 and Iraq in 2003. But in 2003 the elections were finally held under yet another electoral law. The new law increased the number of parliamentary seats from 80 to 104, with the introduction of new (but still uneven) electoral districts, and added six more parliamentary seats in a specific quota for women's representation. Held in June that year, the elections themselves returned some opposition representation to the Jordanian legislature, with seventeen seats going to the IAF, including one to Hayat al-Musayni, its first female candidate. Five independent Islamists were also elected.[18]

Despite the return of the opposition to parliament in 2003, struggles between the regime and opposition parties continued to center around electoral reform, with the latter demanding the abolition of the one-person, one-vote system and the redrawing of electoral districts, all of which had been designed to curb the potential power of opposition parties. By 2007, however, the regime was even less inclined to respond to opposition demands and seemed in fact to be highly concerned with electoral successes of Islamist movements elsewhere in the region, from Hamas in Palestine to Hizbullah in Lebanon. With these security concerns in mind, the 2007 elections, presided over by then–prime minister Ma'rouf al-Bakhit

(2005–2007), were perhaps the most egregiously rigged contests of the post-1989 period. The regime had been especially alarmed by the al-Qa'ida terrorist attacks in Amman in 2005 and by the electoral success of Hamas in the Palestinian territories in 2006 and seemed determined to prevent Islamist inroads at all costs.[19] That strategy may have worked, with Islamist candidates winning a mere 6 out of 110 parliamentary seats, but it also undermined the legitimacy of the electoral process and of the resultant parliament itself. Even the monarchy seemed eventually to acknowledge this legitimacy deficit, as it later dismissed the entire parliament two years before the completion of its term.

With new elections scheduled for 2010, the regime yet again introduced minor amendments to the parliamentary electoral law, without, however, changing the actual voting system as demanded by the opposition.[20] As in the past, the elections were conducted on a one-person, one-vote basis, prompting the IAF to boycott the poll. Most leftist parties, in contrast, chose to participate in the elections, but with almost no success. In fact, not a single opposition party candidate won a seat outright in the new parliament. The only exceptions were Abla Abu Elbeh, the secretary general of the leftist Hashed Party, who secured a seat as one of the twelve MPs elected on the women's quota. Similarly, Wafa Bani Mustafa, who at the time was seen as moderately Islamist but who was perhaps better seen as simply an independent candidate, was elected after she defied the IAF boycott and won a women's quota seat.[21]

As this discussion has illustrated, opposition parties have since 1989 had limited success in securing representation in the Jordanian parliament. Leftist parties have been particularly ineffective, leading one democracy activist to dismiss them as "somehow Left without being progressive. They are old Left. Just oppositionist as a career. They still act like they are an opposition in exile. They don't know how to work inside the system, even when they are in it."[22] The Islamist movement, on the other hand, had a larger popular following, was better organized, and had greater success in past elections but still regarded the various electoral laws as specifically aimed at minimizing Islamist representation, power, and influence in the Jordanian legislature.[23] For more than two decades, regime and opposition parties were at loggerheads over the rules of the electoral game, with the latter pressing for a return to a bloc vote system or (even better) a shift to a proportional representation (PR) system based on party lists. Opposition parties on the political left and right insisted that they remained weak precisely because of Jordan's various electoral laws, but they struggled to form an effective, unified, cross-ideological opposition coalition.

Opposition Parties and Cross-Ideological Cooperation

The literature on cross-ideological cooperation in the Middle East suggests that leftist-Islamist cooperation and alliances are indeed more likely in the contemporary period than at any time in the past; yet scholars differ on how viable, effective, or durable such alliances and coalitions can be in Arab politics. While Browers has argued for the importance of cross-ideological cooperation trends in the region, Cavatorta has challenged this, noting the difficulties in practice of actually achieving cooperation, especially in the cases of Morocco and Tunisia.[24] The Jordanian case actually illustrates both trends: attempts at greater leftist-Islamist cooperation, for example, but also limitations to effective opposition coordination or unity.[25]

Within Jordan, despite differences in ideological and even religious orientation, opposition parties of all shades actually agree on several key political issues, thereby providing a plausible basis for unified action and the formation of broad-based reform coalitions. Most have been sharply critical of the peace treaty with Israel, for example. They have demanded that the regime cease normalizing relations with Israel, and some even demand the abolition of the treaty itself.[26] Within domestic politics and policy, the country's opposition parties also insist that future prime ministers and cabinets should be drawn from parliament in a truer model of a parliamentary system, rather than royally appointed, pending only the formality of parliamentary approval, and, most crucially, they spent decades demanding major changes in the electoral laws.

Despite this unified set of opposition demands toward the Hashemite regime's policies, and in contrast to regime–opposition dynamics elsewhere in the region, especially after 2011, opposition parties focused mainly on public policy and the direction of the state (including demands for democratic reform) and rarely challenged the state itself as a Hashemite monarchy. Yet Jordan's various opposition parties and movements have often found themselves more likely to agree on foreign policy issues rather than on domestic ones, especially regarding the situation in the Palestinian territories and Iraq.[27] Anti-imperial and anti-Zionist themes have tended to pervade the discourse of secular and religious opposition parties alike, for example. Indeed, regional political issues have on many occasions united not only the opposition but also many current or past regime elites themselves. The U.S. invasion of Iraq in 2003, for example, was opposed by state and society in Jordan, regime and opposition alike, albeit to varying degrees. Ninety well-known Jordanian political figures even signed a public petition, presented to the king, condemning the U.S. war as aggression and in effect putting the monarchy itself on notice not to soften its opposition to the invasion, regardless of the depth of the U.S.-Jordanian alliance.[28]

These patterns among opposition parties changed radically during the Arab uprisings, however, as Jordan's traditional opposition forces suddenly found themselves differing profoundly on foreign policy issues. They remained opposed to the peace treaty with Israel, and they remained harsh critics of the U.S.-Jordanian alliance, and of imperial powers in general. But they divided sharply over the Arab uprisings and specifically the civil war in Syria. While the Muslim Brotherhood and other Islamist movements opposed the Asad regime in that war, leftist and Pan-Arab nationalist parties were more likely to support the secular Asad regime especially against Islamist rebels and Salafi Jihadist movements. As the war worsened and dragged on for years, the gap between secular and Islamist opposition forces continued to widen. As one democracy activist, who, like many younger activists, was critical of both the traditional left and Islamists, put it:

There is also a certain sense of waiting for what will happen in Syria. It divided the opposition. Some of the Jordanian opposition backed Bishar, because he and they take an anti-U.S., anti-Israel, and anticapitalist stance. This includes the old socialist Ba'athists or Arab left. Their main focus isn't necessarily prodemocracy but antiprivatization and Jordanian foreign policy. . . . The Secularists are sometimes so terrified that they end up supporting an authoritarian regime, while the Islamist discourse links secularism and liberalism, as though Ben Ali and Mubarak were liberal.[29]

Still, this was a major departure from past stances among opposition parties, when they were more likely to agree on foreign rather than domestic policy.

Besides general agreement on foreign policy issues that they have almost no hope of affecting, and some convergence on domestic reform demands, could opposition parties agree on key issues and perhaps work together as a broader reform coalition in pressuring the regime into liberalizing reforms? The record for political opposition in Jordan shows that opposition parties and independent activists have at times splintered and at times worked together. In her analyses of political activism in Jordan and elsewhere in the Arab world, Ellen Lust has emphasized the importance of context and structures between government and opposition. We can expect opposition to increase during economic crises, for example, but will this opposition work together or in competition? Lust argues that the answer depends on whether the regime itself has excluded all opposition or divided its opponents between loyalist and radical camps. In the former case, opposition parties should be expected to coalesce against the state, whereas in the latter, the divide-and-rule regime stratagem should be expected to work.

Prior to the 1989 liberalization process in Jordan, all political parties were illegal, and hence all were excluded from the system, even though the regime had a decades-long understanding with the Muslim Brotherhood so that the latter operated as essentially a loyal opposition. But as the economic crisis of 1989 hit, opposition forces from the secular left and the religious right were able to mobilize together to push the regime toward greater reform.[30] Elites from these and other opposition elements, along with conservative royalist forces, participated in the 1989 elections that followed, and later in the 1991 crafting of the National Charter (al-Mithaq al-Watani). The charter attempted to clarify the relationship between regime and opposition, allowing for legal opposition activism and greater pluralism in public life, in return for loyalty to the Hashemite monarchy. The National Charter was not so much a legal code as a general set of guidelines, however, as it did not have the force of law. It is therefore better seen as a framing document intended to establish new norms and parameters for loyalty and opposition in Jordanian politics.

But the shift in electoral rules prior to the 1993 election undercut opposition strength in parliament, paving the way for the regime to make peace with Israel, without an opposition majority in parliament blocking ratification of the accords. The regime's move to curb parliamentary opposition, however, only led to greater opposition coordination both inside and outside parliament itself.

A first step toward cooperation in the new multiparty era was taken in 1993, when leftist and Islamist parties held a joint press conference to protest the latest electoral law in the kingdom.[31] Cross-ideological cooperation among opposition groups increased in 1995, when the IAF and seven left-ist parties formed the Anti-Normalization Committee. While the opposition had failed to block the signing of a peace treaty with Israel, this committee was determined to prevent any normalization of relations between various sectors of the two societies.[32] In addition, the committee called for greater political liberalization and domestic reform. The regime's response, however, was quite the opposite, as it moved to repress dissent and counter the opposition bloc.

Regime hostility seemed to help further unite the opposition coalition, which expanded later in 1995 to include thirteen opposition parties through the Higher Committee for the Coordination of National Opposition Parties (HCCNOP). The committee was intended, then and now, to be a forum bringing together all opposition parties in an effort to coordinate and pool their efforts for reform and democratization. As will become apparent below, while the HCCNOP remained the most prominent party-driven reform coalition in the country, numerous additional groups, organizations, and coalitions—often with overlapping membership—had emerged on the Jordanian political scene since the 1990s. Although varying in number and composition, these additional forces should not necessarily be seen as rival or replacement organizations to the HCCNOP but rather as multiple and mutually reinforcing efforts at opposition coordination in the kingdom.

In 1996 yet another economic crisis—and another IMF austerity program—led the HCCNOP to call for a rejection of the IMF measures, especially the lifting of subsidies on bread and other staple foods. In the bread riots that followed, the opposition coalition maintained its pressure on the regime to shift away from its faith in neoliberal market reforms, arguing that privatization and austerity measures were helping some in the wealthy elite while harming average Jordanians.[33] In 1997 the HCCNOP called for major changes in the electoral law, including equal population districts and the abrogation of the one-person, one-vote system in favor of the previous bloc vote system. When these demands remained unmet, the opposition called for a national boycott of the 1997 elections, yielding—as mentioned above—a new parliament with few opposition voices (including only a handful of independent Islamist activists and leftist figures that had broken ranks with the boycott coalition).

In 1998 opposition parties sought to further institutionalize and broaden their coalition by forming the Conference on National Reform (CNF), drawing together leftist parties, the Islamist movement, and independent opposition figures. In short, the newly formed conference was intended to broaden opposition coordination beyond the forces hitherto represented within the HCCNOP, to include nonparty opposition activists as well as the traditional parties.[34] For many years, opposition parties and activists have met continually to discuss their interests, goals, strategies, and tactics, sometimes within the framework of the HCCNOP and sometimes through the broader CNF. But the Arab uprisings and especially the Syrian civil war brought much of this coordination to a standstill.

Despite these organized efforts to unite the country's political opposition and even institutionalize it in a reform coalition, there were still significant areas of difference between and within opposition forces that rendered such cooperation difficult to sustain, even without the intervening events of the Arab Spring. The Islamist movement played an important leadership role within the HCCNOP, for example, but it was also more than willing to break ranks from the opposition coalition, depending on the issue. As Janine Clark has shown, this often turned on gender issues and questions about reforming laws that especially affected women, such as personal status laws, divorce laws, and laws regarding violence against women in the name of "honor crimes." In general, the Islamists proved to be both moderate and reactionary. The Muslim Brotherhood and IAF remained moderate in the sense of believing in reform and greater democracy, but they were by no means moderate in terms of policy and legislation.[35] So for instance, the movement opposed progressive attempts to change all the above laws, finding itself therefore in opposition to the monarchy itself but allied with secular royalist and conservative political parties.

The leftist parties were themselves divided on these issues, but in general a broader pattern emerges: on democracy and liberalization, the opposition reform coalition often seemed to be more progressive than the monarchy, but on social legislation, often the monarchy was more progressive than the opposition parties. Similarly, most opposition parties opposed the Hashemite regime's introduction of a quota in 2003 to guarantee women's representation in parliament, but the Islamists soon had to reverse field, when the first woman elected under the quota was herself an Islamist. Since then, opposition parties have attempted to use the quota to their advantage by putting forward candidates they hope will then secure a seat.

In 2010 a broad range of opposition parties and nongovernmental organizations (NGOs) together called yet again for major changes in the electoral law, preceding the 2010 elections. Facilitated in part by the National Center for Human Rights (NCHR), which was led by former prime minister Ahmad 'Ubaydat, the reform-oriented parties and NGOs called for a one-person two-vote, or mixed electoral system, in which citizens could vote for an individual district representative and also for a party list at the national level. While this was seen as an opposition demand, it actually echoed the unimplemented designs of the royally established National Agenda Committee. Still, together the political opposition parties and movements formed an ad hoc umbrella group: the National Coalition for Reform (NCR).[36] Informal and little institutionalized, the newly formed group included the previous groups and coalitions noted above (including most members of the HCCNOP) while expanding to also include independent activists and representatives of prodemocracy NGOs. Although Ahmad 'Ubaydat formally "led" this particular coalition, its members viewed him as effectively the main coordinator of the movement, but not as in any way in charge of the elements within the coalition itself.[37]

Bringing together a broad range of opposition groups and activists, the ingredients seemed to have come together once again for a fairly unified and comprehensive reform coalition, with clear policy proposals for electoral change and the potential to pressure the regime toward meaningful reform. Yet the regime, to quote one opposition activist, "is really skilled at killing momentum."[38] Despite months of opposition activism, reform proposals, and extensive discussions across the Jordanian public sphere, the state issued the new electoral law, with the same gerrymandered districts, and no party lists or proportional representation whatsoever.[39] Thus, although the opposition was unified and well organized and presented viable policy alternatives, it remained yet again largely ineffective in actually achieving its desired reform objectives.

One of the reasons Jordan's opposition has been so ineffective in pressuring the regime for democratic change may lie in the fact that, aside from the Islamists, most political parties carry little support in society. Indeed, while some democracy activists are active party members, most are not, and many Jordanians see the parties as weak and perhaps even as an obsolete form of opposition.[40] "We have fifty political parties," noted one Jordanian analyst, "but ask any Jordanian and most can't name even one."[41] The parties are generally viewed as ineffective, and it is that very weakness of the parties and the party system that has led many nonparty reform activists to be openly scornful of the parties. As one such activist writer suggested, "The Islamists and leftists, they are covered in dust."[42] Others, such as writer and activist Hisham Bustani, have argued that the problem with the opposition is even more endemic. Bustani asserts that the traditional opposition parties amount to an "official" opposition that had far too many links to the regime itself.

The time therefore appeared to be ripe for an alternative opposition, beyond that of the traditional parties, which—again aside from the Islamists—would be able to mobilize widespread popular support and thus more effectively challenge the authoritarian state. Bustani argued that elements of an alternative opposition did emerge in the Arab Spring era in the form of groups such as the Jordanian Campaign for Change, better known as Jayeen—a mainly nonparty-based reform coalition—although he argues that even this group might be problematic owing to regime connections for at least some "opposition" elites, and limited in its mass appeal because of its emphasis on a unitary (and seemingly East Jordanian) national identity. For Bustani, even these newer coalitions were inherently limiting owing to their own (in his words) "isolationist vision." He explains the alternative opposition as follows:

> What are the constituents of this "alternative opposition"? Its main elements include the Jordanian Social Left Movement, the Jordanian National Initiative, the National Progressive Current, the National Committee of Military Veterans, the Jordanian Writers Association, the Nationalist Progressive Current, in addition to very small groups such as the Democratic Youth Union, the Philosophy Society, the Socialist Thought Forum, the Assembly of Circassean Youth, and the Association Against Zionism and Racism. All the above-mentioned groups (with the exception of the National Progressive Current, the National Committee of Military Veterans, and the Nationalist Progressive Current) form the so-called "Movement of the Jordanian People." And all those groups (without exception) form "The Jordanian Campaign for Change—Jayeen," and are closely allied at both the politics and logistical levels.[43]

While many activists in both the "official" and "alternative" opposition are dedicated to genuine democratic reform, others seem to be using the movements as ways to counter other elites and to get themselves back in office. Worse, Bustani argues, is the tendency for opposition coalitions like the Jordan Campaign for Change to adopt the regime's own Jordanian nationalist rhetoric and to emphasize a Jordanian national movement that is distinct from a Palestinian movement, thereby alienating much of the Jordanian population.[44]

In the Arab Spring era, Jordan therefore had not one but several reform coalitions with overlapping memberships and objectives, including party-led movements (such as the HCCNOP), nonparty-led reform movements (such as Jayeen), and combinations of both (such as 'Ubaydat's National Coalition for Reform).[45] While they all agreed that democratic change was essential, the question remained whether they were talking about the same reforms. I turn to this question below. For as the Arab uprisings continued to shake the Middle East to its foundations, all the parties, organizations, and coalitions mentioned above took to the streets in an attempt to turn their organizational and institutional opposition groups into a kind of de facto national "street coalition" for change.

The Arab Uprisings and the Traditional Opposition in Jordan

As noted above, the 2010 electoral law and parliamentary elections were disappointing for those concerned with real reform and liberalization, but they did yield for the Hashemite regime the type of parliament it seemed to prefer: with a clear majority of members of parliament not from opposition parties but rather "independents," whose backgrounds were loyalist, royalist, often tribal, and mostly Transjordanian. Yet the new government of Prime Minister Samir Rifa'i, appointed for a second time by the king in December 2010, barely had time to exhale before the Tunisian and Egyptian revolutions toppled long-standing dictators. In Jordan, as noted in chapters 1 and 2, the ripple effects and demonstrated efficacy of people in street activism in Tunis and Cairo led to marches and demonstrations that brought thousands into the streets in Amman and other Jordanian cities and towns. Like the demonstrations across the Arab world, Jordanians too marked theirs with heavy loads of patriotic symbolism while demanding democratic change.

Jordan's mass protests for democratic reform echoed calls that opposition parties and civil society groups had been making for years. A

Jordanian journalist covering the protests, and supportive of democratic reform efforts, summarized the emerging opposition consensus: "What needs to change? We need to bring back checks and balances, and to respect the original constitution. It envisioned that the parliament would do two main things: legislate and hold government accountable. But over time, it really does neither, and power shifted almost entirely to the monarchy."[46]

After years of struggles over the nature of elections and election laws, opposition demands thus shifted to the nature of parliament itself. As noted previously, many Jordanians viewed parliament as merely a pro-Hashemite tribal assembly. All democracy activists, regardless of ideological, ethnic, or religious background, seemed to agree that in addition to electoral reform, parliament too needed to change and become a more genuine legislative body, which, in turn, implied changes regarding the nature of government, of governance, and of the balance of power in the state itself.

This suggests, in other words, that in addition to diverse grievances, there were also coherent and consistent sets of demands that most opposition forces (and even many regime reformers themselves) agreed on. This chapter has examined the roots and organization of traditional opposition in Jordan and has emphasized obstacles to opposition unity, but for all the diversity of the coalitions, parties, and groups noted above, both old and new coalitions and activists agreed on at least the following set of reform demands:

1. Parliament should be a body that actually legislates rather than simply implementing cabinet initiatives or royal decrees.
2. Government should be drawn from the elected representatives of the people; that is, it should be a more truly parliamentary system rather than a royally appointed government separate from parliament.
3. Major changes were needed in the electoral system, especially to empower the opposition and build national political parties.
4. There should be fewer restrictions on media, press, and publications, including a shift away from timid and often self-censored reporting, and an end to Mukhabarat interference in the media and in public life in general.
5. There should be an end to corruption and the establishment of a more independent judiciary to hold the corrupt accountable for their actions.

6. Electoral districts should be equal in size rather than gerrymandered (although this remains controversial and not a point of complete consensus among democracy activists).

Jordan's electoral districts have historically been gerrymandered to be unevenly representative, designed to increase rural representation (and hence usually conservative, proregime, East Jordanian communities), while limiting urban representation, since the largest cities, such as Amman, Irbid, and Zarqa, have large Palestinian populations. Given Jordan's complicated identity politics (discussed in more detail in chapter 5), the ethnic implications of redistricting have significant power implications. This particular reform question therefore remains problematic for at least some opposition groups, and even more problematic for more conservative forces in the state itself. Elites within the regime that feel threatened by significant change, especially those in the state security apparatus, will sometimes exploit opposition differences by stoking these fears, for example, of a shift from East Jordanian to Palestinian empowerment, in an effort to prevent the emergence of single, unified, and truly national coalition for change in Jordan.

In my own personal observations of Jordanian politics over more than thirty years, I would argue that the pattern is for antireform officials, state-backed media, and self-described loyalists to insist that prodemocracy activists are an ethnic or religious threat to the identity of Jordan. In short, antireformers try to create disunity by exploiting social divisions and fears, and then (ironically) accuse their opponents of threatening "national unity." Indeed, there is no more pervasive phrase in the antireform lexicon than invoking national unity against opponents, putting them instantly on the defensive, and effectively challenging their loyalty and patriotism.

While the reform demands listed above all suggest political changes, it is worth underscoring that in Jordan and across the Arab world, part of the revolt against the status quo seemed to be not just a revolt against particular governing systems but also a rejection of neoliberal economic policies. These are associated in the minds of many across society with enriching the already wealthy while removing the previous social safety nets of large public sectors with greater guarantees of employment and social welfare. In the Jordanian context, these economic policies have also had profound ethnic implications—given the traditional predominance of Palestinians in the private sector and East Jordanians in the public sector. While leftist and Islamist parties have for years regarded neoliberal reform with suspicion and even overt hostility, in more recent years even traditionally proregime conservatives have joined the chorus against this particular type of economic reform. Conservative East Jordanian nationalists have increasingly charged their own regime with corruption and selling off Jordan's national assets in the name of short-term profits.

Indeed, economic grievances were a large part of the motivation for the "southern movement" in particular; that is, largely nonparty-based activism outside of the capital, Amman, and located in towns such as Kerak, Ma'an, Tafilah, and Dhiban. The activities of what was originally seen as a "southern movement" (and thereafter known as the Hirak, discussed in detail in the next chapter) overlapped with the "alternative opposition" alluded to by Bustani above but included largely independent youth organizations established as local opposition movements, such as the Kerak Popular Youth Movement, the Free Tafilah Movement, and the Ma'an Popular Movement for Change and Reform.[47] Each of these groups expressed particular pride in the role of the (largely East Bank Jordanian) South in creating the political reform revivals of both 1989 and 2011, and each focused in particular on the problems of privatization, Amman-centric investment and development, and especially government corruption related to all the above.[48]

Opposition to economic liberalization thus certainly carried the potential to unite otherwise disparate ideological forces, such as leftists, Islamists, and secular nationalists. But paradoxically, it is also just as likely to create deeper fissures in Jordan's already-established political fault lines, such as Palestinian and East Jordanian identity politics. As Nicolas Pelham has noted, this has led to a kind of reversal, in which some conservative East Jordanian nationalists became harshly critical of the regime, while Palestinians in Jordan's business community found themselves in the role of defenders of the monarchy.[49] In short, anti-neoliberalism has at times brought together a very broad group of activists, for reform *away* from privatization and toward a revitalization of the social welfare role of the state. Yet the ethnic politics inherent in the same controversial issue carry the potential to tear that very coalition apart.

Ultimately, whether reformers and democracy activists in Jordan can unite effectively or not, the Arab Spring protests suggested that widespread discontent spanned almost all sectors of Jordanian society, implying that much needed to change in terms of both political and economic reform in the kingdom, for the security and well-being of both state and society. Yet as this chapter has shown, Jordan's wide-ranging political opposition has had a long history of organization and activism but with little effect on government policy. The state, in turn, has long practiced a politics of inclusion and cooptation of some opposition while allowing others to vent some level of frustration and actively attempting to divide still other groups.[50] But many of these mechanisms—from cooptation to division to coercion—are now all too familiar to opposition forces. And given the large presence of increasingly politicized and active youth in public demonstrations in Jordan from 2011 onward—youth who very often identified with *neither* the state *nor* its traditional opposition forces—it was also clear that older methods were no longer enough to contain opposition. "The palace also seems to always see challenges even when they are actually opportunities," noted one Jordanian journalist. "They could embrace and even lead reform efforts. But they do not. The times have changed, and the tools of rule need to change with them."[51]

Also emphasizing change, a veteran reform and democracy activist noted the importance of *generational* change in the expanding Jordanian reform movement, and the extensive use of social media—especially Facebook, Twitter, and blogging—to organize demonstrations and activism. This was a problem, she noted, not only for the regime but also for opposition parties:

> The parties are not near people's hearts and minds. That's why they have these Facebook groups. That's their political parties. It is like an election, people signing up and "liking" and agreeing to support a figure or group or demonstration. Social media is their device to convert and share their aspirations. But the Mukhabarat are also now trying to infiltrate social media groups. But people just aren't afraid anymore. Measures that used to scare people just don't now. They are sure that they are smarter than the regime. They are just not afraid.[52]

At the height of the Arab Spring, Jordan's youth movements continued to expand to include virtually every town and city in the country. In addition to the southern movements, therefore, youth movements also emerged in northern towns like Irbid, Jerash, Mafraq, and Zarqa. Yet while each movement saw itself as independent, many also overlapped in membership with the youth wings of various political parties. So there was some connection between youth movements and the political parties of the "traditional opposition," but there was also considerable independence. Still, as journalist Taylor Luck pointed out, "many of the popular movements are caught in a love-hate relationship of dependence with traditional opposition parties and professional associations."[53] Many youth movements drew on the organization and logistical experience of organized parties in order to generate public support for their demonstrations, even as they remained independent organizations.[54]

Continuity and Change

Jordan's traditional political opposition, rooted in leftist, Pan-Arab nationalist, and Islamist political parties, predates the Arab uprisings by decades. So the movements and parties themselves were clearly not new. But some of the political dynamics that emerged within the opposition were indeed new and different.

Opposition forces have historically struggled to assemble a meaningful and united front for change, especially when differing often profoundly on domestic social issues, but they have often agreed on foreign policy issues—especially in their opposition to Israel, U.S. policy, and Western imperialism more generally. Unfortunately for these movements, these are exactly the types of "high politics" issues they are least likely to influence. Opposition parties increased their attempts at unity at the outset of the Arab Spring, sensing the opportunity that had finally arrived. But the Arab uprisings, and especially the devastation of the Syrian civil war, soon created sharp fissures within Jordan's traditional opposition parties. Many in Jordan's opposition parties had spent years hoping and waiting for a moment exactly like the Arab Spring—a moment of genuine grassroots popular mobilization, of people in the streets, of protests and demonstrations aimed at real reform and change. But now, when it should have been "their moment," opposition groups struggled to unify, as they had so often in the past. Yet the nature of the split was the opposite of the usual pattern: this time they were more united on domestic reform demands but divided on regional and foreign policy. They were more energized and more active than at any time since the 1989–1993 reform era, yet opposition parties oscillated between moments of unity and coalition building, on the one hand, and moments of rupture and disunity, on the other, especially when they split over the question of the Asad regime and the Syrian civil war.

Still, opposition party activists from across the ideological spectrum marched in the various demonstrations of the early Arab Spring years and succeeded in their attempts to pressure the regime to unseat its own recently appointed government. As noted in chapter 2, in response to the 2011 unrest, the monarchy attempted to respond to the opposition by dismissing the government, but it then put in its place one that was even more conservative—shifting from Prime Minister Samir al-Rifa'i to Prime Minister Ma'rouf al-Bakhit. The appointment of Bakhit was profoundly disappointing to democratic activists who had hoped for a reformer. In typical Hashemite politics, however, the king also appointed a more progressive veteran political leader (and one of the most influential Palestinian Jordanians in the kingdom), Senate Speaker Taher al-Masri, to head the National Dialogue Committee on reform. Masri urged the regime to engage opposition forces directly.

Both the new prime minister and the king met with leaders of the IAF and Muslim Brotherhood in an effort to cool domestic tensions and also discuss the possibility of Islamist figures taking government cabinet posts and joining the National Dialogue Committee (the Islamists refused on both counts). The regime was in full crisis mode, attempting to mollify both traditional bases of support and traditional sources of opposition. But the time-honored techniques of reshuffling cabinets, blaming previous governments (rather than the monarchy) for failure to implement reform, and issuing royal calls for more reform would ring hollow unless followed by real reform.[55] Indeed, in 2011, with Arab Spring demonstrations in full swing, the National Center for Human Rights issued a statement stressing that the lack of real reform in the kingdom amounted to "the gravest danger to the safety and security of society and to national unity."[56]

In May 2011 yet another opposition coalition emerged in Jordanian politics, but one that had the potential to bridge many of the parties, groups, and movements discussed in this analysis. The National Front for Reform, led by former prime minister Ahmad 'Ubaydat, brought together the Islamic Action Front, all the leftist parties discussed above, and the Jordanian Women's Union and intended to bring under its umbrella the various youth movements as well. "They [the youth movements] can be closer to the street than people our age and at the level of our political experiences,"

'Ubaydat argued, "but they also need us and we need them."[57] The youth movements represented a new form of political opposition and activism in Jordanian politics, and indeed still other movements emerged, many drawing on Jordan's vast youth population. Chapter 4 turns to these newer forms, as activists found alternative ways to mobilize and to add entirely new dimensions to Jordanian politics.

CHAPTER IV

The Hirak and Changes in Political Activism

As protests swept the country in 2011–2012, new forms of activism emerged in Jordan, including the largely youth-led protest groups collectively known as the Jordanian Popular Movement (al-Hirak al-Sha'bi al-Urduni) or the Jordanian Youth Movement (al-Hirak al-Shababi al-Urduni) but usually referred to simply as the Hirak. The former refers to all the grassroots activism that emerged across Jordan, starting especially with labor movements, while the latter is subsumed within this but refers more specifically to the proliferation of youth-based local and regional protest movements. The rise of the Hirak phenomenon is perhaps the most unique feature of Jordan's Arab Spring experience. As shown in chapter 3, more long-standing forms of opposition—in leftist parties and in the Islamist movement—were also active in Jordan's protests and in political activism. But these were also the traditional focal points of political activism in the kingdom. This chapter turns to newer forms of activism, including the rise of the Hirak and grassroots opposition movements beyond that of the traditional political parties in the Hashemite Kingdom.

Despite the general public image of Jordan being "quiet" during the Arab Spring era, the kingdom actually saw extensive activism, especially on the part of a younger, mobilized generation that had a great deal to say. These protests ranged from fierce opposition to neoliberal economic restructuring to protests against economic austerity measures. They included a resurgent workers' rights movement and labor activism that, as

Fida Adely has shown, in many ways served as a precursor to all of Jordan's grassroots mobilization during and after the Arab Spring.[1] They also included issue-oriented movements, such as the campaign against a Jordanian gas deal with Israel, environmental activism including efforts to save Berqesh forest from state-led development, and a campaign against state plans to develop nuclear power plants in the kingdom.[2] Jordan's Arab Spring experience may not have involved revolution or civil war, but it was by no means "quiet" or docile. This chapter first turns to the rise of the Hirak, then to dramatic changes and splits within the Islamist movement, and finally to alternate approaches to activism, including single-issue movements and the question of effective grassroots activism in the kingdom.

The Challenge of the Hirak

As many Hirak activists are quick to note, Jordan's Arab Spring protests in 2011 began not in the capital, Amman, but in southern Jordan, much like the protests of 1989.[3] Southern activists in both eras prided themselves on rising up to save a Jordan that they believed had lost its way. Hirak protesters seemed to be mainly of East Jordanian origin, with Palestinian Jordanians eventually joining in as well, but never in proportion to their overall numbers in Jordanian society. Some Jordanians use the term *Hirak* to refer specifically to the youth movements, but others use it more broadly to describe all these forms of organization—youth movements, labor organization and strikes, and new leftist and progressive activism.[4] This is, of course, entirely valid. In this section, however, I will focus mainly on the youth-led movements from the governorates as the main examples of the Hirak.

As noted in chapter 2, Jordan's Hirak protests began in the South—in Dhiban, Tafilah, Kerak, and Ma'an—but soon spread across the country to northern sites like Irbid, Ajlun, Jerash, and Mafraq. At its high point in 2012, it almost seemed as if every town, village, and city had its own version of the Hirak. The protests expanded not just geographically but also ideologically, as the traditional opposition of leftists and Pan-Arab nationalist parties joined in, as well as the Muslim Brotherhood and Islamic Action Front. When all these movements were present, the protests were diverse indeed and numbered in the thousands. But often, activists argue, the Mukhabarat—Jordan's intelligence service—would find ways to divide the movements, thwarting a larger and more potent coalition, usually by attempting to get specific Hirak groups to pull out of a protest, citing Islamist or Palestinian influence. Sometimes these divide-and-defuse tactics worked; sometimes they did not. And sometimes divisions occurred not because of Mukhabarat machinations but because opposition groups divided themselves.

The fact that the regime took so much trouble to focus on the Hirak suggests just how troubling they found the movements to be. The traditional leftist and Islamist opposition they felt comfortable handling—that was the kind of regime-opposition maneuvering and sparring that they were used to. But this was different. Hirak activists and security forces sent to contain them were often from the same backgrounds, families, clans, and tribes. As the previous chapter made clear, Jordan's traditional political opposition spans the political spectrum from left to right, religious to secular. But it was the Hirak that was the new addition and in many ways the force most troubling to many in the Hashemite regime.[5]

The story of the rise of the Hirak, however, is partially one based on the political economy of social change in the Hashemite Kingdom. As noted in chapter 2, in 1989 Jordan had experienced a severe economic crisis after years of descending ever further into debt. The regime turned to the International Monetary Fund for emergency financial support. The austerity programs that followed required the government to lift subsidies and led almost immediately to riots as Jordanians protested the sudden dramatic rise in prices for basic foods and commodities. But this was also part of a much larger picture in which a decades-long economic, social, and political structure seemed to be coming to an end. Since the 1950s, and especially in the aftermath of the Jordanian civil war of 1970–1971, King Hussein had established Hashemite regime security on the basis of extensive state support for key East Bank tribal communities. Jordanian citizens from these communities, in turn, came to make up the overwhelming majority of officials in the government bureaucracy and also in the police, army, and intelligence services. As the public sector became ever more extensively East Jordanian over the years, the private sector became correspondingly more and more the domain of Palestinian Jordanians.

This "ethnic division of labor" was neither official nor absolute, but at least in general terms it did characterize much of Jordan's political economy and social structure for decades. The events of 1989 challenged this, and in many ways Jordan continues its transition—economically but therefore also politically and socially—to increasing neoliberalism and privatization, from 1989 to the present. King Hussein started this transition in 1989, reluctantly and essentially under duress. He simply saw no other way to keep the kingdom afloat financially. So the difficult economic medicine of structural adjustment would be taken, but it would challenge the social and political bases of Hashemite rule itself. This therefore amounted to a major structural shift in Jordan as a state, society, and economy, and it immediately affected the politics of protests. This matters even today, because while King Hussein reluctantly pursued a neoliberal agenda, his son and heir, King Abdullah II, has done so enthusiastically. King Abdullah sees economic development, privatization, free trade, foreign investment, and an active tourism economy all as vital to the modernization of Jordan and as the keys to its long-term prosperity. In both cases, the economic agenda has had social and political consequences, which have in turn had transformative effects on political opposition in the kingdom.

Hirak groups emerged in every city and almost every town across the kingdom, seeing themselves as *Sha'bi* (popular or people's movements) as well as *Shababi* (youth).[6] They emerged in specific cities and towns and also in the heartlands even of the most influential tribes and tribal confederations, including the Bani Hasan and Bani Khalid in the North, the Bani Sakhr in central Jordan, and the Bani Hamida and Huwaytat in the South.[7] The activists were mainly young people in their twenties who—like their counterparts across the Arab world—used social media platforms like Facebook and Twitter as well as SMS phone messaging to organize and communicate with one another. They were tech-savvy youth who therefore could not be dismissed as old-guard "dinosaurs" blocking state reform efforts. Although some in Jordan did just that, dismissing the Hirak as simply delinquents who specialized only in burning tires and blocking roads in the South. But the Hirak also had defenders among older people, including some in the media, in older opposition movements (including some leftist party activists), and even in government and the security services.

Even the name used to describe these organizations is telling: al-Hirak (*the* movement, implying active mobility or mobilization) as opposed to simply Hirakat (movements). The groups were locally organized and hence emerged as grassroots movements, but they also saw themselves as part of a broader national and even regional phenomenon. They were inspired by the democratic impulses of the original Arab Spring. But the roots of Jordanian activism, and even of the Hirak, predate the regional protest movements of 2011 and can be seen in the earlier levels of resurgent tribal and East Jordanian activism throughout the reign of King Abdullah II, such as the labor activism and strikes within Jordan's phosphate industry, the port of Aqaba, and the successful attempts to establish a national teacher's union.[8] Hirak groups and many of these other forms of activism pushed back against neoliberal economic policies that shifted major state industries to private investors, changing the working conditions, opportunities, and livelihoods of local communities.[9]

While Hirak is usually used to refer to mainly East Jordanian youth activist movements, the Hirak are nonetheless sometimes still hard to describe ideologically, and they don't fit a standard left–right continuum. In terms of economic populism and prodemocracy activism the movements sounded leftist, but when some of them turned to identity politics (many but not all avoided this trap) they sounded more right-wing and even ultranationalist. They sometimes associated with leftist and nationalist parties but usually in the sense of temporary organization for particular events. Even when a particular Hirak group identified or organized with one of Jordan's "left" parties, this still didn't necessarily provide ideological clarity, since many leftist parties and figures in Jordan—such as the late columnist and activist Nahed Hattar—were quite right-wing regarding identity issues.

Hirak members seemed to be mainly secular, East Bank, tribal activists. But to be clear, none of the more than thirty Hirak groups represented only a particular tribe. Many members had a tribal affiliation and identity, but the groups tended to be organized for a particular town, city, or region rather than for a specific tribe. Other movements, like the Jordanian Social Left Movement, had a more national focus and had emerged as early as 2007, several years before the Arab Spring protests began.

The activism of Hirak youth, and indeed that of their elders, is often dismissed as "only" economically based. But it would be a mistake to see it as motivated solely by economic self-interest. Some in the regime and in the Jordanian political and economic elite dismiss the Hirak as little more than hooligans or unemployed and directionless youth protesting largely for the sake of protesting. But the Hirak comprised more than three dozen different organizations, some large, some small, some very active, some short-lived and ineffective. Those that were more organized and engaged in multiple protests were part of deeper levels of anger and anxiety within Jordanian society. They were in effect a new generation of activists tapping into grievances similar to those of their 1989 predecessors. But as in 1989, their complaints were about political as well as economic issues.

Both generations of protesters—in 1989 and 2011 onward—were harshly critical of the kingdom's neoliberal agenda. That economic agenda had profound social and political consequences, including rising unemployment among the very communities that had previously been assumed to have unassailable loyalty to the Hashemite state. This was an oversimplification and overassumption in any case, but in the context of the neoliberal impact especially on South Jordan (and the corresponding development emphasis on the capital, especially West Amman), it was even more questionable. Their detractors tend to assume that they can easily be bought off with government jobs or privileges, but Hirak activists emphasized that they were not just looking for economic handouts or even a restoration of the social safety net in the kingdom.[10]

Most important, the Hirak were more diverse than they might appear to be, representing multiple movements rather than a single movement. The Kerak Popular Youth Movement, the Free Tafilah Movement, the Ma'an Popular Movement for Change and Reform, the Popular Movement in the North, and many others were very different and continually changing. Numbers of participants rose and fell frequently, and organization remained deliberately loose. Hirak groups tended to prize their openness and flexibility, but this also meant that linking up and organizing at a truly national, rather than local, level were quite daunting. The strengths of the Hirak movements themselves were therefore also their weaknesses. They remained local rather than national organizations, and most were inclusive in terms of decision making. So while they were truly grassroots activist organizations with democratic impulses, this could be used to divide them and prevent a broader national opposition coalition of the Hirak from forming, much less a cross-ideological or cross-organizational coalition that might have included Hirak, leftist parties, Islamists, and other activist organizations such as the retired military officers or Jordan's growing labor movement.

Many Hirak activists seemed uninspired by the various traditional forms of opposition discussed in the preceding chapter and were particularly wary of being implicated in or linked to Islamist movements. This really was a new generation of activists.[11] Still, many youth remained uninterested in the older, established opposition groups, from leftist parties to the Islamists, seeing them as largely failed attempts at opposition and change. Similarly, many parties themselves might have revived their own flagging fortunes if they had tapped the emerging strength of Hirak youth. Yet many party activists shunned the Hirak, while many youth activists felt that the older parties had had their day. In such cases, each tended to view the other as potentially infiltrated by, or serving the whims of, the Mukhabarat. On the occasions when Hirak activists and Islamist activists attempted to coordinate for particular protests or demonstrations, Hirak youth often complained that the Islamists didn't share their inclusive approach to decision making, with Islamist organizational structures decidedly more hierarchical than horizontal. In that context, Hirak activists often argued that Islamists simply wanted to borrow Hirak numbers and nationalist credentials while hijacking the protests and attempting to bring other groups in— not as allies but rather as subject to Islamist directives.

While Hirak activists were mainly East Jordanian, many with tribal roots, some Palestinian Jordanians were involved as well.[12] The latter group appeared to be greatly outnumbered by Transjordanian activists, and while they shared motivations, they were often careful to minimize their own apparent roles in order to avoid the traditional regime tactic of deriding protest movements as "just Palestinian." Even as Palestinian Jordanians sometimes tried to lay low amid their Transjordanian counterparts, Hirak movements in general tended to opt for overt displays of patriotism. These were not just symbolic. While activists did want to prevent the regime from questioning their patriotism (another time-honored tactic of regimes countering protesters), they were also quite authentic in their patriotic attachment to Jordan. Their motivation, in fact, was improving the country.

As they engaged in protests, the Hirak tended to mix extensive patriotic symbols—flags, nationalist songs, and even the *dabke* national dance—with overt challenges to the monarchy itself. And here they crossed red lines that older generations of protesters and activists would not have challenged. Hirak activists tended to be quite clear regarding their own Jordanian credentials, but some questioned those of the monarchy. While most called for reform (chanting *ash-sha'b yurid islah al-nizam*—"the people want reform of the system"), some were more directly challenging (chanting, as in other Arab states, *ash-sha'b yurid isqat al-nizam*—"the people want the overthrow of the regime"). Some even chanted *malik* rather than *nizam*, meaning the king rather than the system. Others called explicitly for the monarchy to stay but for the king to abdicate the throne.[13] Those who took this rather daring line of opposition also challenged the line of succession. Some preferred (and chanted to that effect) that King Abdullah abdicate in favor of his half-brother Hamzah (the son of former Queen Noor), rather than in favor of the current line of succession from the king to his eldest son, Crown Prince Hussein (the son of current Queen Rania). This was, of course, dangerous ground for any opposition movement to dare to tread. Many Hirak groups and protests steered clear of this level of direct challenge to the regime and focused instead on issues of economic and social justice.

While Hirak activists remained sharply critical of the kingdom's neoliberal development agenda, they were even more focused on the issue of corruption. The Hirak were therefore more than just angry East Jordanians who felt economically and politically disenfranchised. This is part of the puzzle, to be sure, but only a part. Many of the movements began by talking about economic rights as part of a sustained critique of neoliberalism and privatization and regime economic development priorities. Most also emphasized political rights, inclusion, and democratization. But the movements also broadened these themes to talk in terms of al-'Adalah al-Ijtima'iyya, or social justice. Their main focus and main complaint was, and remains, corruption in public life. And in this, at least, they mirrored the views of most Jordanians.

Complaints about corruption pervade Jordanian political discourse. Almost all Jordanians complain about it. While leftist, nationalist, and Islamist opposition forces decried corruption but tended to do so obliquely, some Hirak groups turned their anger on the regime itself and, more specifically, the monarchy. Some accused the royal family of directly profiting for years from the sale of state enterprises in the name of privatization. They called out the king, the queen, and regime elites in general for profiting at the expense of the Jordanian people and for selling the country's limited assets to the highest foreign bidders. As noted in chapter 2, it was in this context that some Hirak protests turned quite personal, chanting, dancing, and denouncing "Ali Baba and the Forty Thieves"—a clearly disparaging reference to the king, his family, and the royal entourage.

While these direct and personal challenges to the king and the queen were jarring in the context of previous norms or even "scripts" regarding acceptable opposition in Jordan, they also echoed those of older generations of critics who had crossed similar red lines as recently as 2010 and 2011. These direct personal insults, in short, could not be dismissed as simply those of overzealous and politically clueless youth, since similar charges had come from powerful and influential military veterans and tribal sheikhs.

As noted in chapter 2, retired military officers and tribal sheikhs had issued manifestos criticizing the regime and demanding changes. Hirak activism therefore followed other significant challenges to the regime from the regime's own traditional support base, including tribal sheikhs and military veterans, and also came in the context of rising labor activism in the kingdom as well as region-wide prodemocracy youth activism.

The Hirak therefore drew on all these lines of activism while also emphatically maintaining their independence from previous forms of opposition and even from one another. Even as press reports tended to follow the rise and fall of levels of protest in the capital, Hirak activists frequently held local demonstrations throughout the country, coordinating with other Hirak groups to make sure that the protests were on the same days and at the same time, but otherwise acting independently of one another. In general, as the Arab Spring wore on, demonstrations in Irbid and Zarqa were often led by Islamists, those in Amman by Islamists at times allied with leftist and nationalist parties, and those in Dhiban, Kerak, Tafilah, Ma'an, and elsewhere often by the Hirak.

While Hirak activists were critical of the regime's economic agenda and accused it of corruption, they also echoed their youthful counterparts across the Arab world in calling for democratization. The Hirak joined other opposition movements, including the traditional opposition, in calling for liberalization and democratization and demanding real rather than cosmetic change. Many activists in the Jordanian Hirak concluded that Jordan had ultimately opted for the latter. The regime maintains that its top-down reforms are extensive, and that these include a number of landmark reforms such as new laws on parties, elections, municipalities, and decentralization, an independent electoral commission, amending the constitution, and creating a constitutional court. But critics in the Hirak and elsewhere across Jordan's opposition spectrum maintained that these were surface-level changes only, and that power in the system remained tightly controlled by the monarchy. On this point, at least, groups as varied as the Hirak and even Jordan's oldest opposition movement, the Muslim Brotherhood, agreed.

Dividing the Islamist Movement

By 2013 a Jordanian regime that seemed confident (perhaps even overconfident) that it had survived the Arab Spring seemed to turn its attention away from grassroots activist movements like the Hirak, refocusing on more traditional forms of opposition, such as the Brotherhood, but with a view to weaken and divide the movement. In doing so, the Hashemite regime was by no means as draconian as many of its Arab allies, particularly Egypt, Saudi Arabia, and the United Arab Emirates. Each of these allied states had been deeply alarmed at the rise of Islamist movements, mainly through elections in places like Egypt and Tunisia, in the early period of the regional Arab Spring. Following the coup d'état in Egypt in July 2013, each of these three Jordanian allies banned the Muslim Brotherhood entirely, with Egypt engaging in violent repression against the movement. Despite allied pressure to follow the same course, the Jordanian regime chose a less directly confrontational path, encouraging an emerging split within the movement. Jordan's Islamists had long been divided between what are known as hawkish and dovish strains, the former following a harder line toward the regime while the latter was more reformist and interested in dialogue with the regime.

This division was also rooted, in part, in identity politics, with the hawkish wing more heavily Palestinian and insisting on maintaining ties to Hamas, while the dovish wing was more heavily East Jordanian and preferred a national rather than regional approach, with an Islamism rooted in Jordan itself and not in the broader question of Palestine. The ideological split within the Islamist movement therefore predates the Arab Spring by many years. But during the Arab Spring era, the split took a more dramatic turn and became more solidly institutionalized. Even just prior to the regional uprisings, the intra-Islamist rift had been challenged several times by the usual question of elections and participation or boycotting. In April 2008 the dovish wing had lost internal elections for secretary-general of the Muslim Brotherhood by a single vote. Moderate figure Salim Falahat lost to more hardline leader Hammam Sa'id. This followed a failed national electoral campaign in which the Islamic Action Front had contested the parliamentary elections of 2007 with little to show for it. The controversial decision to participate, and its failed outcome, only led to more fighting within the movement over leadership and direction.[14] The divided movement, led then mainly by hard-liners, opted to boycott elections in both 2010 and 2013. But in the interim, the reformist Zamzam movement had emerged. Its leaders, including prominent figures such as Ruhayl al-Gharaibeh, were ousted from the Muslim Brotherhood but soon pursued their own movement, leaving the original Brotherhood behind.

By 2015 the dovish wing of the Brotherhood had built on its already established Zamzam reform initiative by leaving the older and official movement, cutting ties with the regional Brotherhood, and establishing a new Jordanian Muslim Brotherhood Society that soon gained licensing approval from the state as a legal national group. This also meant that the older, larger, original version of the Muslim Brotherhood was suddenly a group without legal standing in Jordan. So while other Arab states such as Egypt, Saudi Arabia, and the UAE eliminated the Brotherhood entirely from legal activism in public life, Jordan shifted from one version of the Brotherhood to two. The state seemed to actively encourage the split, and indeed activists in the original movement remain convinced that the entire episode was engineered by the Mukhabarat.[15]

Both movements thereafter struggled with each other over recognition, finances, and membership—and even over connections to the still-legal political party, the IAF, whose members were from both versions of the Brotherhood. By 2016 the state crackdown became more extensive. In March the regime informed the unlicensed version of the Muslim Brotherhood that it would not be permitted to hold internal elections for its own leadership posts. Weeks later, in April, security forces began closing down Brotherhood offices, first the Amman headquarters and later regional offices in Mafraq, Madaba, and other cities. One of the movement's prominent hardline leaders, Zaki Bani Irshayd, was at that time already in prison for online comments criticizing Jordan's ally the United Arab Emirates for its own crackdown on the Muslim Brotherhood.

The regime accurately emphasizes that Jordan does indeed still maintain a legal version of the Muslim Brotherhood; it is just the unlicensed version that is subject to the crackdown. But Jillian Schwedler noted even regarding the 2010 version of this cold war between the Islamists and state that "the regime has almost systematically alienated the Muslim Brotherhood and the IAF at a time when it should be striving to encourage moderate Islam, not because it can necessarily turn those moderates into full-fledged liberal democrats, but because supporting moderate Islamists can deny radical Islamists the constituency support-base that they need to flourish."[16] That advice seemed even more urgent in the latter years of the Arab Spring. However, with the downfall of the Muslim Brotherhood in Egypt and elsewhere and the rise of militant jihadi movements just across Jordan's borders, the regime seemed inclined to continue still farther down the path of confrontation with an Islamist movement that some in the palace regarded as outdated at best and subversive at worst.

But the various versions of the Muslim Brotherhood remain just one of several lines of division across Islamist movements in the kingdom. Other Islamists, for example, had long ago shifted from the Brotherhood toward a more Salafi Islamist trend. This trend, in turn, was divided between "quietist" factions that eschewed political participation and violently activist versions that saw hundreds and perhaps thousands of Jordanian Salafi jihadists cross the border into Syria to join the Syrian civil war by fighting with either Jabhat al-Nusra (an affiliate of al-Qa'ida) or the "Islamic State" (also known as ISIS, ISIL, or Da'esh). Still other Islamists—almost the opposite of the jihadis—turned in a more reformist direction, engaging the state (with strong state backing) and following the *wasatiyya* trend of Islamist centrism, leaving the Brotherhood behind and participating in parliamentary elections, even in 2013 when the Brotherhood was still boycotting the polls.

Yet despite being divided into two different versions of the Muslim Brotherhood, all of Jordan's major Islamist movements (aside from the Salafis) returned to the ballot box in 2016, contesting the polls and forming lists in multiple districts. The IAF competed in twenty out of twenty-three districts, winning seats in all five districts in the capital, for a total of ten seats overall, and an additional five for "allies" on its *Islah* (reform) lists. The other Islamist movements managed to gain five seats each, so even divided into three movements, all were represented under the dome of parliament. In contrast, only one member of parliament in the 2016 election came from a leftist political party, and none came from any of the Hirak movements, since the age of eligibility for parliamentary office remained thirty, in a country in which more than half the population is under twenty-five.

The Decline of the Arab Spring Protests

In some respects, the renewed focus of the regime on thwarting the various levels and types of Islamist opposition was also a measure of the decline of the Hirak. Even as early as 2013, many in Jordan felt that the Hirak was over. Activists in the Hirak had been co-opted or arrested or had simply faded away, they argued, but in any case it was over. That may be far too optimistic an assessment on the part of those who dismissed Hirak activists as country rubes who could easily be intimidated or even bought. Hirak is, after all, a collective term for disparate groups that weren't actually a collective. They had national motivations in terms of prodemocracy, anti-corruption, and antineoliberal activism, but they never organized at a national level or as a singular national organization. But despite the decline in their levels of activism over the years, that local focus could easily reignite, especially in response to economic austerity (as in the riots and protests of November 2012). "The Hirak isn't over," noted one Jordanian analyst, "it's sleeping. And it could come back."[17]

While the levels of protests among Hirak, Islamists, leftist parties, and others clearly declined from 2013 onward, this didn't amount to an endorsement of the regime's position regarding the depth of reform in the kingdom. To the contrary, Jordan's diverse array of opposition forces may differ on many things, but almost all rejected the "reform drive" as superficial rather than meaningful. For some, the decline in activism is not acquiescence but simply disillusionment. Others are holding their activism in abeyance, seeing Jordan in a particularly vulnerable situation, especially amid regional wars, the massive influx of refugees, and the threat of terrorism from ISIS and other jihadist groups.

Yet these activists did not accept the status quo. Rather, they were self-consciously holding back, arguing that now is not the time to push the regime or the system too much. The question, of course, is this: when *is* the time? Should Jordan manage to weather its many regional storms, these activists hope to revive their protest movements and to push the regime for further political change—for greater democratization, for genuine efforts to combat corruption, and for a shift in economic priorities that includes more support for those across society who seem to be left behind even as development projects press forward.

Part of the decline in protest activism on the part of the Hirak and other groups was based on these types of assessments of the lay of the land. Some became disillusioned and moved to less political pursuits. Some held back, waiting for the return of greater levels of activism and opportunities for change. A few may have joined the state itself, muting their previous criticisms. But coercion also played a role. As noted previously, the regime has, for the most part, prided itself on its "soft security" approach to protests and demonstrations. But security forces acted swiftly when Hirak activists were deemed to have crossed acceptable lines. Activists who denounced the king, burned or tore up his picture, or who too publicly and too personally challenged the king, queen, or royal family were arrested. Some were tried in the State Security Court rather than in the civilian court system for allegedly undermining the regime itself.[18] This combination of factors served to dampen the activism of the various Hirak groups. But the crackdown, arrests, and trials of Hirak members also led to international criticism, including from organizations such as Human Rights Watch.[19]

But the Hirak were also influenced by regional politics and by some of the same factors that were splitting the opposition across the country. In addition to co-optation, coercion, and even disillusionment, opposition forces also declined in effectiveness when they split over the conflict in Syria. As noted in chapter 3, leftist and nationalist political parties supported the Asad regime and thought the Hashemite regime should have too. Islamists in the Muslim Brotherhood and Islamic Action Front, in contrast, called for the ouster of the Asad regime and for support for Islamist rebels. Many in these traditional opposition parties hoped that their more youthful counterparts would follow their lead. But Hirak activists had no single unified position on these issues, and as the many fissures across Jordan's various traditional opposition movements steadily deepened, so too did those in the newer grassroots and Hirak movements, presumably much to the pleasure of the regime's own domestic security apparatus. To quote one high-ranking figure in the Hashemite regime, referring explicitly (and somewhat sarcastically) to the many splits and sources of division, "Thank God for the opposition."[20]

Before the decline and fracturing of these movements, the various opposition forces had indeed attempted to form a national coalition, more than once. But each attempt failed, and regional events only made their disagreements worse, leaving the opposition factionalized and deeply divided. They split over the Syria crisis and then split again over the issue of whether to participate in or boycott the 2013 national parliamentary elections. One activist summarized the opposition activist dilemma in this way:

> There is no common agenda whatsoever. The political parties represent very few. Some want an electoral law based on population, while others want to preserve East Jordanian districts. Even on just the basic electoral law, there is no agreement. So groups rarely define "reform" to keep it ambiguous and get larger numbers at the demonstrations. And "large" here is in the thousands, not the tens of thousands. So you have demonstrations, but no unified agenda, while we have clashes over Jordanian identity itself.[21]

In 2011–2012 the regime seemed mainly concerned with reining in Hirak activism, while from 2013 onward the emphasis changed to a more traditional anti-Islamist stance, ranging almost across the board, from efforts at undermining the Muslim Brotherhood to thwarting more severe security threats such as those from al-Qa'ida and ISIS. Yet aside from the very real fears regarding Salafi jihadist terrorism, the regime had tended to focus on traditional forms of opposition in the form of leftist, Pan-Arab nationalist, and Islamist parties and movements.

The weakness of the traditional opposition, however, in addition to their own ideological differences and organizational disunity, is their own elite makeup. The traditional opposition parties and organizations are mainly elite based, and while they spar with the regime, they often struggle to gain the most mundane connection to Jordanian society. The entire struggle, at times, appears to be between regime elites and opposition elites. Yet for the all the faults or weaknesses of the youth movements, labor movements, and other newer forms of activism in Jordan, these were all more organically rooted in Jordanian society. None were as deeply elite-based as the traditional opposition of either the secular left or the religious right. And as such, they still retain the potential for more genuine grassroots mobilization. They may need only a spark to do so.

Still, Jordan's opposition tends to remain divided in terms of goals, priorities, and forms of organization. But the clear organizational disunity may mask the fact that even these disparate groups agree on at least a few important factors. The grievance list here will sound similar to the complaints enumerated toward the end of the previous chapter on traditional opposition. Even here, with the more alternative and grassroots opposition movements, there is consensus that corruption is the main problem affecting Jordanian politics and society and that this needs to be dealt with seriously. Most activists believe there should be more checks and balances between political institutions, with a strengthening of the role of parliament, but also one that is itself transformed by more fair and representative electoral laws, though there is little agreement regarding how that is to be achieved. Most continue to view parliament itself with disdain, so they are thinking here of an altogether transformed institution—one that has yet to emerge. Activists also tend to agree that the judiciary should be more independent and that political dissent should not be curtailed or subject to intervention by the Mukhabarat or the State Security Court. They all call for a return to a more free and open media, again without state interference. And many call for a more constitutional monarchy. They are also united in their pervasive lack of trust in the regime and the ruling elite. Many feel that 2011–2012 should have been the moment for real and lasting change to match the regime's own rhetoric about its reform program. But that moment, they argue, has passed. The question is, what is to come next?

Beyond the Arab Spring: Prospects for Political Activism in Jordan

Some of Jordan's strongest democracy advocates pursue their activism in ways that do not include parties, elections, street demonstrations, or other protests. Jordan has, for example, also seen extensive online activism, community organization, and single-issue activism.[22] The Arab Spring era saw a rise in online activism and citizen journalism across the Arab world, and Jordan was no exception. These were consummately democratic forms of activism and participation in public debate. Even when the streets are silent, in the sense of no protests, there is often much more going on in online dialogues and forums. Even at the height of Jordan's Arab Spring protests, as is true of most societies, most people were not actually out protesting. I am not, however, suggesting here that this large segment of Jordanian society amounts to a "silent majority." Majority yes, but not in any way silent, especially if one simply examines Jordanian social media. Jordan's political dialogues take place not just in the streets, in cafes, in state institutions, or in editorial pages but also and especially in social media forums. During the Arab Spring era, these included extensive Jordanian presence on Facebook, Twitter, Instagram, Snapchat, and Whatsapp, to name just a few. Jordan's Arab Spring saw the rise of extensive levels of youth activism, both in the streets and in cyberspace, from blogs to Twitter to Facebook groups. This included expanding public-sphere discussions on virtually all topics, in cyberspace, in print, and in person. Activists organized countless events that were then tweeted, posted, and live-streamed. From the king himself to the most ardent grassroots activists, Jordanians are a tech-savvy lot, and especially in the Arab Spring era they were not shy in making their voices heard.

Like other Arab countries, Jordan saw a rise in citizen journalism. Jordan's innovative 7iber project, for example, engages in multimedia online journalism. 7iber (or *Hiber*, the Arabic word for ink) was actually established in 2007, before the Arab Spring. The group has, from the outset, remained deeply committed to internet freedom and digital media. During the Arab Spring era, 7iber activists also launched what they called the "hashtag debates"—gatherings of citizens for open democratic discussions of controversial and important issues. These included public discussions on reform, social media, the constitution, and even such controversial topics as the role of the Mukhabarat in Jordanian life. The activists tweeted their reactions during the debates while also receiving questions, via Twitter, from those who could not participate in person. Debates were live-streamed to maximize the audience, including a session in which activists engaged in a wide-ranging discussion with Jordan's former head of the National Agenda for Reform, Marwan Muasher.[23]

Youth interested in engaging in serious political discourse established Maqha Amman al-Siyasi (the Amman political coffee house)—a coffee house style of informal meetings for political discussions, also known as Le Café Politique. Like the hashtag debates, Café Politique sessions used social media to draw in virtual participants and live-stream events. The group's Facebook page provided a forum that often led to rigorous and politically diverse online discussions about political and social topics. "The purpose of this forum," the group wrote, "is to provide a virtual Salon of thought-provoking dialogue. Focusing on the Jordanian and Arab narrative, our aim is to include a diverse spectrum of political ideologies."[24] Hirak and other activists sometimes criticized liberal Amman-based activism as elitist and Amman-centric—and even more specifically, West Amman-centric, referring to the wealthier side of the capital city. But many in each of these groups were rigorous in their attempts to maintain inclusive and pluralist networks that crossed ethnic, religious, and sometimes class lines.

Groups like Taqaddam (Progress) sought to create a liberal, democratic, and progressive current in Jordanian society and, very importantly, to create a political space for secular political discourse in Jordan. With a base especially in the Amman liberal business and professional communities, Taqaddam worked to carefully and methodically build a program. It intended to move beyond discussion, to play an active and progressive role in Jordanian public life, but was not in a rush to form a political party or to field candidates in elections. At least not yet. One activist noted that the goal was to create a meaningful and effective liberal current, but liberal in the social and political, rather than economic, sense. The latter version, in the form of neoliberalism, had earned a bad name in much of Jordanian society and represented much of what people were actually protesting about. So the group would emphasize its progressive orientation, liberal in all but name. It would be based on "social and political liberalism, on individual rights and liberties," noted one activist. "There are so many people who feel this way, but each of us feels alone."[25] Taqaddam aimed to bring progressives together but to remain progressive in a broadly conceived sense, rather than being more narrowly ideological. The group met frequently, working on multiple tracks for a broader platform that covered politics, the economy, culture, education, environmentalism, media and information technology, and social issues. Activists hoped to expand their membership, including geographically, and slowly but surely create a space in Jordanian politics for secular, progressive, and reform-oriented Jordanians.[26]

Still other activists turned away from broader forms of organization toward specific issues, seeing these as perhaps more achievable. Some of these campaigns were relatively small and focused, such as the active grassroots campaigns against nuclear power (near Mafraq) or to save the Berqesh forest (near Ajlun). But others, such as the national campaign against gas from Israel, seemed to reactivate the street protest movement, assembling broad-based coalitions of supporters. The campaign against Israeli gas, in fact, seemed to reenergize a fairly diverse cross-section of Jordanian political activists, bringing protesters back to the streets in the largest-scale demonstrations since the Arab Spring.

In September 2014 Jordan's National Electric Power Company (NEPCO), in accordance with the wishes of the Jordanian government, signed a letter of intent with Noble Energy, a U.S. energy company based in Houston, Texas. The agreement called for Jordan to import natural gas from the Leviathan oil field in the eastern Mediterranean—an oil field controlled by Israel, but one that many Jordanians view as being rightfully Palestinian. The deal was designed to account for at least 40 percent of Jordan's liquefied natural gas needs, guaranteeing a steady supply of gas from Israel.

Jordan remains not only an aid-dependent country but also an energy-dependent state, so Jordan's government hoped that the deal would shore up the kingdom's energy needs. The deal was intended to replace the kingdom's previous reliance on sources such as Egypt and its frequently sabotaged pipeline across Sinai. The deal faced multiple obstacles, including

Israel's own antitrust authorities concerned over growing energy monopolies. Economic circumstances also changed when Jordan opened its own liquefied natural gas (LNG) terminal in Aqaba, thereby opening the kingdom to any number of possible suppliers. But within Jordan, aside from the economic motivations behind the deal, what was striking was the depth of resistance to the deal itself, and the reemergence of a broad and democratic opposition coalition for the first time since the early days of the Arab Spring.

On March 6, 2015, at least a thousand protesters marched in Jordan against a proposed deal in which the kingdom would purchase most its gas from Israel.[27] The Jordanian government had made initial moves to purchase large amounts of gas from Israel, leading to outrage among many in Jordanian society, especially as the announcement came shortly after the end of the Israeli-Hamas conflict in 2014, which had involved the Israeli bombardment of Gaza. Activists argued that Jordan would effectively be subsidizing the occupation of Palestinians in Gaza by purchasing Israeli gas. This ultimately led to the slogan of the emerging protest movement: "The gas of the enemy is occupation." Activists argued that the slogan has a dual meaning, implying that by buying Israeli gas, Jordan is subsidizing Palestinian occupation, but also implying that Jordan itself is being "occupied" by giving Israel so much control over the kingdom's energy sources.

The movement was well organized and drew together liberals, leftists, nationalists, and Islamists. It wasn't a movement that immediately hit the streets, however. Instead, grassroots activists gathered for a meeting to plan a response. Rather than protest, they focused first on research. The government hadn't been particularly forthcoming with information, so data and details were needed. A coordination committee worked with Platform, a London-based think tank, to get the details of the deal itself, including how Jordanian taxes would effectively go to Israel via the gas purchases. The coordination committee presented its findings in a press conference, setting the stage for the committee to become a movement.

On December 28, 2014, the campaign held the first of several national conferences against the deal. Individual activists and civil society groups were joined by professional associations, leftist and Pan-Arab nationalist political parties, labor organizations and trade unions, women's rights organizations, Hirak youth activist organizations, and the influential organization for retired military veterans. The coalition also included the Jordanian version of the Boycott, Divestment, and Sanctions (BDS) movement, but this was also just one of more than thirty organizations represented.[28] The coalition thus ranged from progressive, leftist, and liberal forces to Islamists, and even centrist and nationalist political parties. These included the Islamic Action Front, both of Jordan's two Ba'thist parties, as well the Stronger Jordan Party and many others. While Islamists have been part of the movement, they have been a relatively small part. Top Muslim Brotherhood leaders came to some marches, for example, but did not mobilize their entire rank-and-file membership. This in turn, gave many leftist and progressive movements confidence in their own efforts, since they were succeeding in turning out significant numbers even without the Islamists. "This is the first 'unified' campaign since the Arab Spring broke up the ranks of unified work on major issues like normalization," said organizer Hisham Bustani.[29] Another activist put it this way: "Things are picking up. . . . I think there is a small opening within the public sphere, for the traditional opposition amongst leftist parties and professional unions, and their traditional causes to create some sort of dynamic, in partnership with various Hiraks around the country."[30]

The campaign had quickly become, in fact, one of the most diverse movements within Jordan since the start of the regional Arab Spring. Both traditional forms of opposition and newer forms such as the Hirak have tended to be overwhelmingly male in leadership and in terms of overall membership or participation. The campaign against buying gas from Israel, in contrast, included many women as demonstrators and as key leaders. It also brought together Arabs and Circassians, Muslims and Christians, secular and religious activists, and Jordanians of multiple different social and economic backgrounds. By bringing activists back to the streets, the campaign even influenced members of parliament to take up and debate the measure publicly, with many activists attending in the galleries of the parliament. MPs ultimately voted 107 to 13 against the deal in a nonbinding resolution. Since parliament remains a weak institution in Jordan, it didn't have the authority to change Jordanian national policy, but the demonstrations and the vote seemed to be enough to shelve the issue at least momentarily.

"We also tried to redefine the relationship between the citizen and the state," said Bustani. "We talk about the *taxpayer*, about the taxpayer's money, about *our* money and how it is being used." These goals were underscored not only by the specific protest actions of the movement but also by its emphasis on research, on facts and data, and on getting this information to the general public. "The idea is to respect the audience," Bustani said, "to empower them, and to get them the information they need."[31]

In September 2015 the coalition moved beyond marches and protests to stage a unique event: a public tribunal that put the gas deal itself on trial. Working with members of the bar association and with many prominent lawyers, activists held a trial, complete with prosecution, defense, judges, and jury.[32] While these actions drew much attention to the campaign, other measures also gathered support across society, including from many Jordanians who were not otherwise involved in the movement at all. The most popular of these was the move to turn off lights (and hence tie the gas deal to the generation of electricity in Jordan) simultaneously across the country for one hour each week. This took place for several weeks in succession and garnered the participation even of people who considered themselves nonpolitical. The selective "blackouts" generated a public-sphere discussion and some level of popular engagement with the campaign, far beyond the activists themselves.[33]

Government officials and critics of Jordan's assorted opposition movements often argue, with some accuracy, that many movements are strong on criticism but weak on presenting viable policy alternatives. The movement against Israeli gas was therefore also unique among many activist groups in presenting the government with a host of alternatives, including specific alternative suppliers. This is especially worth noting because Jordan's own development strategies have called for diversifying its sources of energy, from the development of wind and solar power to investment projects (with Russia) for nuclear power plants. The latter choice is itself controversial and has generated its own activist movement in an attempt to thwart Jordan's pursuit of nuclear power.[34] But both campaigns—against Israeli gas and against nuclear power—represent alternative forms of activism within modern Jordanian politics.

Despite feeling that they had achieved real success, pushing the state to look into alternative energy suppliers, many activists and citizens across Jordan were stunned in September 2016 when Israel and Jordan announced they had signed the gas deal after all.[35] The move came immediately after the 2016 elections but before the new parliament convened. Predictably, the movement revived once again, bringing activists to the streets to protest the new deal, arguing that Jordan was not only subsidizing occupation but also making itself vulnerable to the whims of the Israeli government. The state, in turn, may have weighed the risks of raising energy prices (and triggering riots like those of November 2012) against what it viewed as the more manageable risk of bringing protesters back out into the streets. The protests weren't just about energy policy, however, but also about Jordanian sovereignty, Palestinian rights, the regime's priorities, and the question of having a public voice in an important matter of public policy. Very importantly, the anger over the issue also extended well beyond that of the protesters gathered in any particular demonstration.[36]

Naseem Tarawneh, a well-known Jordanian writer and blogger (the Black Iris of Jordan), questioned, however, whether the movement was itself falling for the usual pattern of rising and falling activism in Jordan, one that may be quite acceptable to the state. "There's a cyclical nature in which social protests unfold in Jordan that isn't just vexing, it has a dizzying déjà vu effect," he wrote. There is a danger, he argued, that external catalysts like Israel can provide a false sense of unity, and divert activism away from perhaps more pressing problems within Jordan itself. He continued:

> When you throw Israel into the mix of any unfolding national con-versation, what you usually get is noise. It's like throwing a blinding spotlight on to the madding crowd; the emotional sentiment and reaction is understandable, but also knee-jerk, automatic, and there-fore predictable. Raising questions even runs the risk of being seen as digressing from the default setting of being anti-Israeli. And therein lies our problem: Israel is the easiest and safest distraction for the masses. It quickly mobilizes people into a state of frenzy, and once that's initiated, the countdown begins until its final demise; until it's a distant memory. The clock is reset, and the process is repeated when necessary. The gas deal is simply a case that exemplifies the problem like nothing else has in Jordan since the Arab Spring began.[37]

Perhaps a broader test, then, would be if opposition activism were able to mobilize in similar ways but on distinctly different issues.

Still, the goals of the movement against Israeli gas included not only affecting Jordan's development trajectory and energy policies but also reviv-ing a public-sphere space for still broader citizen activism and effective democratic participation in Jordanian political life. "The campaign against the gas deal is a new kind of Jordanian protest movement," noted a key participant. "The activists in the movement have moved beyond slogan-eering, conducting serious research on the deal and entering into informed policy debates about energy security and the development of the national energy sector." The same activist noted that the movement specifically tried to move beyond the "mobilization repertoires" used by activists in the past. In doing so, they attempted not only to influence a specific policy choice but also to transform political activism and even political participation more broadly conceived. "We want people to rethink government and citizenship," noted one activist.[38]

Previous attempts at unified and democratic opposition have often been rooted in deals between aged opposition elites, but this was a grassroots movement that was both deeper and wider than many of its predecessors, drawing on people from different ages, classes, religions (Muslims and Christians), and ethnic backgrounds (including Transjordanians and Palestinians, tribal and non-tribal Jordanians, Circassians and Chechens). The movement, in short, bridged the many identity divisions across Jordanian society.

Continuity and Change

There is no shortage of activism (or of anger) in Jordan. Overall, for all the diversity and indeed division among forms of activism in Jordan, one thing that most activists share is frustration. Reform, however defined, has not proceeded as they had hoped. Most activists see Jordan continuing to pursue its standard neoliberal economic development agenda, most see corruption as a persistent and unresolved issue, and most see political reform as barely more than cosmetic change. So despite all the reasons noted above for the decline in protests, demonstrations, and public activism, this remains a key overall point: none of the issues that originally brought people to the streets in 2011 has been clearly resolved. Protest and demonstrations may have declined after 2012, but Jordan's political debates, policy struggles, and indeed even its economic, social, and political crises have all continued.

Chapters 3 and 4 have shown extensive levels of proreform and prodemocracy activism in Jordanian politics but with little success in achieving reform. In addition to an ever-expanding number of NGOs, civil society groups, trade unions, and professional associations, Jordanian politics has seen decades of opposition activism and coordination involving established left-wing and Pan-Arab nationalist parties as well as the larger and more popular Jordanian Islamist movement (including Jordan's two Muslim

Brotherhoods, the Islamic Action Front, and independent Islamists). In addition, newer reform movements emerged, from coalitions such as the Jordanian Campaign for Change to the many Hirak groups as well as increasingly pervasive youth and social media activism. But for all their presence, activism, and attempts at coordination, Jordan's reformers and democracy activists are more pluralist than a single reform coalition and to date have had limited effectiveness in achieving reform and change.

Yet in some ways, observing Jordanian reform struggles is like watching two coalitions maneuver and spar with one another. One is a tighter, narrower, conservative, antireform coalition embedded in key institutions in the state itself. The other is a set of movements for reform and hence is a broader, more diverse, and highly pluralistic set of groups that constitute a coalition in only the loosest possible sense. These include the traditional opposition rooted in Islamist, leftist, and nationalist parties, as well as the series of youth movements and forms of activism discussed in this chapter. This general image, however—of two sparring sets of coalitions—would seem to suggest a distinct advantage for the antireform coalition so deeply imbedded in the regime itself. But what is also most noticeable in the sparring between these two large sets of forces is that they sometimes appear to belong to two different eras.

The king's own former leader of regime reform efforts, Marwan Muasher, emphasized in his report for the Carnegie Foundation that the problem is not unique to Jordan but can be found throughout the region. Entrenched elites oppose reform, he argues, because they occupy "a privileged position that would be compromised by merit-based systems, rather than ones based on clientelism and patronage." In the specific case of Jordan, he adds, the ruling elite, and especially antireform elites, need to realize that they are deluding themselves but no one else: "The political elite must recognize that the only way they can retain power is by sharing it, and governments will have to acknowledge that substituting serious implementation with reform rhetoric fools no one."[39]

Meanwhile, the layer of fear does seem to have been lifted in Jordan and across the Arab world, and in some ways it is represented by the contrast between tweeting, blogging, and Facebooking activists, on the one hand, and the crude physical and brutal methods of the *bultajiyya* (thugs), on the other. The image of that contrast should serve to remind outside observers also that most Jordanians are under thirty. Most have been hearing about reform promises and campaigns all their lives. Many, but not all, are tapped into broader regional and global networks, are well educated and literate, and are not shy about voicing their political views. The future, they feel, is clearly theirs, and many hope that it will be a future of reform and democracy in Jordan. That does not mean, however, that they are particularly optimistic. And they certainly aren't naïve.

Yet many activists, especially the youth who were so inspired in 2011, became disillusioned over the years that followed, and they had little to no confidence in the reform process or the rhetoric or intentions of the state. Some of the king's own advisors are themselves dedicated reformers, while others seem to come from precisely the opposite camp. But the reformers remain emphatic that the king is still with them and has simply been thwarted at seemingly every turn by an old elite inherited from his late father and a newly entrenched elite that is, ironically, largely of his own making. The two largest parts of the regime's ruling political elite might therefore also be seen to include more specifically an old-guard, largely East Jordanian elite rooted in the bureaucracy, security services, and armed forces, and a newer elite (which arose with King Abdullah's accession to the throne) of more business-oriented technocrats, including both East Jordanians and Palestinians.[40] Among more grassroots reform activists, in contrast, there is considerably less faith that the monarchy is really with them. For most, their instincts remain reformist rather than revolutionary, but they retain little hope that meaningful change is coming soon.

CHAPTER V

Identity Politics, Real and Imagined

M any discussions of Jordanian politics, almost regardless of the specific topic, eventually arrive at identity politics.[1] Many note, for example, the importance of identity politics within Jordan, especially noticeable in the form of a private sector that is largely Palestinian and a public sector or state institutions that are dominated by Jordanians of East Bank origins. As economic liberalization and privatization continued in Jordan, shrinking the public sector and empowering the private sector, many historically bedrock proregime communities felt increasingly left out of the kingdom's development plans. Tribal East Jordanians have long been seen as the core supporters of the Hashemite regime, but as Jordan experiences often dramatic economic, social, and political changes, such expectations regarding loyalty or regime support can no longer be assumed.

As previous chapters have shown, the regime has come under considerable criticism from East Bank tribal leaders, veteran military officers, and largely East Jordanian youth movements in the form of the Hirak, in addition to criticism from Islamists, leftists, and liberal democracy activists. When uprisings rocked the Arab world in 2011, Jordan's youth-based Hirak movements emerged throughout the kingdom, but most often in tribal East Jordanian communities.[2] Many protesters felt that Jordan's neoliberal reform process had gone too far, and that it had undermined the social safety net as well as their own prospects for jobs and livelihoods.[3] To some extent, the Arab Spring protests in general seemed to echo the earlier 1989 era of protest, when most (but certainly not all) of those hitting the streets seemed to be Transjordanians, and hence were read by some in the regime as far more alarming than the "usual suspects" of Palestinian- or Islamist-based protests.

As noted in chapter 4, identity politics did reemerge as at least part of the debate surrounding the challenge of the Hirak. Yet struggles over national identity, rights, loyalty, and citizenship have been part of Jordanian politics since the foundation of the state. So the key issue for this chapter is not that identity politics itself is in any way new but rather precisely how and to what extent it matters for understanding Jordanian politics during and long after the Arab Spring. One of the conclusions of this chapter is that Jordanian politics cannot be reduced to the simple binary of Jordanian-Palestinian divisions; yet this fault line—for all its artificiality—is nonetheless often activated and even manipulated especially by reactionary elements in Jordanian politics in their efforts to thwart reform and change. Despite its artificial nature, in short, identity politics—and especially the abuse of identity politics—remains the Achilles' heel of Jordanian politics.

This chapter attempts to explain how and why the resurgence in identity politics in Jordan was well under way long before the Arab Spring began, and also how it has affected, and been affected by, the protests, demonstrations, and political changes during and after the Arab Spring. I will first turn to the very idea of identity politics: what does identity even mean in the Jordanian context, or, *who*, really, are the Jordanians? This may sound like a rather basic question. But it is actually a complicated one, and many debates on other topics in Jordan seem to continually return to this issue, with some Jordanians having a broad, diverse, and inclusive answer to the question "who is Jordanian?" while others have narrow visions and hence fear for the survival of a Jordan they feel may be slipping away.

Jordanians, Palestinians, and National Identity

Jordan as a country was drawn on the map by British imperial officials and named after the Jordan River. Many decades later, the Jordan River remains in many ways the political symbol of the main ethnic dividing line within Jordanian politics: between those whose origins are traced to the West Bank of the river, namely, Palestinians, and those whose origins lie in the East

Bank of the river. The latter group is alternatively referred to as East Bankers, Transjordanians, or East Jordanians. Whether Palestinians are a minority or majority in Jordan remains a highly contentious issue. In the absence of clear statistics, most analysts assume that Palestinian Jordanians constitute either half the Jordanian population or perhaps a majority.[4]

There is general agreement in the literature on identity politics in the kingdom that this line between Palestinians and East Jordanians can be one of the deepest fissures in Jordanian politics but that it is also but one of many levels of identity within the kingdom.[5] Jordan is mostly Arab but includes also Circassian and Chechen minorities; it is mostly Sunni Muslim but includes also Christian and even Druze minorities. In addition, tribal politics continue to matter profoundly, and many studies of identity in Jordan focus extensively on the tribal aspects of the formation and maintenance of national identity within the East Jordanian community.[6] Indeed, while there are at times tensions between East Jordanians and Palestinians, there are also many fissures within the East Jordanian community itself, especially between and within clans and tribes, as these too reassert their separate identities.[7] Tribal politics has, for example, seen a rise in intergenerational conflict, as youth movements have increasingly sought to find their own path, without routine deference to tribal leaders.[8] There are also vast differences regionally between tribes, whose economic fortunes and political influence vary considerably. It is therefore important to bear in mind that East Jordanian or Transjordanian is not actually a unitary category. It is, rather, an artificial social construct whose salience varies. Finally, Transjordanian does not necessarily equate to tribal, which in turn does not necessarily equate to bedouin.

In her study of identity politics, Luisa Gandolfo emphasizes multiple identities rather than a single Jordanian identity: "The identities of Jordan bind individuals to their history and origin, fracturing the monolithic 'Jordanian' identity into a kaleidoscope of major and minor *ethnies*. Incorporating Palestinian-Jordanians, Palestinians, ethnic Jordanians and bedouin tribal Jordanians, in addition to the Chechen and Circassian communities, identity is augmented by faith. In turn, the Christian and Islamic identities distill into denominations and sects."[9]

Jordan is, in short, more diverse than it sometimes appears, and "national identity" in the Hashemite Kingdom includes various levels of ethnic, religious, geographic, or regional identity. Modern Jordanian and Palestinian national identities both emerged only in the twentieth century.[10] Both refer to predominantly Arab peoples, with Sunni Muslim majorities and significant Christian minorities. Even among the artificial constructs of national identities, this remains an artificial "ethnic" distinction. As Hisham Bustani argues, this insistence on separate identities limits both peoples' options and futures, hindering a united reform movement and playing into the hands of antireform regime elites.[11]

Yet, like so many artificial constructs, these identities are vividly real and very meaningful to many actual Palestinians and Jordanians and are even reinforced in the educational system.[12] While Palestinian national identity has been deeply affected by the struggle with Israel, Jordanian national identity has been more deeply intertwined with the creation of the state itself as a Hashemite Kingdom. As part of the League of Nations Mandate System, Britain created the Emirate of Transjordan in 1922, which in 1946 became the independent Hashemite Kingdom of Jordan.

The Hashemites themselves hailed originally from neither west nor east of the Jordan River but from the Hijaz in what is now western Saudi Arabia. The Hashemite family had ruled Mecca and its environs but were defeated and expelled by the rival al-Sa'ud family as it consolidated its control over much of Arabia after World War I (leading to the creation of Saudi Arabia in 1932). As allies of Britain in the war, the Hashemites, having lost their original seat of power in Mecca, were rewarded with the newly established monarchies in both Transjordan and Iraq. The latter monarchy was overthrown in a bloody military coup in Baghdad in 1958, but the Hashemite family retained and strengthened its rule in Jordan, in large part due to the loyalty of the Jordanian army, and also due to strategic alliances with key tribes.

With the monarchy and armed forces as the foundational institutions of the state, Jordanian national identity has been deeply affected by the Hashemite alliance with the tribes of Jordan in creating the kingdom, and by royalist sentiment and service in the state security forces.[13] Yet within Jordan, this has always been problematized by the Israeli-Palestinian conflict since Jordan absorbed waves of Palestinian refugees in the wars of 1948 and 1967 and in the years between. Unlike most Arab countries, Jordan in 1950 extended citizenship to Palestinian refugees. The Hashemite Kingdom of Jordan as it has developed since independence in 1946 is therefore a combined legacy of British imperial designs (establishing Jordan in the first place), regional wars, repeated refugee flows, and, of course, Hashemite rule.

The tensions following the Arab-Israeli war of 1967 led to perhaps the lowest point in Jordanian history: the civil war of 1970–1971. That conflict, better known as Black September, saw the defeat of Palestine Liberation Organization (PLO) guerrillas at the hands of King Hussein's Jordanian army. For Jordanians who recall that disastrous moment in the country's history, some bitterness remains, with dramatically polarized perceptions. Hence many in Jordan remember the event either for Hashemite brutality in suppressing the PLO and the refugee camps or for Palestinian disloyalty and subversion against a country that had given them sanctuary. But even five decades later, there is little middle ground on the issue.[14]

Today, despite a troubled history, both Palestinian Jordanians and Transjordanians can be found among the country's ruling elite. Jordan is a kingdom of both East Bankers or Transjordanians as well as West Bankers or Palestinian Jordanians. Yet these are not entirely separate communities, as intermarriage is common, so many families have roots east and west of the Jordan River. In addition, neither community is in any way unitary. While some Palestinians continue to live in destitute camps attached to major urban areas, for example, others live in plush villas in upscale neighborhoods such as Abdun in West Amman. Similarly, East Bank Jordanians range in fortunes and circumstances from poor villages in the South to the height of wealth and power in the kingdom. Some have bedouin roots, but most do not. Still, even the many East Jordanians whose roots were in sedentary towns, villages, and agricultural communities at the time of the state's founding in 1946 maintain tribal—if not necessarily bedouin—links. Tribe and tribalism continue to matter in Jordanian politics, as many Jordanians take very seriously the support network of family, clan, and tribe.[15]

East Jordanians have historically dominated the civilian and military aspects of the public sector—the police, the armed forces, the government bureaucracy, and the intelligence services (Mukhabarat). From the founding of the state to the present, the security forces have been recruited heavily from among the tribes, East Jordanian villages and urban communities, and Circassian and Chechen minorities. Indeed, many in the security forces (both military and civilian) see their role as defending the country not only from outside threats but also from internal threats, and protecting Jordanian nationalism itself. "The security sector in Jordan perceives itself as the guardian, protector, and stronghold of Jordanian nationalism in the face of a demographic or political Palestinian takeover of Jordan," writes Nawaf

Tell. "The roots of this perception go back to the Jordanian-Palestinian confrontation of 1970–1971."[16] With the demographic balance in mind, the kingdom even abandoned national military conscription in 1992, maintaining thereafter a volunteer professional army—and one that is overwhelmingly East Jordanian.

In contrast, Palestinian Jordanians correspondingly constitute much (but by no means all) of the private sector.[17] There are, of course, exceptions, as more young East Jordanians forgo military or civilian government service to go into business themselves, especially in the current climate of economic privatization. More and more sons and daughters of the government, military, and intelligence elite can be found in private business and the professions, mirroring socially the shift in the Jordanian economy itself. But historically, Jordanian politics featured this de facto ethnic division of labor. Correspondingly, nationalists from both communities can and often do claim that their group built the country, and each is partially right. One is referring to national military and civilian service and governing institutions, while the other is referring to developing the economy through private enterprise and entrepreneurship.

In his study of identity politics, Adnan Abu Odeh writes: "The de-Palestinianization of the security apparatus has triggered a self-perpetuating divisiveness. Transjordanians look on Palestinian-Jordanians as disloyal or, perhaps, as permanent subjects, and thus see no reason why they should be part of officialdom. . . . Since the authority of the state in Jordan is felt most strongly through the Transjordanian-dominated security apparatus, the Palestinian grassroots feel that the state is not theirs." He argues further that there are also material aspects that underpin real and perceived divisions, which sometimes vary dramatically between social classes.

The exclusion of Palestinian-Jordanians from the public sector means not only reducing their employment opportunities but also depriving them and their families of the fringe benefits that go with government jobs, such as health insurance and subsidized goods (food, clothing, and appliances) to which the army, security personnel, and civil servants are entitled. This fact arouses the resentment of Palestinian-Jordanian lower-middle-class families, just as the ration given by UNRWA to Palestinian refugees arouses the resentment of Transjordanian lower-middle-class families.[18]

Abu Odeh's views remain controversial in Jordan. Many scholars see them as too deterministic, too binary, in what may better be understood as a complicated mosaic. But some in the regime were angry that he aired his views at all, especially in a book published in the United States. Abu Odeh was expelled from the Jordanian Senate after the publication of his book.

Still, the economic dimensions of identity politics remain vitally important, and they underscore the cross-cutting issue of social class. As another Jordanian analyst noted: "The division here is not just Palestinian-Jordanian. Mainly the issue is rich-poor: the haves and have nots. Jordanians and Palestinians are on the inside, in the top elite, and on the outside too."[19] Despite the fact that each community has its rich and its poor, there remains a tendency for each to see the other group as the wealthy one. One Jordanian analyst argued that "Jordanian identity has a class conflict within it, especially among those who resent rich Palestinians and want them out, so that the wealth will be Jordanian. They even think that Palestinians living in camps are somehow hoarding wealth."[20] Such conservative East Jordanian nationalists therefore resent what they see as Palestinian inroads in the state itself. Correspondingly, many Palestinians—regardless of income and class—see themselves as less empowered politically. "Palestinians complain about being underrepresented in the public sector or in high positions in government. They want *wasta* and don't have it," noted one commentator, adding, "but they don't want to change the regime or the state, they want to be in it. Jordanians want to get into the private sector for more money and wealth, but Palestinians want to get into the public sector for more influence."[21]

National Unity or Divide and Rule?

The Hashemite monarchy has insisted for decades that it has had enough of this emphasis on two distinct communities within one state. Historically, the regime has demonstrated no tolerance for displays of Palestinian nationalism, usually seen as at the expense of Jordanian nationalism. The latter, on the other hand, is strongly encouraged but tends to be wrapped in royalist symbols that make Jordanian nationalism difficult to separate from Hashemite identity. Yet the regime has also shown little patience for ultraconservative nativist Jordanian trends that tend to be overtly hostile to Palestinians.

It is worth remembering here that the Hashemites aren't originally from the territory that is now Jordan either. But many, including in the Jordanian state, see that as more of an asset than a liability because even with the tribal emphasis within state institutions, it would be more divisive if the Hashemites represented one of Jordan's many tribes or other groups in society. Instead, the monarchy has always presented itself as the unifying force bringing together multiple communities—Palestinians and East Jordanians, urbanites and bedouins, Muslims and Christians, secularists and Islamists, and Arabs as well as Circassian and Chechen minorities—and of course as the force uniting the tribes themselves into something larger: a state and a nation.

Like his father before him, King Abdullah II refers to Jordanian society as a family (with the king as head, of course) and frequently calls for national unity in the face of numerous challenges. The regime also emphasizes its Islamic credentials as Al al-Bayt—that is, that the Hashemites are of the house of the Prophet Muhammad and are direct descendants. They may have lost Mecca long ago to the rising power of the Saudis, but they maintain ties to Jerusalem's Muslim and Christian Holy places and see themselves as custodians of these sites, including the sacred Islamic sites: the al-Aqsa Mosque and the Dome of the Rock. In nationalist terms, they also emphasize their role as leaders of the Great Arab Revolt against the Ottoman Turkish Empire. On June 2, 2016, the Hashemite monarchy sponsored a series of lavish celebrations of the hundredth anniversary of the revolt, underscoring it as a consummately Hashemite and Jordanian event. And indeed, in terms of the state, nation, and loyalty, these two concepts—Hashemite and Jordanian—are often closely intertwined in everything from state holidays to postage stamps to the various denominations of the national currency (the dinar). The regime has in the past tied itself to this key event but has emphasized it still more over time, including even developing a tourist spectacle in which visitors can see reenactments of bedouin cavalry attacking Ottoman Turkish positions (and a train) as part of a tourism event in Wadi Rum.

It is worth quoting the Royal Hashemite Court's press release from the 2016 celebrations since it conveys the state vision of how the Arab revolt underpins both Jordan's regional importance and also Jordanian national identity itself. It also gives a clear sense of the sheer scope of the event. According to the Royal Court:

His Majesty King Abdullah II, the Supreme Commander of the Jordan Armed Forces—Arab Army (JAF), on Thursday, attended a grand military parade in which 1,000 military personnel participated at the newly-built Al Rayah parade ground, located at the Royal Hashemite Court. The parade, which was the culmination of the Kingdom's celebrations of the Great Arab Revolt Centennial and the Arab Awakening anniversary, was held in the presence of Her Majesty Queen Rania Al Abdullah, His Royal Highness Crown Prince Al Hussein bin Abdullah II, Royal Family members, senior officials and 5,000 guests. Among the audience were families of some of those who participated in the Great Arab Revolt and families of JAF martyrs. The parade coincides with the anniversary of the passing away of the Great Arab Revolt leader, Sharif Hussein bin Ali, who fired its first shot on 10 June 1916. The Revolt not only ended four centuries of regression, it also ushered in a restoration of the Arab Nation's spirit, identity and sovereignty.

Events like this underscore the importance of the royal and state connections to the armed forces, which in turn are also part of the national identity and image of Jordan itself that the state wishes to project.

In terms of internal identity issues, however, from the perspective of many elites within the regime, the Hashemite strategy is not a matter of divide and rule but rather a deft royal policy of pluralism and inclusion. This can be seen in the appointment of prime ministers and cabinets, in which Palestinians will be included; however, East Jordanian majorities will usually be maintained. Royal cabinet appointments are also mindful of geographic differences and tend to carefully include figures from different regions of the country and from various influential tribes. Similarly, Jordan's elections in 1989, 1993, 1997, 2003, 2007, 2010, 2013, and 2016 were designed to yield loyalist proregime parliaments with East Banker majorities, based on gerrymandered districts created to maintain a power imbalance that did not match the demographics of the Palestinian-Transjordanian balance, and certainly not of an oft-alleged Palestinian majority.

Many conservative Transjordanian nationalists agree strongly with this strategy. Their insistence on maintaining a Transjordanian majority is based in part on their fear that Israel will attempt to "solve" the Palestinian problem by making Jordan the "alternative homeland" (al-watan al-badil). As one nationalist put it: "There is a danger of Palestinian empowerment in

Jordan making the Israeli 'Jordan is Palestine' argument real. Of making it viable. Even having more Palestinian government ministers does this too. We can't let this get past or even to 50 percent representation—we lose Jordanian identity at that very moment."[22]

While the monarchy sees itself as the bridge linking Palestinian Jordanians and Transjordanians, many critics suggest that the opposite is often true. Opposition activists, for example, argue that the regime offers intermittent cosmetic reforms simply to buy time, but, in the words of one activist, that it is really engaged in "an agenda of permanent conflict resolutions, with the regime as facilitator." The same activist added, "In Bahrain, the regime is forming its identity against an 'other'; in Jordan, the regime is the barrier between identities."[23] In contrast, the monarchy itself would strongly dispute this characterization and in fact make the opposite argument. The regime does indeed talk at length (complete with extensive marketing and billboard campaigns) about national unity, including such campaigns as the "Jordan First" (*al-Urdun Awalan*) program or the "We Are All Jordan" (*Kullina al-Urdun*) campaign. These are but two examples of the recurring emphasis on branding for both the regime and the country. The state, in short, has repeatedly launched marketing campaigns toward its own citizens, often emphasizing unity amid diversity, and a national identity that is tied together by Hashemite rule. Critics, however, nonetheless argue that divide-and-rule strategies also remain part of the state's tactics and strategies, especially when it is challenged. As even one Jordanian official suggested, "The regime talks unity but opens fissures in response to any opposition."[24]

But if so many Jordanians reject ethnic identity politics as divisive and out-of-date, why do we so often see upsurges in identity politics, in which many Jordanians actually identify with ever smaller units—not Jordan but East Jordanian or Palestinian, or even smaller units such as region, tribe, or clan? The roots may lie considerably earlier, as the Jordanian public sphere practically erupted into debates about identity, nation, and nationhood in response to a series of key policy and regional changes. Specifically, when King Hussein in 1988 officially "disengaged" from the West Bank, relinquishing Jordanian claims on the territory (lost to Israeli forces in the war of 1967), this was truly a game-changer in the Arab-Israeli conflict and peace process. But it was also a game-changer within Jordanian domestic politics since it led to raging debates about who, exactly, was Jordanian as opposed to Palestinian. Were these inherently separate identities?

Or inherently linked? The initial debates also coincided with Jordan's earlier political opening and liberalization process, including a more open and pluralist media, which made the Jordanian public sphere that much more vibrant at the time.[25] The debates, in turn, grew still more extensive with each new move and change in Jordanian-Palestinian-Israeli relations, especially the Oslo Accords of 1993 between Israel and the PLO, the landmark Jordanian-Israeli Peace Treaty of 1994, and the Declaration of Principles of 1995 (for solving the Israeli-Palestinian conflict), signed by the Israeli government and the PLO.[26]

The more recent upsurge in identity debates has also been influenced by external events as they affected Jordan's domestic scene, as well as by the communications revolution triggered by the internet and the rise of online media in the kingdom. Jordan, it should be noted, has such an extensive online presence that there is more Arabic content from Jordan on the global internet than there is from almost any other country. The new identity debates were therefore triggered once again by regional events and facilitated by new media.

Several events in particular had a deep impact on Jordan's domestic politics, including the collapse of the Arab-Israeli peace process and rising fears in Jordan that Israel would attempt to turn Jordan into the alternative Palestinian state. Identity politics were also heightened by yet another surge of refugees and migrants into Jordan, this time Iraqis fleeing the U.S. invasion of Iraq in 2003 and the political chaos and violence that followed. Conservative nationalists, already worried over Palestinian inroads into Jordanian politics and society, feared that the Iraqis would become a new permanent refugee community—in effect, the new Palestinians—perhaps further diluting the position of East Jordanians in the Hashemite Kingdom. All these fears were amplified by the increasingly pervasive nature of electronic media, creating a kind of cyber public sphere in Jordan that defied past state controls in place for print media, radio, and television.

Many democracy activists argue that the electoral laws themselves had an enormous impact on identity politics within the kingdom, contradicting state unity campaigns by encouraging people to think in ever smaller units, including tribes. As author and activist Hisham Bustani argues:

Whereas the notorious 1993 one-man-one-vote elections law . . . tremendously strengthened the tribes and turned them from social units into political ones, the continuous detribalization at the top of the regime's bureaucracy was doubtless placing the regime on a collision course with the tribes. By detribalization here, I do not mean "Palestinianization." Many of the new guards are of eastern Jordanian descent, but they lack tribal connections and influence.[27]

This new elite is especially associated with the transition to King Abdullah II, even though the transition began earlier, and they are sometimes referred to within Jordan as "the digitals."

Even as external events and new technologies changed Jordan's politics, the kingdom's own neoliberal policies of privatization and structural adjustment also led to dramatic social (and hence political) disruptions in the Jordanian body politic. As privatization proceeded, state industries were sold, and the possibility and reliability of government employment correspondingly declined. With limited economic opportunities, more and more Jordanians were feeling physically and geographically displaced, especially those that migrated from the more rural South to urban centers in the North. A member of the Jordanian Senate noted the social tensions emerging from these changes: "Palestinians dominate the cities, and the higher levels of Palestinian wealth are very clear. As East Jordanians migrate from villages to the cities, they see this, but then live in poorer neighborhoods and even slums, and it only adds to their grudge."[28]

While many Jordanians do not hold these binary views regarding the two communities, nationalists often do, disagreeing even on how Jordan got to this point. Consider, for example, the following two interpretations of Jordan's development, each from an influential opinion maker in the kingdom. The first is from an interview with a prominent Palestinian Jordanian official.

The West Bank and East Bank united in 1950 and became one state, and Jordanian citizenship was given to Palestinians as well as Jordanians. They became an integral part of the kingdom. They had higher levels of income, education, and sophistication. East Jordan was underdeveloped and underpopulated. Together, the two groups built and developed the country. The 1967 war led to many new refugees. . . . In 1973 was the beginning of the oil revolution at the same time as the rising hardships of occupation in the West Bank, and also the weakness of the Jordanian economy. Many Palestinians migrated to the Gulf for jobs and they were well qualified. They were educated and enlightened, and they worked not as laborers but as managers and engineers, while Transjordanians were working in the public sector in Jordan, in the military, and in government. Palestinians sent money home and helped to develop Jordan and make it flourish. And Arab leaders poured millions into Jordan because of the Palestinians. And this country became as you see it now. . . . But the tribal parts of society are not used to private enterprise and even to labor. Many see it as beneath them. Unlike tribal culture, which limits what people are willing to do, Palestinians invested capital, developed banks and businesses and companies. The Jordanians remained running the state.

In contrast, this second viewpoint is from an interview with a prominent East Jordanian figure.

We are not opposed to Palestinians. We live with them. They are our friends and neighbors. We are married to them. We grew up with them. But we don't want to be a minority here. The big fear is of course that Israel tries to make Jordan the Palestinian state. But in some ways it already happened, not by Israelis but by Jordan. This is another version of the alternative Palestinian state. Palestinians dominate the economy. Now they dominate the government too. There are foreign pressures to increase their representation. Not just from Israel. From the U.S. and from international NGOs. But we built everything. It's not fair. We are marginalized in our own country. . . . We have no chance in the private sector. Most East Jordanian families entirely rely on the public sector. Most work there. So speaking out can destroy your family's livelihood. It's confusing. We aren't used to being in the opposition. But everything has changed overnight. Overnight it's all different.

East Jordanian nationalists, such as the one quoted above, argue that they are losing not only economically but also politically. The de facto monopoly on state employment no longer seems secure; hence they wish to prevent what they perceive as further Palestinian inroads on the state itself. In short, in the view of conservative East Jordanian nationalists, the private sector is already lost, and the state is all they have left to protect:

In our community, we all do national service. We serve in the army, the police, the intelligence services. We have always been willing to sacrifice our lives—and we have—for the state and for the regime. And now? Fight for who? Are they fighting for us? We can't even trust the big East Jordanian government men to fight for us. They will lose. The Palestinians are now getting peacefully what they tried to get in the civil war in 1970. They failed then, but they are winning now.

In a discussion with several Jordanian nationalists, one argued that "the Palestinians play the victimization card, and it pays. But it is important not to tip the demographic balance here." Another agreed, adding, "This is our country, not theirs. Theirs is Palestine." One of the nationalists in this discussion thought about his own comments for a moment and then continued: "But we are still here. We won't be silent forever. Especially as more and more of us become poor and marginalized. Not forever." Some of the more conservative nationalists I met with invoked a specific comparison, seeing their plight as similar to that of Sunnis in post-Saddam Iraq, a once-dominant group now marginalized in their own state.

Yet because of these extreme views, it is too often forgotten that East Jordanians as a whole are not synonymous with conservative or ultraconservative East Jordanian nationalists. And in 2011 and 2012 East Jordanians appeared to constitute the majority of prodemocracy and proreform demonstrators. Some even complained of the *absence* of Palestinians demonstrators (aside from those in the traditional opposition such as the Islamist movement and many leftist parties). It is perhaps ironic that Palestinians, so long reviled for being too active and too likely to take to the streets, were now being accused of being too docile.[29]

Despite all the economic, social, and political dislocations that have led to the current climate of heightened ethnic identity politics and have reinvigorated old debates about what it means to be an "authentic" Jordanian, it is important to note that most Palestinians and East Jordanians do not match the polarized and stereotypical images of their detractors, nor do they support this kind of bigotry. There are, to be sure, those with extreme views in each community. "We have a Jordanian Likud here," noted one activist, "but we have a Palestinian Likud too."[30] Unlike most Jordanians, hard-liners tend to enforce old binaries and reinforce stereotypes of whichever group they see as the "other" in Jordanian politics. Some Palestinians, for example, are disdainful of East Jordanians, seeing them as less educated, tribalistic, backward, and chauvinistic. Similarly, some East Jordanian nationalists view Palestinians as one of two social class stereotypes: either poor, ungrateful, disloyal, and perpetually complaining refugees draining state resources, or rich business moguls with an eye on profit but never on the national good. The latter set ironically mirrors old anti-Semitic stereotypes from Europe, in which Jews were so often victims of both ends of the class divide.

Yet contrary to these stereotypes, Jordanians of all backgrounds tend to be well educated and literate, and it is extremely important to note that most Jordanians would find such stereotypes insulting and offensive (as they of course are). Still, these ethnic rifts and sometimes polarized views matter because they can be manipulated by cynical and even unscrupulous reactionary elites—especially if they wish to break up protests, demonstrations, activist movements, and even state-led reform efforts in order to prevent change.

Identity Politics and the Arab Spring Demonstrations

Despite the ethnic and identity dynamics enumerated above, most demonstrators in 2010 and 2011 seemed to take to the streets without identity politics as their prime motivator. But many *shabab* (youth) movements that marched in West Amman were quite diverse and included Transjordanians and Palestinians, Muslims and Christians, Arabs and Circassians, men and women. Demonstrations arranged by the Islamist movement and other opposition parties often started downtown, near the al-Hussein Mosque, and included many Palestinians of various social classes, in addition to East Jordanians. For that reason, some state officials saw the first type of demonstration as nonpartisan and national in focus, while the second was often seen as ideological and Palestinian rather than Jordanian.[31]

As the demonstrations grew and the numbers swelled, however, there were de facto mergers of all the groups. And in that broader and more inclusive capacity, they gathered numbers, strength, and momentum and certainly caught the attention of the regime. Outside the capital, the makeup of protests and demonstrations varied considerably by location. Not surprisingly, East Jordanians made up the great majority of protesters in southern towns like Tafilah, Kerak, Ma'an, and Dhiban and saw their movement initially as a southern revival, much like the movement in 1989 that led to the political liberalization process in the first place. In the North, in cities with large Palestinian populations like Irbid and Zarqa, Palestinians were more likely to join East Jordanians in the demonstrations.

Rifa'i or Rifa'i?

In chapter 2 I noted the discussions in Jordan comparing the events of 2011–2012 to those of 1989. It is a comparison worth pursuing a bit further since in April 1989 most Palestinians and East Jordanians I spoke to routinely described then–prime minister Zayd al-Rifa'i as the consummate regime insider. Many saw him as an antireform, antidemocratic, Jordanian nationalist, notoriously hostile to demands for greater Palestinian empowerment. If identity politics came up at all regarding the prime minister, it was to emphasize his family connections across the northern border to Syria and what most viewed as his anti-Palestinian politics. In the 1989 episode, as antiausterity and antigovernment riots spread across southern Jordanian towns and cities, crowds chanted for the fall of the Rifa'i government. They got their wish and more, as Jordan embarked on a liberalization process.

Many years later, in 2011, as demonstrations spread across the same southern towns and the capital, protesters once again called for the ouster of the Rifa'i government. Only this time it was a different prime minister from the same family. In 2011 Jordan's prime minister was Samir Rifa'i, son of Zayd, scion of a powerful proregime family and fourth in the family line to serve the Hashemites as prime minister. This time, however, he seemed to be viewed as the archetype of what many East Jordanians were complaining about: government ministers who were actually neoliberal and technocratic Palestinian businessmen. When the king complied with protesters' demands, firing the entire cabinet, he replaced them with an East Jordanian former career military officer from the influential Abbadi tribe, Ma'rouf al-Bakhit. Ministerial portfolios changed, but little else did. Complaints about the nature of governance itself, in other words, were not addressed by the government shift. "The reshuffle of the Rifa'i government did neutralize some people for a short time," argued one democracy activist, "especially the generals and some of the tribal leaders. They wanted a government of tribal East Jordanians. They got them. But now? There is no real difference."[32]

Still, the change in government was emblematic of several broader problems: First, identity politics tends to be allowed to obscure more meaningful discussions of reform and change. Second, identity itself is fluid. Had the Rifa'i family changed ethnicity between 1989 and 2011? Many people I spoke with in 1989 emphasized the roots of the family in northern Jordan near the Syrian border and spoke with suspicion of the family's Syrian connections. In 2010 and 2011, in contrast, many noted accurately that the family had roots west of the Jordan River as well. Both Zayd and Samir al-Rifa'i see themselves as patriotic Jordanians with a long history of loyal service to the state. Yet comparing these episodes illustrates the tendency in politics for detractors to use identity issues seemingly to "change" an opponent's ethnicity to undermine that opponent's legitimacy in Jordanian public life. In 2010 and 2011, for example, many of his hardline detractors saw Samir Rifa'i as the embodiment of Palestinian inroads into the levers of power within the government itself.

This is in contrast, of course, to the allegedly purer roots of many East Jordanian families, especially those who proudly uphold their tribal backgrounds. And here we get to the real heart of the matter. Put simply, ultranationalist Transjordanians view themselves as pure Jordanians, often adding *mi'a bil-mi'a* (100 percent), and hence see themselves as more patriotic, and *more Jordanian*, than much of the rest of the country, which includes refugees, immigrants, and other "guests"—all of whom are seen as less authentic and merely as temporary denizens of the kingdom.

Yet these tribal and clan lineages predate the Hashemite Kingdom itself, and most families therefore have roots both within Jordan and across its various borders. This includes most obviously, and perhaps ironically, the Hashemites themselves, who migrated after World War I from Hijaz (in what is now Saudi Arabia) to Jordan before assuming control there and establishing the British-backed monarchy. For that reason, while the regime has historically stressed the importance of the tribes in creating and building the state, the Hashemite kings have nonetheless simultaneously rejected the kinds of nativist, exclusivist, and inherently narrow visions of Jordanian nationalism associated with figures such as Ahmad 'Uwaydi al-'Abbadi.[33] Yet similar arguments over identity can be found on the left in Jordan as well, including among some who marched in the Arab Spring demonstrations. "Just a few years ago, talking identity was blasphemous in progressive circles. Now it's valid," noted one prominent leftist activist and analyst. "But these are all fabrications. Jordan was a fabrication. All families have roots across borders."[34]

Manifestos and the Monarchy

If some East Jordanians were feeling more and more displaced within their own country, a key political question is, of course, who do they blame for this turn of events? Some conservative nationalists blame the Palestinians and what they see as a new Palestinian business elite taking over not only the private sector but also the state. Some blame the regime, while others see the two as increasingly indistinguishable, arguing that part of the problem was the excessive influence of what they viewed as the (Palestinian) Queen Rania on the (East Jordanian) King Abdullah. This was clear in the various manifestos in the early months of the Arab Spring, in which tribal leaders and retired military officers—all Transjordanians—criticized the monarchy and especially the queen directly. Queen Rania had, by that point, become a kind of lightning rod of controversy for many East Bank nationalists. Some tribal leaders—the Bayan of the 36—even publicly denounced what they saw as her too active role in Jordanian politics and policy. In doing so, they crossed all previously established red lines in Jordanian politics. The retired military officers (while not attacking the queen directly) went on record warning the monarchy against selling the state off to allegedly corrupt Palestinian business people.[35] A high-ranking Palestinian Jordanian government official stressed the urgency of the rising tensions: "I told His Majesty the King, they are angry. They are your army. They are your security. You have to do something about it."[36]

Perhaps oddly, the anger at the queen actually crossed various identity and even ideological fault lines, as the Islamist movement joined the public critiques.[37] While all detractors insisted that their critiques had nothing to do with the fact that Queen Rania is a well-educated, charismatic, multilingual, Palestinian-Jordanian woman, they each seemed to find in her a fault emblematic of national-level problems.[38] This is in sharp contrast to Queen Rania's international reputation, where she is better known for her YouTube, Twitter, and Instagram presence, and for her efforts in support of children and in eradicating global stereotypes against Arabs and Muslims. But Queen Rania also has many supporters within Jordan itself, who view these various complaints as little more than sexism, veiled in false patriotism or self-righteous but ultimately fake religiosity.

It is difficult to separate the lines of tension here since the complaints draw on ethnic, class, and gender divisions. It is likely that all play key roles, and that the queen presents simply an easier target for regime critics than directly attacking King Abdullah himself, and therefore this mirrors in some respects the region-wide trend of male leaders' wives under ever closer public scrutiny in the era of the Arab Spring and beyond.[39] For ultraconservative East Jordanian nationalists, however, their main complaint is the issue of alleged Palestinian political influence in the palace itself.

Most Palestinian Jordanians would of course find the argument about excessive Palestinian influence in Jordanian governance to be utterly laughable. Rather, they see themselves as routinely disenfranchised, underrepresented in government and even more underrepresented in the military, security, and intelligence services, and yet continually discriminated against in everyday life as they interact with the governing East Jordanian bureaucracy and these same institutional power centers on a daily basis. Despite this, many Palestinian Jordanians have experienced a kind of role reversal, in which they sometimes find themselves defending the monarchy against hardline East Jordanian nationalist critiques.

In April 2013, when King Abdullah returned to Jordan from Washington, D.C., again having worked to shore up U.S. support for Jordan in an increasingly volatile regional environment, he was met by yet another opposition manifesto, this time signed by a thousand opposition figures.[40] Previous manifestos (discussed in chapter 2) from tribal leaders and retired army officers had harshly criticized the regime's domestic economic and political agenda. The new manifesto, whose signatories included leftists, nationalists, Hirak representatives, and trade unionists, as well as tribal leaders and retired army officers, decried plots to undermine Jordanian sovereignty, condemned the neoliberal economic policies of the state, and once again rejected either confederation between an independent Palestine and Jordan or, even more emphatically, allowing Israel to exercise a "Jordan option" in solving the Palestinian issue at Jordanian expense.[41] The latest manifesto, in short, took a fairly strident tone regarding identity politics.

On many of these issues, left- and right-wing opponents within Jordan were sounding increasingly similar. Both sides used increasingly nativist or "isolationist" terminology in their critiques of Jordanian policy and identity politics. In the manifesto of 2013, the opposition statement launched into familiar critiques of the kingdom's foreign policy but also harshly criticized the regime's policies more broadly. The statement warned ominously about "plots" and "conspiracies" to undermine Jordan's sovereignty and identity as a state. The authors accused the regime of failing in its internal and external policies, resulting in "despair and frustration" for Jordanian citizens and "leading to increased levels of poverty and unemployment, deteriorating basic services, education, health and social welfare."[42] This scathing assessment of the kingdom's neoliberal economic development policies included a denunciation of the roles of the IMF and World Bank and condemned corruption in governance and especially in the process of economic privatization.

In many ways, the new statement echoed earlier manifestos, one from tribal leaders and another from retired military officers who had questioned the regime's path and priorities. Even as attempts emerged regionally to revive the long-moribund Arab-Israeli peace process, the "Manifesto of 1,000" pointedly rejected two feared outcomes: confederation between an independent Palestine and Jordan (as part of a future settlement of the Palestinian question) and, even more emphatically, any hint of Jordan becoming an "alternative homeland" for the Palestinian people. To be clear, however, while some on the far right of Israeli politics do indeed speak of a "Jordan option," there is no part of Jordanian society, government, or the monarchy that desires to make Jordan the alleged alternative homeland. Senate President Taher al-Masri, in an interview with *al-Hayat* in 2013, reiterated the view of most Jordanian government officials (whether of Palestinian or East Jordanian origin), stating: "The idea of an alternative homeland is completely unfounded in reality. Jordan is Jordan and Palestine is Palestine."[43]

Al-Shabab versus al-Bultajiyya

As I have argued in preceding chapters, Jordan's demonstrations and demonstrators especially during the Arab Spring were many and diverse. Perhaps the most inspiring proreform, prodemocracy, and pronational unity moment came in the form of the 24 March Shabab Movement, only to be broken up with violence by what are known throughout the region as *bultajiyya*, or proregime thugs. Like their counterparts in Tunisia and Egypt, Jordanian youth activists organized extensively through social media, including a March 25 Shabab Facebook group.[44] Through Facebook, Twitter, instant messaging, texting, phone calls, and direct discussions, they attempted to harness the momentum of weekly Friday protests to create a larger and broader exercise in direct democracy. The March 24 Shabab Movement was diverse, inclusive, pluralist, and decidedly democratic.

On March 24, 2011, youth and other activists established a sit-in at the Ministry of Interior Circle and successfully brought together Jordanians who spanned ethnic, class, gender, and religious divisions. The protest was part prodemocracy demonstration and part patriotic rally. As in Tunisia and Egypt, the demonstrators—most of whom happened to be East Jordanians— carried national flags, wore flag face paint, played nationalist and patriotic songs, and made clear in every possible way that they were calling for real reform, not regime change. Many wore on their heads or draped over their shoulders the red-and-white-checked keffiyeh that is so deeply associated with Jordanian identity. For Jordanian democracy activists, as great a day as March 24, 2011, was, March 25 was a nightmare. On that day groups of *bultajiyya* began taunting and insulting the proreform activists and soon turned to pelting them with stones, before charging the demonstrations and breaking them up altogether. In the mayhem that followed, one man died reportedly of a heart attack, while scores were injured.

But why? Many reform activists believed that these antireform youths were mobilized from rural tribal areas and brought to Amman.[45] Despite the clear Jordanian and Hashemite nationalist symbolism, the *bultajiyya* viewed the demonstrators as subversives, as revolutionaries, and *as Palestinians*. In that moment, in short, the issue of Palestinian versus East Jordanian turned not on ethnicity or background but rather on perceived loyalty versus disloyalty. To protest or demonstrate at all seemed to be read by the *bultajiyya* (and by whatever antireform part of the state apparatus that had presumably sent them) as a sign of disloyalty to Jordan.

Ironically perhaps, but very importantly, in this and many other events, it was the prodemocracy demonstrators who reject the binaries and divisiveness of identity politics, while many of their opponents, from *bultajiyya* to antireform government officials, often saw the divisions as all too real, despite the fact that it was their own actions that made them so. As one veteran democracy activist noted: "The March 25 incident was shocking. It was a dangerous response. They opened the door to a more dangerous threat by remobilizing from the regime itself the Jordanian-Palestinian issue."[46] Another Jordanian analyst, however, cautioned that one should not read too much into the episode. While decrying the brutality of the incident, she also compared the levels of coercion to those of other Arab countries: "Still, we don't have killings here. It's not like Syria, or Yemen, or Libya. We don't have snipers."[47]

As brief as it was, the March 24 idea in many ways created in real life the kinds of unifying slogans that the regime has been using for years—such as "We Are All Jordan" and "Jordan First." On that day in the Ministry of Interior Circle, Jordanian youth and others made those slogans momentarily real, until proregime thugs destroyed them. As this analysis has shown, the pervasive power of the politics of identity, ethnicity, and nationalism can be used—and on many occasions in Jordanian history has been used—to divide and rule, or even to bludgeon the democratic opposition into submission. Yet the prodemocracy movement remains and even continues to expand. Fortunately for the regime, the proreform (rather than revolutionary) sentiments of March 24 remain as well, at least for many activists.

Continuity and Change

Jordanian-Palestinian relations are a feature of Jordanian politics, but they are not the defining feature. This chapter has examined them in depth precisely to avoid overly simplistic or essentialist understandings regarding ethnicities, identities, and political life in the Hashemite Kingdom. Jordan is a country with East and West Bank roots, and a state that is home to Arabs, Circassians, and Chechens, as well as (religiously) home to Muslims, Christians, and even a small Druze community. While Jordan is therefore more diverse than it is sometimes credited for, this chapter has focused mainly on the East Jordanian and Palestinian Jordanian aspects of identity politics in the kingdom before, during, and after the Arab uprisings.

The regional Arab Spring came at a time of resurgent political activism in Jordan, ranging from elite-level government and opposition struggles over elections and electoral laws to grassroots activism, starting with labor movements and later including youth movements like the Hirak. But Jordan's protests also came at a time of resurgent identity politics within the kingdom, including, at least for some Jordanians, rising tensions between Palestinians and East Jordanians, and even between and within tribes in Transjordanian communities.

To be clear, however, Jordanian politics is not simply a contest between powerful East Jordanian elites and poor, disenfranchised Palestinians living in urban refugee camps—or as one Jordanian analyst put it, "This is not a country just of Palestinian refugees and Transjordanian bigots."[48] Nor is it the reverse: a struggle between rich Palestinian business elites and poor, disenfranchised tribal East Jordanians. One can find all the previous dimensions within Jordan, but these are also cross-cutting social cleavages. They are, in short, intersectional.

Jordanians of both Palestinian and East Bank origins can be found among the country's poorest citizens, and also among its richest. Sometimes the dividing lines in Jordanian politics are between ethnic identities, but sometimes they are between tribes, sometimes between ideologies, and sometimes between regions, religions, or genders. Yet often a deeper dividing line is economic: between rich and poor. Still, there is an instrumental utility to invoking and even engaging ethnic identity divisions, at least for those opposed to reform and change. The cynical invocation of identity politics nonetheless has a long history of success in terms of dividing potential opposition coalitions for greater economic or political change.

Many Jordanians choose not to reinforce these old binaries. But some, especially in corridors of power and even more especially those who oppose reform and change, do precisely the opposite. So despite the perhaps more enlightened attempts to craft a new national narrative and move beyond old ethnic fault lines, these lines are nonetheless continually reintroduced for political purposes and are often successful in thwarting change. Specifically, identity politics has been used so often in the past as a divide-and-rule tactic, especially by some in the intelligence services, that some Jordanian democracy activists try to downplay identity politics and even their own roots, fearing that legitimate democratic activism will be manipulated by hardline, antireform elements in the regime.

Reactionaries in the state have a long history of attempting to label any mass activism as "really" Palestinian, or Islamist, or both. And in each case, the identity labels are used to question the national loyalty and patriotism of the participants. This is, in many ways, an old tactic, but in a twist from its usual usage, even East Jordanian activists sometimes find themselves facing something similar: with their activism at times derided as not really national but simply local, or ethnic, or tribal. It's not that there are no local, tribal, or interethnic tensions or troubles. Rather, what this suggests is that truly national attempts to organize are often met with counterattempts to demobilize such efforts by opening various identity fissures and by reducing any national effort to something smaller—something that can then be accused of harming national unity, and of being less than fully Jordanian.

Identity politics is also, therefore, something of a minefield, so reform and democracy activists sometimes take great care to avoid it. Aside from the Islamists, most of Jordan's Arab Spring era protesters, for example, saw themselves as nonpartisan and nonsectarian, in either the religious or ethnic identity senses of that word. They focused not on the perennial electoral representation questions (especially since they tended to hold parliament in low regard anyway) but rather on a more general return to democratization and against perceived endemic corruption in government. Even more than representation, they wanted good governance, and especially clean and noncorrupt government.

Yet for all its artificiality, identity politics remains the Achilles' heel of Jordanian politics. It emerges across countless topics—from refugee rights, to debates over the rights of children of Jordanian women married to foreigners (discussed in chapter 7), to even the soccer pitch, at least when popular sides like Faisali and Wahdat play each other.[49] Even struggles over electoral laws (examined in chapter 6) turn in part on identity politics. In the various protests over elections and getting greater levels of public voice in political life, many in the opposition called for major changes in Jordan's highly gerrymandered electoral districts, precisely because these districts included urban areas that underrepresented Palestinian majorities and rural districts that seemed to overrepresent Transjordanians. These demands were fairly transparent in their take on identity politics: they simply wanted a more equitable distribution of seats, access, and, potentially, power, or at least greater levels of influence in Jordanian public life.

Most Jordanian democracy activists remain supportive of varying degrees of liberalization and democratization, and while they are willing to march side by side with the Hashemite monarchy, they want the monarchy to side with them too. For that to happen, however, proreform elements in both the regime and the opposition—and therefore in both state and society— need to be careful not to fall into the traps of identity politics (and the cynical manipulation thereof) that have so long derailed prospects for greater liberalization, reform, and change in the kingdom.

CHAPTER VI

Struggles Over Elections and Electoral Systems

W hile part of the Jordanian public-sphere debate focuses on policies and reforms, much of the focus—and much of the conflict between government and opposition—has for years centered on the nature of the electoral process itself. That is, even before wrangling over policy outcomes, political forces within the kingdom have argued over issues of representation in parliament, and hence over elections and electoral laws. So in one sense, this struggle over elections and electoral laws is a perennial feature of regime-opposition interaction and therefore warrants close examination for that reason alone. But as constant as the conflict appears to be, it also features recurrent changes in a different sense: same struggle, new rules.

Given the overwhelming power of the monarchy in the Jordanian political system, and the corresponding weakness of parliament and, for that matter, of political parties, it is perhaps ironic that so much government-opposition energy is used up in battles over electoral rules and elections themselves. But that is also part of the point. Elections aren't just about representation, and parliament is not just about legislation or policy. The struggles themselves are a state strategy, absorbing considerable opposition energy and effort. Changing the electoral rules so often serves to amplify these effects.

From the start of the earlier liberalization process in April 1989 through the years of the Arab Spring, Jordan has seen a new temporary electoral law for every single election: 1989, 1993, 1997, 2003, 2007, 2010, 2013, and 2016. Each time, government and opposition have squared off over issues of inclusiveness and representation, even before getting around to policy disagreements and debates over institutional reform, including questioning whether parliament was an effective institution in the first place. Since most Jordanians (regime supporters and opponents alike) would tend to answer an emphatic "no" to the latter question, both sides have emphasized getting the electoral laws right first, then attending to making parliament a more meaningful institution. But the question of who exactly would be represented in parliament remained a key issue. Fights over electoral laws, in short, have often proven more extensive than the electoral contests themselves.

In November 2010, just weeks before the outbreak of the regional Arab Spring, Jordan held its sixth round of national parliamentary elections since the start of the liberalization process in 1989.[1] The response to those elections, however, served as an indicator of how far things had fallen since their promising start in 1989. Before the elections even began, they were immersed in controversy, as they were held under a new, temporary electoral law that failed to address opposition demands for greater reform. Not surprisingly, many leftist activists joined with Islamists in calling for an electoral boycott. The elections of 2010 certainly represented no hallmark for reform or liberalization in Jordanian history, but they remain important because they are the immediate backdrop to the onset of the Arab Spring protests in Jordan. The elections took place in November, and within weeks Jordanian street protests would mobilize against the government, even—as noted in chapter 1—before their counterparts in Tunisia and Egypt.

So as elections and election debates unfolded in Jordan, what was new and what was perhaps all too familiar? This chapter examines Jordan's struggles over electoral laws, the electoral process, and electoral outcomes, especially regarding three specific elections: 2010, 2013, and 2016. These elections occurred just before, during, and after what is regarded as the Arab Spring. As with the other chapters and key dynamics examined in this book, the analytical emphasis in each case is on what aspects represented continuity and what aspects suggested change in Jordanian politics. The analysis in this chapter starts, then, in 2010 because it is precisely the failure of the elections that year that set the stage for the protests that would soon erupt and sweep across the country.

Backdrop to the Arab Spring: The 2010 Elections

The elections in 2010 seemed poised to fail from the start and in many ways echoed the 1997 campaign: both featured a regime-opposition standoff in terms of the actual electoral law, both were affected by an opposition boycott, and both resulted ultimately in an unrepresentative and ineffective parliament. This was a far cry from the 1989 elections, at the start of the liberalization era, the only election that opposition forces tended to point to with any level of approval or acceptance.

As noted in chapter 3, in the first round of elections that started the 1989 liberalization era, opposition forces scored impressive victories and secured more than half of the eighty seats in parliament, including thirty-four seats for the Islamist movement. Alarmed by the electoral successes of both the secular left and religious right (and especially of the Muslim Brotherhood), the regime changed the electoral laws for the next polls, held in 1993. These changes had the desired effect, limiting opposition representation and specifically ensuring a decline in the number of Islamist members of parliament. The two different electoral systems, in short, led to two very different sets of results.

In 1989 Jordan allowed voters multiple votes for multiple-member electoral districts. Voters in Irbid, for example, had nine representatives, and they could then cast nine votes. In 1993 Jordan shifted to a single non-transferable vote (SNTV) system. That is, it shifted to a one-person, one-vote system—better known in Jordan as *sawt wahid*, one voice or one vote—in which voters cast a single vote yet within multimember districts. SNTV is itself not necessarily problematic, but it does seem to be best suited to a system of single-member districts. This electoral system had two pronounced effects. First, it undercut political parties and hence reduced opposition representation in parliament, and second, it led most voters to revert back to very personalized and even clientelistic voting patterns. With only one vote, voters tended to back candidates based on family, clan, or tribe rather than ideology, qualifications, or policy platform.[2]

Raging debates between government and opposition from that moment onward continually returned to the changes in 1993, with the opposition demanding an end to the one-person, one-vote system, to be replaced with something like the 1989 multiple-vote system or perhaps proportional representation (which opposition parties argued would strengthen the power and roles of political parties). But as early as 1997, twenty-four years before the Arab Spring, government and opposition had already reached such an impasse over the electoral laws that the opposition arranged a boycott. This boycott included not only leftist parties and Islamists but also prominent political figures such as former prime ministers Ahmad 'Ubaydat and Taher al-Masri. The resulting parliament, naturally, had few opposition voices and indeed appeared to be little more than a tribal assembly of sorts, one that could not be seen as representative of Jordanian society as a whole. In each successive election up to that point, therefore—1989, 1993, 1997—parliament saw less opposition representation, but it also became less representative of society in general, and certainly less effective.

Many Jordanians complain that electoral campaigns often lack substantive policy debates, with candidates instead producing fairly innocuous slogans, or sometimes skipping even those and simply plastering districts with their pictures and names. Candidates are often expected to establish large meeting tents, where those who can afford to do so dish out ample amounts of Jordan's signature national dish, mansaf, and meet and greet potential voters. Not surprisingly, candidates in this context are often well-connected tribal figures, financially well-off business people, or both.

After the accession of King Abdullah II to the throne in 1999, opposition forces returned to mainstream participatory and electoral politics, starting with local municipal elections that year. Leftist, Pan-Arab nationalist, and Islamist forces also returned to participate in the next two rounds of national parliamentary elections—in 2003 and 2007. Yet each of these elections was marred by widespread allegations of vote rigging, with the 2007 polls seeming to be particularly egregious. So by 2010, just before the Arab Spring, opposition forces were boycotting again and citing a now-familiar litany of complaints: electoral districts were gerrymandered to be uneven and unrepresentative, the nature of the voting system kept political parties weak and marginalized, and even after elections, governments were not drawn from parliament itself but instead appointed by the palace. Jordan therefore had a parliament but not a parliamentary political system.

The electoral law of 2010 addressed none of these opposition concerns. But it did double the quota for women's representation from six to twelve seats. It also added several seats in mainly urban districts (Amman, Irbid, and Zarqa), essentially to increase Palestinian Jordanian representation. Predictably, reactionary nationalists felt that the changes had gone too far in empowering Palestinians within Jordanian politics, while opposition activists felt that the changes were minor, barely significant, and failed to address their main complaints.³

For all its other issues, however, the 2010 electoral law was also perhaps the most confusing in Jordanian history. It introduced the concept of multiple "subdistricts" within each of Jordan's multimember electoral districts. To make matters more confusing, these were to be "virtual districts" existing within the actual geographic districts. Candidates had to select one subdistrict to run in, while voters could cast their votes in any of the subdistricts within their designated home districts. The law wasn't just confusing, it also seemed to create an even more localized politics than usual, instigating ever harsher levels of competition within these micro constituencies. The election-day dynamics were themselves unsettling, with violence erupting in various locations around the country, including Ajlun, Irbid, Jerash, Ma'an, Mafraq, and Zarqa. These were not pro- and antiregime clashes, however, since the opposition had boycotted the polls. The violent incidents did not stem from Palestinian, leftist, or Islamist opposition but rather from within ethnic Transjordanian or East Jordanian communities. Many of the skirmishes seemed to be loyalist-on-loyalist—or royalist-on-royalist—violence, and in most cases they seemed to be rooted in other inter- and intratribal tensions.

As in previous rounds of elections, voters in 2010 tended to use their sole vote in support of a relative or member of their clan or tribe. For most voters, this was based not on some sense of primordial loyalty but rather was quite instrumental. With only one vote to cast, voters favored candidates they knew and who they felt they could approach for services. This utilitarian dynamic, however, reinforced the public sense that the parliament was a glorified tribal assembly, and for that matter, that *wasta* (or making use of personal connections) was essential in public policy. For these reasons, opposition forces, and especially opposition parties, continued to argue in favor of multiple votes in multimember constituencies. This type of system, they argued, would still allow voters to cast more personalized votes but would also encourage them to use additional votes in different ways, including for parties, policies, and specific platforms.

In 2010, with the introduction of subdistricts, candidates were forced to compete for even smaller slices of the electorate. In some cases, district races in effect pitted rival tribes against one another. In other cases, they provoked intratribe tensions, often along generational lines. But many tribes organize themselves as voting blocs prior to elections. Many hold intratribal meetings to decide what candidates to field or to support. These are, in effect, tribal primaries. But with all this pre-election organization, and tribes often attempting to organize as voting blocs, each voting group goes into an election assuming its vast bloc of voters will assure it of victory. Yet other tribal voting blocs do exactly the same thing, with someone bound to lose. In that type if instance, it is not just a matter of a single candidate losing but rather an entire tribe or clan possibly feeling suddenly marginalized and excluded. For these reasons, most acts of violence over the polls emerged not during the elections but after, as the results were being posted, with supporters of losing candidates claiming fraud and in some cases even attacking rivals, committing acts of arson, or clashing with the police.

Prime Minister Samir Rifa'i (whose father was prime minister during the April 1989 riots) seemed mindful of the potential for unrest. He therefore tried to thwart it by allowing for greater transparency than in previous elections in Jordan. The 2010 polls, for example, allowed for participation by Jordan's own Civil Coalition for Monitoring the 2010 Jordanian Parliamentary Elections, which deployed more than 1,600 election observers around the country. For the first time, the kingdom also permitted international election observers as well, including the National Democratic Institute (NDI) and the International Republican Institute (IRI), among many others. Following the outbursts of violence, the Ministry of Interior tried to dampen rampant rumors of fraud by posting full elections results (rather than just the names of the winning candidates), so that the full tallies—and margins of victory or defeat—were clearly visible for every district and subdistrict.

With the opposition boycott still in place, however, the general outcome was clear from the start and not at all surprising. As expected, most members of parliament (MPs) could have been described as loyalist, tribal, and Transjordanian. There were changes in terms of specific MPs, however, and at least two-thirds of incoming members were newcomers. In effect, even some old loyalists lost to new loyalists. As has been true across Jordan's modern elections, most winning candidates did not represent a political party. As noted in chapter 3, party identification remains low in Jordan, and political parties themselves tend to be small and largely ineffective. Whether parties represent known proregime figures or opposition activists, they are often small and organized around particular personalities, with various platform statements about Israel and Palestine, Arab solidarity, national unity, the importance of Islam in public life, and so on—but few have real platforms based on actual domestic policies or policy stances.

In 2010 no political party candidate won outside of a special quota seat. Leftist MP Abla Abu Elbeh, secretary general of the Hashed Party (Hizb al-Sha'ab al-Dimuqrati, or the People's Democratic Party), secured a seat as one of the twelve MPs elected on the women's quota. That quota also saw the election of the first woman from a bedouin district, Myassar al-Sardiyyah of the northern Badia. Salma al-Rabadi also won on the women's quota, adding an extra seat for Christian representation in parliament. Independent candidate Wafa Bani Mustafa defied the Islamist boycott and won a seat in her home district of Jerash. And Reem Badran, daughter of former prime minister Mudar Badran, became the first woman in Jordanian history to win a seat outright; that is, without any quota. Badran's election meant that the new parliament had thirteen rather than twelve women representatives. The numbers were still small, a mere 13 out of 120 members of parliament, but the female MPs did comprise a very diverse group, representing very different backgrounds and ideological positions. This may have been the only bright spot of an otherwise dreary election.

Having boycotted the polls, Jordan's large Islamist movement remained unrepresented under the dome of the Jordanian parliament. As was the case following previous rounds of electoral boycotts, the lack of Islamist parliamentary representation forced Islamist activism in other directions, particularly in street activism and also within Jordan's many professional associations (for example, for medical doctors, pharmacists, and engineers). Islamists tended to do very well in internal elections within these associations. The Muslim Brotherhood and the Islamic Action Front nonetheless argued that their boycott worked, and they claimed to have kept voter turnout low. The government suggested that overall turnout was around 53 percent. But turnout in Jordan also tends to vary greatly by location. In 2010 the disparities were particularly glaring. Turnout was posted at 73 percent in largely East Jordanian communities like Kerak and averaged around 80 percent in the northern, central, and southern Badia (bedouin) districts. Either the boycott or low feelings of efficacy and interest kept turnout down to a mere 33 percent in Zarqa and 34 in Amman itself, both urban areas with large Palestinian populations.

While government officials insisted that the Islamist movement had only hurt itself by boycotting, many within the movement, both moderates and hard-liners alike, maintained that it had been the right decision. This underscored just how illegitimate and discriminatory they felt the 2007 and 2010 polls to be, and how ineffectual they believed the parliament to be. This is a key point not just for the Islamist movement but also for democratic opposition across the ideological spectrum and throughout the kingdom: it is not just the electoral system that is at issue but also the weakness of the legislative system.

As noted above, critics often dismiss the Jordanian parliament as little more than a tribal assembly. If Jordan's elections produced representatives who truly represented all of Jordan, then the parliament should include tribal figures but should in no way be dominated by them. Yet many Jordanians see the House of Representatives as a bastion of tribal loyalists competing not for policy but for patronage. This is not just a function of public disaffection with the electoral rules; it is also a function of the role of parliament as an institution. Jordan's royally appointed governments initiate legislation, which they then expect parliament to debate and pass. In a sense, it is the executive that legislates, and the legislature is then expected to execute those decisions.

For all their many faults, the 2010 elections provided the immediate backdrop to what would become the Jordanian version of the Arab Spring. And the elections were contested in several ways—before the polls in the form of the Islamist and opposition boycott, during the polls by higher than usual levels of violence and clashes, and after the polls as dissatisfied Jordanians within weeks mobilized in protests to demand the resignation of the new postelection government. In short, political activism actually increased in the postelection period, as many Jordanians pushed for more substantial reform. In lieu of effective elections or parliament, activists instead took to the streets.

The state had focused on refining the act of voting itself, by modernizing and computerizing the process, attempting to cut back on electoral fraud (such as forged voter cards), and posting results online. But many in the opposition pressed for reforms of a different kind. They called for a parliament that was a meaningful assembly, with genuine legislative powers and elected governments drawn from parliament itself. Many called for electoral districts that were equal rather than gerrymandered, and many also demanded the end of the one-person, one-vote electoral system. In making these demands, elements of Jordan's opposition were echoing reforms that had already been put forward in the regime's own "National

Agenda" for reform (to be discussed in chapter 7). But that ambitious agenda had quickly been shelved, leaving all these matters undecided and deeply contested within Jordanian politics.

In my own assessment of the 2010 elections and their outcomes, I wrote this at the time:

> In the aftermath of the 2010 elections, calls for greater change will grow stronger, not weaker, and will include ever larger numbers of people previously considered loyalist, royalist, and even "tribal" Transjordanians, who have already demonstrated their own disaffection with the electoral process and results. Meanwhile, the regime should at least have the parliament it seemed to want: loyalist, royalist, tribal, and mostly Transjordanian. That also means, however, especially in the context of severe economic hardship in the Kingdom, that it will now be expected to deliver. The patterns of violence on election day and the extent of the boycott suggest that time is of the essence.[4]

Weeks later, Jordanian protesters had hit the streets, demanding the downfall of the Rifa'i government and the implementation of a host of political reforms. In the immediate aftermath of the 2010 elections, Jordan's version of the Arab Spring had begun.

The Arab Spring and the Revival of Jordan's Perennial Electoral Law Debates

With the quick toppling of the Rifa'i government, opposition activists felt they had achieved a significant victory. Rather than sit back and exhale from these efforts, activists vowed to keep the pressure on the regime to proceed with more meaningful change. With the appointment of a new government, the regime promised that a series of changes were on their way, including new elections. And new elections in Jordan, of course, meant yet another electoral law. This led at least some elements of the opposition to return to familiar territory: struggling with the regime over electoral laws and eventually elections. The debates, as always, turned on questions of representation, fairness, and inclusiveness—or lack thereof—in Jordan's parliament. But as noted above, activists also wanted parliament to become a more meaningful and effective institution, yet if the institution were going to perform the rare magic trick of reforming itself, then the question of who was represented "under the dome" of the Jordanian parliament carried some level of urgency. So once again, government and opposition found themselves sparring over the design of the electoral system itself.

Little progress was made regarding electoral reform in the next short-lived government, that of Prime Minister Ma'rouf al-Bakhit (February 2011–October 2011). Prime Minister Bakhit, after all, had overseen the disaster of the elections in 2007, so his government had no real credibility to address the issue at all. In fact, Bakhit's appointment seemed designed in particular to reassure some conservative East Bank Jordanians that reform would not leave them behind, and that it would not empower Palestinian Jordanians at their expense. Similarly, many proreform activists (regardless of background) read the appointment of the Bakhit government as a sign that the state would not willingly open the system in line with the populist demands of the Arab Spring.[5]

It was in the next government, that of reformist prime minister 'Awn al-Khasawneh (October 2011–May 2012), that the new electoral law would finally emerge. Indeed, it may have been the struggle over that law that ultimately brought the government down. The prime minister had been charged by the king with shepherding the new laws through parliament, and he did so, but he appeared to be opposed to the very law he was to implement. Khasawneh and his many supporters felt that the electoral law debate had an unwelcome visitor: the General Intelligence Directorate (GID), or Mukhabarat. Activists and reformers across the Jordanian political spectrum decried the interference of the Mukhabarat in the policy process, and indeed many even routinely referred to the new law as the Mukhabarat version, which was more conservative than the one that had been recommended by the royally appointed National Dialogue Committee.[6]

As noted above, opposition activists had for years called for revoking the one-person, one-vote system and replacing it either with the earlier multiple-vote system or proportional representation (PR) based on party lists, or perhaps a combination of both. The new law did not meet the opposition party demands, but it did, perhaps surprisingly, abandon the one-person, one-vote system while also eliminating the bizarre "virtual districts" utilized in the 2010 elections. It also called, for the first time, for an independent electoral commission to oversee the electoral process, which had been especially problematic in both the 2007 and 2010 elections. The new law provided for a mixed electoral system, in which voters would have *three* votes—two for representatives in their multimember electoral districts and a third that would go to a party list at the national level. The parliament would expand from 120 to 138 representatives, including 15 seats to be allotted as part of the "women's quota" to ensure women's representation in parliament. This was an increase from the previous 12 quota seats.[7] Fifteen seats out of the overall 138 would be drawn from the results of the party list part of the election.

This idea of a combination electoral system, including party lists, was new in modern Jordanian politics, and indeed opposition parties had for years been demanding party lists and some form of proportional representation to replace the one-person, one-vote system. They didn't quite get their wish, however, because opposition parties had called for either a straight PR system based on party lists or a mixed system in which half the seats came from PR and parties while the other half came from multiple-member district voting (in effect restoring, for at least half the parliament, the rules from 1989 that had led to opposition electoral successes). Instead, the government was offering a mere fifteen seats, and even adding a five-seat limit for any one political party. The Islamic Action Front, naturally, assumed that this was a deliberate dig at them, and a means to thwart their electoral chances.

Nonetheless, opposition parties, and indeed the overwhelming majority of activists who were not members of any party, saw the stakes this time as particularly high. With new temporary electoral laws preceding every election, these perennial debates were naturally somewhat stale. But this time, if regime promises were fulfilled, future governments would be parliamentary governments, raising the stakes for getting the electoral law right this time, and for that matter, for participation in the elections themselves. But almost immediately after the release of the government's proposed electoral law, tensions between the prime minister and the palace came to a head. Decrying both palace and GID interference in government, including the electoral law itself, Prime Minister Khasawneh resigned, bringing an abrupt end to his reformist government, and with it another electoral law.

The new and much more conservative government of Prime Minister Fayez Tarawneh (May 2012–October 2012) now found itself with the very same charge: issue an electoral law to set the stage for the next national elections even as economic pressures mounted and new (and very unpopular) economic austerity measures pinched Jordanian family budgets, making it harder and harder for Jordanians to make ends meet. This time, however, the new electoral law was issued by a government led by a consummate regime insider. The lower house of parliament quickly approved the bill, while the royally appointed upper house soon seconded the law with no revisions whatsoever.

This seemingly rare intragovernmental efficiency may have proceeded quietly enough within halls of power, but in the Jordanian street the response was anything but quiet. Jordan's street protests seemed to have been wavering or losing steam at that point—indeed, Jordan's political opposition had been quite hopeful about the reformist potential of the Khasawneh government—but the economic austerity program, combined with the new electoral law, served to unintentionally reinvigorate the protest movement. Protesters took to the streets immediately after the government issued its second electoral law in a mere two-month period, under its fourth prime minister in seventeen months.[8]

King Abdullah then surprised observers by calling for a special session of parliament, sending an earlier draft of the legislation back to be amended, and even making the same suggestion as the opposition: adding seats for political parties and national lists. The result was a law that increased parliament from 120 to 140 seats. Now voters would have *two* votes: one would be for a district representative, while the other would be for national-level lists that would include—but were not limited to—political parties. The new law reserved 15 seats to guarantee women's representation, an increase from the previous 12-seat women's quota. Of the 140 seats overall, 108 were to come from the previous district voting format (in effect, the one-person, one-vote system) while 17 would be drawn from the winning national lists, and 15 from the women's quota. Still, this seemed far short of what opposition parties and activists had been asking for, and even short of the problematic law that had been unveiled merely a month earlier.

The palace, in contrast, insisted that the new electoral law was not only important but in fact the next key change in Jordan's overall reform process. In a meeting and discussion one month earlier, King Abdullah had been passionate about his reform vision and about getting the process right. The electoral law, he argued, was in many respects the final piece in the overall political reform puzzle. The kingdom had already unveiled multiple constitutional amendments, a constitutional court, a new law on political parties, and an independent electoral commission. The elections, he asserted, were essential to engage the citizenry in the reform project and launch Jordan into an entirely new era.[9]

The National Dialogue Committee—a royally appointed committee formed after the start of the regional Arab uprisings—had in part responded to Jordanian opposition demands by recommending a mixed electoral system. Prime Minister Tarawneh, in turn, argued that his government produced exactly the kind of mixed electoral system that the opposition had been demanding for almost twenty years. The opposition, however, regarded the new law as little more than the old, much-despised one-person, one-vote system, with a mere handful of additional seats tacked on for parties and national blocs. After all the talk of reform, they contended, the new law looked like the old law with a few vague references to parties attached to it. They rejected the new law, reiterated their demands regarding what an acceptable law would look like, and threatened to boycott the elections to follow—potentially robbing the regime of the legitimacy it sought by having the opposition return to the electoral process.

The task at hand, however, actually consisted of three parts in succession. The electoral law was the first of these, and it hadn't passed the test of the opposition by any means. But the next two steps were just as vital for the overall reform process to be genuine. In addition to improving—and in effect democratizing—the electoral law, the next task was one of process: making the elections themselves more free and fair, and cleaning up the many irregularities that had marred the previous several rounds of polls. Third, and finally, all this was designed to lead to parliamentary representation. But parliament itself was weak, ineffectual, not truly representative of Jordan, and generally the object of ridicule on the part of many Jordanians. This issue wasn't so much about the palace or the regime but rather about members of parliament, and especially their behavior. Some MPs had, for example, made themselves the objects of public scorn by doing everything from routinely skipping sessions, to falling asleep midsession, to even—in one instance—chasing another MP across the building with a firearm in hand. In the era of instant online news and social media, almost every Jordanian knew about these incidents.

But if a more inclusive electoral law could produce not only a more diverse and inclusive parliament but also a higher quality of public servant, then it would be just as important to make parliament relevant again. That would require empowering it and creating more checks and balances between governing bodies, and hence a decline in monarchical power relative to elected institutions. The first task was a matter of the electoral law itself. The second would fall to the new Independent Electoral Commission (IEC), which had the difficult task of making sure that the electoral process itself would be fair, accurate, and free from the rigging that had at times marred electoral results, especially in the recent past. The third task, making parliament an effective institution and creating the foundation for parliamentary governments, was in some ways entirely new to Jordan. Many would maintain that Jordan in the 1950s had stronger parliaments and greater checks and balances between prime minister, parliament, and palace. But for the overwhelming majority of Jordanians, that period was long before they were born. So at least in the lifetimes of most Jordanians, this project was something yet to be achieved. Before any such change could take place, however, the electoral process itself needed to change, and change greatly.

These tasks, however, would fall to yet another government in Jordan. In October 2012 King Abdullah appointed his fifth prime minister since the start of the regional Arab Spring. Veteran politician Abdullah an-Nsour was appointed to replace Prime Minister Tarawneh. Nsour (October 2012– June 2016) was the tenth prime minister since King Abdullah's accession to the throne in 1999. The new prime minister was expected to serve in a transitional role by overseeing upcoming parliamentary elections, after which another prime minister was to emerge in consultation with the new parliament itself.

As noted in chapter 2, Jordanian prime ministers don't tend to stay in office for very long, but even by Jordanian standards, the pace of government turnover in 2011 and 2012 was very rapid indeed. For some Jordanians, this amounted to a fairly weak and all-too-familiar tactic for the monarchy to create the semblance of change without actually having any. But others argued that something different was afoot, that there was a logic to the specific succession of governments, as each was charged with a different task, building from one stage of reform to the next. And in Nsour's case, the next stage would be the elections of 2013 and their aftermath.[10] Having an already-controversial electoral law in hand, however, the next issue on the agenda was cleaning up the electoral process.

Attempting to Reform the Electoral Process

Establishing the Independent Electoral Commission had been a key part of the package of reforms. The question now was who would lead it. The regime had initially looked to engage an opposition figure for this task, figuring that this would demonstrate that the reform process was real. But Ahmad 'Ubaydat, leader of a coalition of opposition parties and organizations—the National Front for Reform—declined the request. Instead of turning from one opposition figure to another, the regime moved toward a more nonpartisan presence in 'Abd al-Ilah al-Khatib and enlisted him as head of the IEC. Khatib was a veteran official, but in a country whose main complaint was endemic corruption, he had a reputation for honesty and integrity. He had previously served twice as Jordan's foreign minister and had also most recently served as the U.N. envoy attempting to mediate a peaceful solution to the conflict in Libya. Khatib took the matter very seriously. He knew his reputation was on the line with what many regarded as a tremendously difficult task, and he had very little time in which to do it. "Time matters," he noted, "but we won't cut corners, because credibility and transparency matter more than a particular date."[11] The commission turned to international expertise to determine "international best practices" for everything from ballots to ballot boxes to polling centers. Khatib knew that the task at hand was a large one:

> People need to be able to vote freely, without anyone stealing their votes. I will try to put in place checks and controls to prevent violation of the law. How? By applying international standards and getting international help for technical support. For example, for registration cards, we can apply international standards. Violations of elections come not just from the state but from candidates buying votes, voters selling votes, traders in the voting marketplace, acting like horse sellers. Fraud can come from all directions. So we need safeguards, steps, measures to prevent all this.[12]

Despite Jordan's many previous elections, the IEC was in many respects starting from scratch. It embarked on a process of reregistering voters across the country and issuing new voter identification cards.

Since the new system called for two votes, replacing the earlier SNTV or one-person, one-vote system, the IEC created two ballots: one for a district representative and one for a national list of candidates. The new system and process, however, also required some explanation. So the IEC embarked on a national campaign, including with online media and instructional videos, showing Jordanian citizens how the new system would work, with two transparent ballot boxes at each polling station—marked gray for district representative ballots and green for national list ballots. Poll workers were trained, and thousands of domestic and international observers were invited to watch every stage of the process from the opening of polling stations through the counting and tabulation of votes. Leading clerics even backed the IEC's efforts by issuing Fatwas against vote buying and selling.

Despite the many misgivings regarding the system, the stakes in the elections seemed to be high, since the king's own statements suggested that the new parliament would participate in the selection of government itself, or at least of the prime minister. Going into the elections, the implication seemed to be that the revolving carousel of governments would finally be over in Jordan. The king had indicated that, ideally, a new government would serve a full four-year term, matching that of parliament. Still, critics contended that the election law retained the old problems of gerrymandered and unequal electoral districts designed to overrepresent rural areas and underrepresent urban areas that were more heavily Palestinian and that also included deeper bases of Islamist support. Opposition groups argued further that parliament remained weak, much like the country's party system, and that the issues of institutional checks, balances, and greater separation of powers remain largely unaddressed, despite the extensive efforts of the IEC.

The elections in 2013 would be the first in the Arab Spring era. As noted earlier, the previous two rounds of elections—in 2007 and 2010—had been marred by extensive charges of vote rigging, and each had produced a lackluster parliament that was disbanded long before its term was up. Faith and confidence in the system, in short, remained very low. So the IEC and the regime had a tall order simply in generating interest and even participation in the polls, which took place while Jordan remained mired in economic crisis. The elections occurred barely two months after the November 2012 antiausterity riots had rocked the country. Those riots (discussed in chapter 2) had been in response to cuts in gas subsidies and hence dramatic price increases on cooking and heating gas just as winter was setting in.

Many Jordanians continued to complain of economic injustices, corruption in government (especially in terms of business deals connected to privatization), and an electoral and governing system that seemed designed to maintain the status quo. Thus many felt that, regardless of changes to either the system or the process, the elections ultimately wouldn't matter.[13] But the Hashemite regime remained emphatic that these elections were different, that Jordan was different. King Abdullah consistently maintained, including in personal interviews, that Jordan was carving a unique path through the regional Arab Spring: that it was a case of a regime reforming itself. The regime emphasized that Jordan was at a key turning point, including a shift toward a truer parliamentary system of governance, and that the elections were a key part of this process.

In an effort to engage public debate and encourage voter participation, the king had published a series of brief political treatises (discussed further in the next chapter) that he described as "Discussion Papers." Just before the elections, the fourth of these discussed a "roadmap for democratic transformation," including a gradual shift toward parliamentary governments. "After the upcoming elections, we will start piloting a parliamentary government system, including how our prime ministers and cabinets are selected," the king wrote. "International experience suggests this will require several parliamentary cycles to develop and mature. The key driver of the timeline for this transition is our success in developing national political parties."[14] Ideally, a prime minister and government would be drawn from the party or parties winning the largest share of seats in parliament. But as chapter 3 made clear, aside from the Islamic Action Front, parties remain small and weak in Jordan, and most Jordanians belonged to no party whatsoever. And in any case, the IAF also chose to boycott the elections. But a transition to a more parliamentary government, the king asserted, would be predicated on the development of national political parties.

In various interviews and commentaries, the king referred to essentially three main parties—"left, right, and center"—that needed to have platforms and stances on actual issues of social and economic policy.[15] That process would take time, so for the immediate future the next prime minister might not actually come from parliament itself but would emerge based on consultations with the largest blocs that coalesced within parliament after the election. If there were no majority bloc or coalition of blocs after the election, then the palace would consult with all blocs before selecting a prime minister.

Even after the elections, however, the king (in his fifth discussion paper) emphasized the responsibility of the parties themselves to reform. They needed to be representative at a national level and have coherent policy platforms in order to be prepared not just for participation in parliament but also for the eventual transition to parliamentary governments.

> Political parties must continue to develop their internal systems and capabilities so that they evolve into well-functioning, professional, platform-based national parties, capable of winning a majority of votes. They must also focus on producing competent leaders who can assume positions in government so as to enable an advanced form of parliamentary government. In parallel, efforts should continue to enhance the performance of parliamentary blocs in the House of Representatives because they can provide impetus towards platform-based national parties.[16]

A key difference, between palace and political parties, remained where exactly the main responsibility was for reform and change. While the regime listed multiple reform achievements, it insisted that parties also reform themselves. The parties, meanwhile, emphasized that it is the electoral system that ultimately decides the party system. So for parties to truly be strengthened—and indeed, they needed to be, otherwise the entire discussion of eventual parliamentary and party-led governments was meaningless—then the laws had to be designed specifically to empower political parties.

Yet at least since the 1950s, political parties have been weak and ineffective features in Jordanian politics. This is in part because of the kingdom's modern political history, in which the regime banned parties for decades, when it thwarted an attempted coup in 1957 and thereafter established martial law. It was only in the 1990s that parties reemerged legally, following the promulgation of the National Charter in 1991. In the 1950s, in contrast, parliamentary life and party activism had been stronger, but decades of martial law and the absence of both parties and elections had hampered the growth of political parties. But in any country, party strength tends to be correlated to the nature of the electoral system, and Jordan's various systems had thus far served to dampen the strength of parties, even after 1991 when they were relegalized in the system. This is one of the reasons that opposition parties remained emphatic that party lists and proportional representation needed to be at least significant parts of Jordan's electoral system. Otherwise, they argued, parties would never get back off the ground in Jordan.

While the king's papers and speeches refer to the need to develop stronger parties, envisioning eventually party-based parliamentary governments and loyal opposition parties forming shadow cabinets, the electoral system had yet to meet these key opposition demands. Only the 1989 system seemed to empower opposition forces (and even then, still short of demands for party lists or PR systems), and calls for its revival have been part of the opposition party lexicon since the early 1990s. Still, the regime argued that Jordan remained on a slow path toward parliamentary governments and that these would be but the latest step in a series of reforms over a two-year period that included amendments to the constitution, new laws on political parties, new laws on elections, the creation of a constitutional court, and the creation of the Independent Electoral Commission. The regime even marketed the 2013 elections as a "national democratic wedding" that would mark a key turning point in Jordanian history and politics.

The Elections of 2013

On election day at one polling station in the city of Jerash, an older woman sarcastically asked poll workers if they hadn't just done this a few years ago. Jordan had elections as recently as 2010, but this was a new and cleaned up system, they assured her, handing her two ballots. This then led to exaggerated and mock horror that she had two ballots in hand. "How do I do this?" She asked. The poll worker politely and with great patience explained the new electoral system once again, raising his voice so that voters waiting in line would also hear the explanation. "I vote one time?" she asked. Yes, he replied. "But I have two ballots." Yes, vote once on each ballot. "You just said to vote once. Now you are saying twice. *Which is it?*" she asked again with mock outrage, to the general amusement of poll workers, voters, and at least one foreign election observer. To his credit, the precinct captain also laughed and with great patience showed the two ballots, the two ballot boxes, and how—with identification cards checked multiple times and a finger of each voter dipped in indelible ink to prevent recurrent voting or other fraud—the process would be decidedly cleaner than in 2007 or 2010.[17]

The IEC was charged with improving the electoral process but had no control whatsoever regarding the electoral system. It did achieve real successes in the former, while the latter would remain a key point of contention.[18] But the electoral system remained the province of lawmakers. So while debates continued about the fairness of the actual electoral *system* in Jordan, the IEC's efforts greatly improved the election day *process*. More than 1,500 candidates contested the 150 parliamentary seats, but the electoral law itself remained controversial and met few of the demands of Jordan's opposition. It included 108 seats to be decided on the district-based one-person, one-vote system—the same system that had led to the last several rather unimpressive parliaments.

The new electoral law maintained the now long-established practice of reserving seats to guarantee representation for particular minority groups. Specifically, this included nine seats for Christians and three for members of Jordan's Circassian and Chechen communities. In these ways, the new system resembled many of its predecessors. The differences this time were that the quota to guarantee women's representation had been increased from twelve to fifteen seats, and that national lists (and proportional representation voting) would decide the remaining twenty-seven. More than sixty national lists competed for those seats, but they therefore split the vote to such an extent that they almost guaranteed that no list would get more than one or two seats.

The Muslim Brotherhood was not among the lists put forward. As has had happened several times in the past, the IAF (the political party affiliated with the Muslim Brotherhood) boycotted the elections. Many leftist parties and youth-led Hirak movements also boycotted. "We are against the elections because they are a theatrical gimmick meant to maintain the government's strong grip on power," IAF leader Hamza Mansour told the media. "We call on all Jordanians to boycott the polls."[19] While many in the opposition did heed the call and join the boycott, others did not. The opposition, in short, was divided. Some Islamists defied their own movement's ban, leaving the Muslim Brotherhood to contest the polls under the heading of the *wasatiyya* or Islamic centrist movement.

Several leftist and Pan-Arab nationalist parties, following a personal meeting with the king, agreed to contest the elections by forming a joint list. This was a far cry from the party politics of the 1950s, when leftist and Pan-Arabist parties (e.g., communists, Ba'athists, Nasserists) tended to compete as arch enemies, while the Islamist movement remained small and largely peripheral. As chapter 3 showed, in the modern period, and certainly from 1989 onward at the very least, the Islamist movement has been the largest opposition force, while leftist parties declined steadily. In 2013 leftist and Pan-Arab nationalist parties joined forces in an attempt to get at least one seat between them in a parliament of 150.

Even with much of the Islamist opposition boycotting the polls, the Jordanian urban landscape was soon covered with posters and banners featuring candidates' faces, names, and sometimes even a fairly innocuous slogan. Democracy activists and even some proreform elements in the palace itself complained about the lack of serious platforms. Platitudes, many argued, outnumbered policy stances by a hefty margin. But there was therefore also a danger rooted in the system rather than the process: that is, that all the announced reforms, and all the extensive IEC efforts, might seem to amount to nothing if the ultimate result was a parliament that looked strikingly like its predecessors. Many reform and democracy activists chose not to run, and many not even to vote, yielding the field to the usual candidates who tend to dominate Jordanian elections. In most Jordanian elections, most candidates are well-to-do men who run as independents (but generally range ideologically from centrist to conservative), often with extensive tribal ties. Even with the changes to the electoral system, it remained predisposed to produce essentially this outcome, and of course it did just that.

On January 23, 2013, Jordan held elections for its seventeenth parliament. Despite all the changes in process, the results were as expected. Still, while most MPs were conservatives, a few genuine progressives were also elected. Eighteen women won seats, which was a record high for Jordan. In addition to the fifteen female MPs elected via the women's quota, three other women won seats (one by leading a national list and two by winning their districts outright).

Because parties are so weak and ineffective, most MPs after any election are independents rather than members of parties. Parliamentary blocs therefore form after elections, not before, and they tend to be fluid and change, so they do not approximate political parties. Since most MPs have no party and no real platform, even the blocs that form in parliament after elections tend to be temporary alliances based on personal connections.

With no bloc, party, or faction with a clear majority, the palace asked blocs to nominate candidates (not necessarily from within their own bloc) to be prime minister. This was new to Jordanian politics. While some blocs and MPs nominated Nsour, then the current prime minister, many others avoided naming a specific candidate at all. Many blocs and individual MPs seemed to prefer avoiding responsibility for naming a prime ministerial candidate, leaving the initiative back where it had always been: with the palace.

Even the symbolism of the consultations themselves was striking: blocs met with the chief of the Royal Hashemite Court, Fayez Tarawneh (who had been prime minister a matter of a few months earlier), but in doing so, the blocs went to the palace rather than having the palace representative visit parliament. Despite all the campaign efforts and complaints, however, MPs either named no candidate or rallied around the same one, leaving the current prime minister as essentially a compromise candidate. It was not exactly a rousing endorsement, but many blocs credited Nsour—as a former MP and cabinet minister himself—with a real understanding of parliamentary life, and with a certain reputation for at least minimal support for reform. For conservative MPs, at least Nsour was not in any way radical. For reformers, he seemed the best available alternative, at least at that moment, and his appointment would spare them from having to deal with a more reactionary figure.

In many ways, the election began and ended with Abdullah an-Nsour. He had been appointed prime minister in October 2012, barely three months before the new elections. Many had expected him to simply oversee the elections as a transitional figure, soon to step down in favor of a new prime minister. Nsour was already Jordan's fifth prime minister in two years, and in a way he was also the sixth, since it was he who was ultimately tapped to head a new government following the elections.[20] Unlike its several predecessors, however, Nsour's new government paralleled the life of parliament itself, serving a full four-year term.

Nsour's reappointment turned out to be one of many signs of continuity amid all the discussions of reform and change. Immediately after the elections, the new parliament elected Saad Hayel Srour to be its Speaker. Srour had served in the post several times before. Along similar lines, former prime minister Tarawneh was appointed chief of the Royal Hashemite Court. Both men were conservative veteran officials. Similarly, the reselection of Nsour as prime minister didn't exactly cry out "change" either. Nonetheless, the regime argued that many parts of the Jordanian political process were actually new and different. Jordanian prime ministers have always been royal appointees, for example, but this time, palace officials argued, marked a major departure from Jordan's past because the new prime minister and government emerged following extensive consultations between the palace and the newly elected parliament. For many in the regime, the elections of January 2013 represented another milestone in reform and in the political development of the kingdom, and even a cautious step toward more parliamentary government.[21]

In his first (three-month) term as prime minister, Nsour had been charged with implementing a series of difficult and unpopular economic austerity measures, including removing fuel subsidies and allowing energy prices to rise in the middle of winter. These had, of course, triggered the November 2012 riots. But some even in the opposition credited Nsour with at least appearing on national television to explain why the measures were essential, and why he was not backing down from them. For many Jordanians, having a prime minister bother to explain and defend his position to the nation was at least something new. Immediately after the riots, Nsour's government was tasked with carrying the country through the next elections, based on an electoral law that he himself had voted against when he was a member of parliament. Now, with a new term as prime minister, Nsour was expected to revisit the electoral law yet again, to eventually present a revised version in addition to deepening the overall reform process.

New Era, New Electoral Law

By the end of the summer of 2015, Jordan's government had announced a new electoral law for the kingdom that sounded strikingly like an old one. In September 2015 parliament had extensive debates over the new law, questioning provisions about districts in particular, but by February 2016 it passed the law with no revisions. The government argued that the new law had much in common with the long lost 1989 version. As noted above, many democracy activists in Jordan, and many opposition parties, had been consistently calling for the return of the 1989 law for the previous twenty-six years. That law, they argued, was more democratic and inclusive than the many that had been passed since. On unveiling the new law, Prime Minister Abdullah an-Nsour alluded to this, saying that the new law was "historic" but also that it was "more or less the same as the always-praised 1989 law." Even opposition movements such as the Muslim Brotherhood suggested that the law was a "step in the right direction."[22] While the new law was indeed different from others that had preceded it—there was, after all, a new law for every election—it was not actually a carbon copy of its 1989 predecessor.

Still, Prime Minister Nsour's government contended that the newest law was but the latest piece in the broader set of reforms that marked Jordan's response to the Arab Spring. The government argued that the law met key opposition demands to drop the SNTV system for the first time in twenty-six years, and that it was "more or less" a revival of the 1989 system. Like that system, under the new law voters would have multiple votes, voting for as many representatives as are allotted to their districts (as in 1989) but also casting a vote for a list of candidates. The 2013 system had introduced candidate lists at the national level, whereas these lists were to be within districts for the 2016 elections. So the 2013 experiment with national lists, which most had assumed would increase proportionally with each election, was instead abandoned after only one election. The new law also included the provision that while voters would vote for candidate lists within their district, the individual candidates they voted on thereafter would also have to be drawn from that same list.

While the government argued that it had met opposition demands by reviving something like the 1989 law, opposition parties rejected this as an altogether different system, and they maintained the call for national (not district-level) lists. Critics of the new law argued that previously heavily gerrymandered districts had simply been replaced by similarly uneven representation based in part on the governorates. The law did provide for increased representation for Jordan's largest cities (28 seats for Amman, 19 for Irbid, 12 for Zarqa), but it retained the tradition of overrepresenting rural areas and underrepresenting urban areas. It reduced the overall number of parliamentarians from 150 to 130, while retaining quotas to guarantee minority representation (9 seats for Christians, 3 for Circassians and Chechens). It also maintained a quota to guarantee women's representation. Activists for women's rights in the kingdom were disappointed that their demand for a quota of 20 seats for women had not been met. But Prime Minister Nsour insisted that keeping the quota at a minimum of 15 seats, with a parliament reduced from 150 to 130 seats, would be at least a marginal increase proportionally if not in absolute terms.[23]

Even after the elections bill passed in parliament, activists continued to challenge it, hoping to trigger changes before it officially became law. MP Wafa Bani Mustafa, part of the reform-oriented Mubadara (Initiative) bloc in parliament, joined many activists in calling for a quota of one seat for women in each of the twenty-three districts, rather than one in each of the fifteen governorates. Other activists pushed the issue further, including Salma Nims, head of the Jordanian National Commission for Women (JNCW). Nims argued that the issues went beyond quotas and included the effectiveness and relevance of the parliament itself. Speaking to *al-Jazeera*, she said: "Historically we have never seen women from a citizenship approach. Women are seen as a minority, as a marginalised group and an add-on to society," rather than as the majority that they actually are. Nims suggested that even a twenty-three-seat quota was really too few: "I think the draft law is actually below our ambitions. We should reach 50/50. We should look at a law that, for example, has women on the lists, that 50, 30 percent of the lists should be women. But the law itself did not provide for that."[24]

Nims and the JNCW emphasized, as did many reform activists, that a larger quota for women's representation would be an improvement, but that the very nature of parliament and parliamentary life also needed to change. But this would require an electoral law that helped strengthen program-based parties. "There's no form of programmatic or political party representation in parliament—it became a service-oriented parliament," Nims said. "You call your MP to get a job, or to have a street paved in your town. . . . If you look at voters who are in their 20s and 30s, they are disillusioned. As a whole, they don't believe in the parliament as having a real role in reform."[25]

The Elections of 2016

Jordanians returned to the polls on September 20, 2016, to elect a new parliament. Or at least some of them did. The election received little attention in international media, and even Jordanians seemed to be less than enthusiastic, with pre-election polls suggesting participation by fewer than 40 percent of eligible voters.[26] The 2016 elections took place via the new and untested electoral system based on proportional representation. Unlike the previous several rounds of elections, however, the polls in 2016 saw the return of the entire democratic opposition, including the Islamist movement. For the first time in nine years, there would be no Islamist or opposition boycott.

Yet even electoral officials were worried about the lack of public enthusiasm and hence feared that a markedly low turnout would cast doubt on the polls themselves.[27] "I'm afraid that there is a real problem of trust among voters," noted Jordanian analyst Osama al-Sharif before the polls. "If there is low turnout, it will send a clear message to the regime. People are fed up with the rhetoric of reform, with rhetoric about parliamentary governments, and with new slogans."[28] Many officials, candidates, and activists alike were predicting 40 percent turnout or less. "No parties are boycotting," said one activist, "But the *people* are boycotting."[29]

Jordan's Independent Electoral Commission, however, disputed these pessimistic assessments and worked to double the turnout prediction of their critics. The IEC put its efforts into a voter turnout and information campaign, explaining the new system and precisely how one votes.[30] This was needed because many Jordanians found the new system to be confusing. With a new electoral law for every national parliamentary election since the political liberalization process began in 1989, explaining each new system was definitely warranted, and the IEC made extensive use of social media and videos to demonstrate precisely how it worked.[31] Civil society organizations and research centers, such as al-Hayat Center and its associated five-thousand-strong teams of observers in the Rased organization, actively monitored the elections, providing additional analysis of the process, the candidates, the lists, and ultimately the outcomes.[32]

With the new system, the government acceded to a long-standing opposition demand by finally abandoning the single non-transferable vote, or one-person, one-vote system for individual district representatives. The new law did away with SNTV, restored multiple votes for multimember districts, and required candidates to be part of district (not national) lists. Voters voted first for a list and then for multiple candidates within that list. The government argued that the law would help foster political parties, as a step toward eventual parliamentary governments. However, while the new system did require candidate lists, these were based within districts, not the country at large. So they were not likely to become the building blocks of national political parties. Instead, many opposition groups found themselves competing against one another within smaller district-level contests.

Many activists were surprised that the new law did not build on its pre-decessor. The 2013 elections had, after all, introduced a two-vote system: one ballot for a district candidate and one for a national list (with 27 seats out of 150 drawn from these lists). Many expected the new law to use pro-portional representation for national lists but expanding over time from twenty-seven seats to half of parliament. That might have eventually helped build national parties, but shifting back to district-level contests was more likely to have the reverse effect. Activist and analyst Hisham Bustani has argued that the new law, like its predecessors, was not about enhancing pluralism or democratization but about sustaining power and the status quo.[33]

Even if many voters remained uninspired, candidates were very active, with more than 1,200 candidates on 226 lists competing for 130 parliamen-tary seats. Some 255 women contested the polls, a record in Jordan, includ-ing two all-female electoral lists.[34] Many lists followed the familiar electoral path of putting candidate names and pictures on large billboards, sometimes with a slogan, sometimes not, but rarely with any actual platform. There were several exceptions to this more generic trend, however. The Ma'an (Together) list in Amman, for example, billed itself explicitly as a "Civil State" (*al-dawla al-madaniyya*) list, arguing for a secular politics and the sepa-ration of religion from government. Running on the slogan "Citizenship, Justice, and Security," the Civil State list also produced a program of prin-ciples and priorities.[35]

In contrast to secular lists like Civil State, however, Islamists returned to the polls, but in the form of at least three different movements. In 2013 the Islamic Action Front and Muslim Brotherhood had boycotted (again), leaving the field to an alternative Islamist movement—the Islamic centrist or Wasat Party, which many see as in effect state-allied Islamism. But this time Wasat had to compete against the much larger, well-organized Mus-lim Brotherhood. Yet as noted in chapter 4, Jordan's MB had split into two movements.[36] The newer, government-approved Muslim Brotherhood Society formed several lists, related to the Zamzam reform movement, which in turn had recast itself as the National Congress Party. But by far the largest of Jordan's several Islamist movements was the one rooted in the original, unlicensed version of the Muslim Brotherhood and its related political party, the IAF. They formed the National Coalition for Reform (Islah) and fielded lists of candidates in twenty out of twenty-three dis-tricts. The various Islamist lists downplayed Islamist rhetoric and slogans and made sure to include tribal, Christian, and other non-Islamist candidates on their lists in an attempt to maximize their appeal.[37] Jordanian elections have often seen tribal-backed candidates sparring with Islamist opponents, but the new law seemed to have triggered multiple tribal-Islamist alliances, at least for election day.

There were some surprise ousters of MPs in the 2016 elections—including of multiple reform advocates. These included reformers as diverse as MPs Rula Hroub, Hind al-Fayez, and Mustafa Hamarneh. Hamarneh, elected to parliament in a Christian seat for Madaba in the 2013 elections, was the main organizer of the Mubadara bloc in parliament that gathered a set of MPs backing greater reform and change. Unlike most parliamentary blocs, Mubadara worked on specific policy papers and legislative proposals. They took their roles as MPs quite seriously, in other words, whereas most blocs had no consistent policy positions whatsoever. Hroub was also known as an outspoken reform advocate and had been particularly vocal as a critic of the regime's gas deal with Israel. Fayez was so well known for her outspoken views—from Pan-Arab nationalist causes to domestic reform efforts—that an incident within parliament in December 2014 went viral both on video and in terms of countless memes, often with the Arabic hashtag for "sit down Hind." In it Fayez was interrupted repeatedly during a parliamentary debate, which culminated in neighboring ultraconservative MP Yahya Saud attempting to shout her down and to bluster "sit down Hind" as he railed against the women's quota. Before the 2016 elections, Fayez had also spoken out against the gas deal with Israel and against regime plans to develop nuclear power in the kingdom. In one of the most bizarre incidents from the 2016 elections, ballot boxes from her home district in the Badia vanished, only to be returned later, leading to considerable speculation about rigging of the results. As different as these three MPs were, all three were nonetheless associated strongly with reform causes, and all three lost their seats in 2016, causing at least some activists to question the results. Some saw these outcomes as legitimate electoral results, some as the result of yet another problematic electoral law, while others worried that the Mukhabarat had interfered with the results, preventing outspoken reformers from returning to parliament. There was no way to definitively confirm or deny any of these interpretations, but the fact that they were fairly open and common points of conversation does at least suggest that faith in the process was, once again, problematic.

While some Jordanians argued over the electoral results, many others ignored the process entirely. Overall, in fact, perhaps the most glaring issue in 2016 was the low participation rate, suggesting that many Jordanians were not interested in the fine points of electoral law or of the elections themselves and in a sense made a statement by not voting at all. Ultimately, pre-election polls turned out to be correct, with roughly 37 percent of voters casting ballots. "By not participating," noted one Jordanian analyst, "Jordanians *are* participating, but in a negative way, sending a message that we are not on the right track."[38] Still, the return of the opposition—including multiple streams of Islamism—to Jordanian elections was perhaps the most important aspect of the elections. Postelection tallies showed the IAF winning ten seats, with its list allies gaining an additional five. This was a small proportion of parliament's total seats (130), but the IAF had gained more seats than any other party or list. The Zamzam- and Wasat-led lists gained five seats each. Twenty women gained seats, more than in any other Jordanian election—fifteen through the quota, and five outright. Several of these were affiliated with the IAF, however, leading many women's rights activists to worry that this may not have been a landmark victory, if several MPs ultimately worked against an agenda for women's rights.

Continuity and Change

As the debates over Jordan's many electoral laws show, the electoral system and the system of governance have often proven to be key points of contestation in Jordanian politics, at least between government and opposition elites. These struggles therefore suggested both changes and continuities in Jordanian politics. On the one hand, electoral struggles, electoral laws, boycotts, weak parties, and questions of uneven representation and for that matter limited parliamentary power are all perennial aspects of government-opposition struggles in Jordan. On the other hand, every new election generates a new law, a new system, and a new conflict over the changed rules of the game. This chapter has shown that much of the debate between regime and opposition before, during, and after the Arab Spring has been over the nature of these changes.

Yet even a freer and fairer electoral process, and a parliament more representative of all of Jordanian society, would be changes of limited impact if power remains concentrated almost entirely in the monarchy. Many Jordanians support the monarchy, but they also reject cosmetic reform and strongly support greater pluralism and democratization in the kingdom. Shifting some real power from the monarchy to parliament, the prime minister, and the cabinet would move reform beyond simply cleaner elections. This would also create conditions for greater accountability in governance via a more genuine separation of powers between branches of government.

Outcomes in Jordanian elections depend on the nature of the electoral law itself, the cleanliness of the electoral process, and, very important, whether the opposition chooses to participate in the process or to boycott the polls. Islamists and many leftist parties had boycotted the elections often over the past several decades. For both government and opposition, debates will continue regarding the electoral system and the electoral process, but also about the role of parliament in public life. Both the regime and the opposition have talked of eventually forming genuine parliamentary governments, although they clearly have very different timetables for this. For the regime, this is to be a lengthy process that will take years but without a precise endpoint. Opposition parties, in contrast, were hoping that the answer would have been after the 2013 election. But since it did not happen then, or even after 2016, they therefore see this as long overdue.

Regime emphasis, in contrast, tends to be on the need for developing modern political parties, but in doing so the monarchy in effect puts the burden of reform on the opposition itself. If they can manage to reform themselves and assemble genuine nationally representative parties with clear platforms and stances on a host of policy issues, then the process can finally proceed toward parliamentary and more representative government. But opposition parties from the secular left to the religious right continue to argue that it is the electoral system that needs to change first, creating the conditions for strengthening political parties in Jordan, with the same stated goal in mind: real parliamentary governments and greater separation of powers between palace and parliament. Whether the opposition chooses to participate in future elections, or to remain reformist rather than take a more revolutionary turn, depends in part on these structural factors: the electoral system, the electoral process, and, most important, governance itself and whether Jordan shifts (even if slowly) toward genuinely parliamentary governments.

As much debate as the various electoral laws have triggered among Jordan's many proreform constituencies, however, political opposition during and after the Arab Spring era took a major turn by moving beyond the perennial electoral law debates. The electoral laws matter, to be sure, since they determine who has a real chance of representation and who does not. But as the preceding chapters have suggested, opposition forces have also rallied over a diverse set of demands that may seem disparate or even muddled to less democratically minded forces in the kingdom but in actuality represent a fairly clear program. In terms of institutional reform, prodemocracy and proreform activists call for a shift in power from the palace to elected representatives and to representative parliamentary governments, for checks and balances between the legislature and executive authority, and for a more independent judiciary. Activists across the political spectrum also call for a reduced role for the Mukhabarat in daily life and an end to corruption in government and business, especially in the context of the country's long-standing economic privatization program.

As Jordan's usually low voter turnout percentages suggest, many Jordanians are much more concerned with the broader political and economic reform process than they are with elections. Even as people in government and the opposition reengage one another over each cycle of new electoral laws and new elections, numerous Jordanians couldn't be less interested. Many see those struggles not as the core elements of politics but almost as theater, and as a recurring sideshow diverting attention away from more meaningful questions about deeper issues of reform and change. The next chapter turns to the broader question of reform in the Hashemite Kingdom, beyond struggles over electoral laws and elections, to examine the more comprehensive question of reform before, during, and after the Arab uprisings.

CHAPTER VII

Rebooting Reform

State-led reform initiatives, and indeed state and societal struggles over the depth and breadth of reform in Jordan, did not begin with the 2011 Arab uprisings or the regional Arab Spring. Jordan has seen various reformist eras, so the term *islah*—reform—is one that has dominated Jordanian political debates for decades. But that is also precisely why the term has lost meaning over time for many Jordanians. Is it, after all, just a word? Or are there real and meaningful changes to point to? These questions turn on broader social and political perceptions regarding the social and economic status quo, the regime itself, and ultimately, of course, the state of reform in the kingdom. Regarding reform, many Jordanians ask quite bluntly: is it real? Does the latest reform campaign (whatever and whenever it is) represent actual change, or is it all-too-familiar reformist rhetoric masking nothing more than continuity or politics as usual?

For Jordan's Hashemite regime and its many supporters, reform is a slow but clear and steady process, one that can list myriad accomplishments. The Jordanian state, in fact, tends to refer to Jordan's "reform march" as a set of actions, each building on its predecessors. But many proreform activists see more continuity than change. They are quite familiar with reformist rhetoric and terminology but tend to see reform initiatives as repetitive—as similar to prior initiatives, simply adorned in new slogans. Numerous advocates of greater change in the kingdom see not a steady reform march but rather "déjà vu all over again." Questions of the depth or lack of depth of reform lie at the heart of Jordanian political debates, and indeed at the heart of any analysis of Jordan's past, present, and future. For these reasons, this chapter takes a deeper look at these questions, to examine Jordan's struggles over reform and change before, during, and beyond the Arab uprisings.

Patterns of Reform and Reaction Before the Arab Spring

Of Jordan's many previous eras of reform, perhaps the most important was the political and economic liberalization process that followed widespread popular unrest in the kingdom in April 1989. King Hussein's motivations may indeed have been defensive at the time, but the results were significant. The regime initiated a liberalization process that included the revival of elections and parliamentary life in Jordan.[1] From roughly 1989 to 1993, Jordan's liberalization looked to be the most promising and the most extensive reform process in the entire Arab world. The process expanded in that period to include the lifting of martial law (which had remained in place for decades), legalization of political parties, loosening of restrictions on the media, and—from 1989 onward—multiple rounds of national parliamentary elections.[2] That reform period was for many a turning point in Jordanian political history, and one that is still regarded as almost a golden age of reform within the kingdom.[3]

In 2011 and after, reform activists attempted to revive the spirit and effectiveness of that earlier reform era. Many Jordanians continued to differ, however, on the real meaning of the 1989–1993 reforms. For some, the period was the high water mark of Jordanian reform efforts that had since gone astray or at least stagnated. These Jordanians felt that reform efforts had fallen into a more than two-decade slumber, with 2011 providing a wake-up call for both regime and opposition as well as the impetus for reviving the reform movement. But others also wondered if the earlier era was itself a kind of historical anomaly and hence the exception rather than the rule in terms of reform and government-opposition relations in the kingdom. For this more skeptical outlook, revival of reform was a much taller order, and perhaps even a fool's errand doomed to the same outcome as its predecessor.

Each of Jordan's earlier rounds of reform was preceded by some level of economic crisis. The jolt of 1989 had, after all, been prompted by the stringent demands of an IMF economic austerity program. The harsh economic medicine of the austerity measures triggered riots that quickly turned political as well. The protests and riots of April 1989 shook the foundations of the Jordanian state. Some activists, then and now, still refer to that moment as a "Jordanian Intifada." King Hussein responded by sacking the prime minister and cabinet and promising the wave of political reforms noted above. In the years afterward, the political reforms may have wavered, but the economic liberalization process proceeded apace, remaining every bit as controversial as it was in 1989.

Still, despite these controversies, economic liberalization in Jordan has remained regime policy, with its associated implications for both foreign policy and domestic politics. Political reform, in contrast, has often faltered, stalled, stagnated, and at times regressed. There is a pattern, in short, of rising and falling reform efforts that suggests continuity even amid apparent change. Over the past several decades, for example, Jordan has experienced both liberalization and deliberalization in its political life, as the state has at times retreated from earlier reforms.

This was especially clear in the aftermath of Jordan's peace treaty with Israel in 1994.[4] King Hussein had presided over the 1989–1993 political opening, but by 1994 Jordan was on the verge of a breakthrough peace agreement with Israel. Like the earlier Egyptian-Israeli peace treaty in 1979, this one would be a bilateral peace treaty between two states but would leave the question of Palestinian sovereignty, independence, or statehood unresolved. For these reasons it was and is controversial in both Jordanian and regional politics. For King Hussein, the peace treaty would be a final grand foreign policy achievement in his long career. By that time, the king was suffering from cancer, and quiet and discreet discussions regarding a future succession had already begun. Having ruled Jordan for more than forty years, King Hussein could secure a peace treaty with Israel against any potential domestic or regional opposition. But the king's successor would likely not be in a similar position. In a sense, the king was already paving the way for a succession by trying to stabilize the single most difficult aspect of Jordan's foreign relations: its relations with Israel. Jordanian-Israeli peace also carried profound implications for Jordan's most important foreign relationship: with the United States.

The peace treaty earned Jordan a top spot among U.S. foreign aid recipients, with the United States increasing economic and military aid to the Hashemite Kingdom, following a brief but difficult rupture in

U.S.-Jordanian relations over the Gulf War in 1991. In the Gulf conflict, Jordan had angered the United States and many of its Gulf allies as well when it refused to join a U.S.-led coalition against Saddam Hussein's regime in Iraq. Jordan had attempted to straddle the fence between its own belligerent allies—the United States and Iraq especially. But that strategy instead led to ruptures in Jordanian ties with key allies like the United States and Saudi Arabia, and accordingly temporary losses of foreign aid and oil at concessionary prices. It even led to the expulsion of thousands of Jordanian citizens from Saudi Arabia and Kuwait. For Jordan, the peace treaty with Israel wasn't just about peace with Israel but was also intended to bring Jordan back in from the cold, and especially to reestablish its formerly firm alliance with the United States and the military, political, and economic support that went with it.[5] With all these considerations in mind, King Hussein showed little to no patience for opposition to the Jordanian-Israeli peace treaty, and thus Jordan's much-heralded "political opening" of 1989–1993 began to close.[6]

In 1999, however, when the succession did occur—from King Hussein to King Abdullah II—it appeared that the door of reform might be opening once again.[7] King Abdullah II took office at a moment when both Jordan's domestic and regional politics seemed to be remarkably stable. Keeping with the broader political liberalization program, the new king allowed municipal elections to take place as scheduled in July 1999. It seemed that for the first time in years the kingdom might finally be able to move beyond its difficult geography and its various security concerns to renew, consolidate, and even expand the reform process at home. The period of internal and external stability turned out to be even briefer than expected, however, and since 1999, regional and domestic security concerns have more often than not outweighed attempts at greater domestic political reform.

In September 2000 in the West Bank and Gaza, the perceived calm was shattered by the second Palestinian Intifada or uprising against Israeli occupation. The Jordanian government worried about the impact of the Intifada, and the Israeli military crackdown, on Jordan's own domestic stability and security. This included fears that Israel might expel thousands and perhaps even millions of Palestinians to Jordan. Similar fears have recurred over the years, accompanying every renewal of Palestinian resistance and Israeli military response.

A year later, on September 11, 2001, with the Intifada still raging, al-Qa'ida terrorists attacked the United States, killing almost three thousand people and leading to a massive U.S. military intervention in Afghanistan, a state then led by the militant Islamist Taliban movement, which had hosted al-Qa'ida on Afghan soil. The Jordanian regime joined most of the world in condemning the 9/11 attacks, but it also supported the U.S. invasion of Afghanistan (to topple the Taliban regime and expel or destroy al-Qa'ida). Most Jordanians shared the regime's revulsion at the 9/11 attacks. But the U.S. military intervention in Afghanistan, and Jordan's support for it, was far more controversial and served to widen the gap between government and opposition. That gap grew still wider when, in 2003, U.S. President George W. Bush ordered an even more massive U.S. invasion, this time of Jordan's eastern neighbor, Iraq.

Jordan's regime had warned the United States repeatedly of the folly of such an operation—that it would destabilize the region, including many U.S. allies, and ultimately lead to more terrorism and a boon to jihadi movements. These warnings, of course, turned out to be accurate, but the Bush administration heeded none of them. Within Jordan, however, the government-opposition divide expanded, as Jordan (while opposed to the war) continued to stand by the U.S. as a key ally and benefactor. Wedged between the Intifada to the west and the U.S. war in Iraq to the east, Jordan found itself essentially in security mode, with reform no longer a top priority. Not only was the kingdom caught between escalating conflicts, but it also had to absorb waves of hundreds of thousands of Iraqi refugees fleeing the U.S. invasion and the widespread unrest, insurgency, and terrorism that followed.

This suggests a recurring pattern, in which a key change in domestic politics leads to renewed reform efforts and renewed hopes—in 1989, in 1999, and in 2011—but then regional turmoil around the kingdom serves to dampen domestic reform initiatives, either by postponing reform measures or by serving as a convenient excuse for the efforts of antireform elites. Security concerns have consistently served to derail the opposition goal of greater democratization in Jordan. Yet economic liberalization—especially in the form of privatization—has tended to continue regardless of regional instability or insecurity. As noted above, these economic priorities have had profound social and political impacts. As the state sector declines in size, so does the social welfare component of previously reliable state employment.

Jordanians complain consistently, and with good reason, about rising food and housing prices, unemployment, underemployment, and poverty, while also complaining about the issue of corruption among business and government elites. In 2011, as had happened before, these economic frustrations fueled social unrest and motivated many Jordanians to mobilize politically and press the state to return to its long-promised political liberalization and reform program.[8] Yet antireform hard-liners, especially in the Mukhabarat, have for decades used security concerns as their main argument against opening the political system to greater public participation.

Proreform activists, however, argue that this type of security-oriented antireform message relies on a kind of reverse logic. Reform advocate and later parliamentarian Mustafa Hamarneh, for example, speaking two years before the Arab uprisings, noted: "To say if we open up, we sow instability is a statement I flatly reject. I believe it's the other way around; the lack of opening up sows the seeds of instability."[9] Regime obsessions with security concerns, in short, often (and ironically) actually undermine security. As suggested in chapter 1, within the field of comparative politics, then, this mirrors the international relations theory concept of the "security dilemma," in which states in the international arena unwittingly undermine their own security even as they try to enhance it. Authoritarian and semiauthoritarian regimes often do much the same thing in state-society relations, building their security apparatus and even fortress-like regimes but thereby also undermining their domestic legitimacy and ultimately their security vis-à-vis their own societies.[10]

In an analysis of stalled reform in Jordan written as early as 2003—eight years before the Arab uprisings—the International Crisis Group (ICG) suggested that Jordan was suffering a "deficit of democratic representation" and that this might provide the spark for real conflict in the kingdom. But the same report also remarked on the weakness of Jordan's political opposition, arguing that "too often, opposition parties and civil society have contented themselves with vacuous slogans and unrealistic proposals that do not resonate with the people and further undermine the credibility of political action." Analyzing rising tensions and unrest in the kingdom, the ICG noted that governmental reform efforts seemed to focus mainly on procedural democracy—that is, the act of elections—without providing meaningful channels for genuine participation, transparency, and accountability.[11]

Almost a decade before the Arab Spring, while investigating recurring unrest and violence in the southern town of Ma'an, the ICG argued: "Nevertheless, the regime's Achilles' heel is the feeble bond of trust between most citizens and the state. Meaningful relationships are based primarily on family or tribal loyalties, with religion also an important social glue. The state, however, is largely absent from these relations, being broadly perceived as non-transparent, unresponsive and unaccountable."[12] The report also cited King Abdullah himself, who was quoted in an American newspaper as early as 2002 stating that "the leadership of the Middle East don't understand that 50 percent of the population is under eighteen, and if they don't get going to create some means for real participation for these young people, they are going to have serious problems."[13] That was good advice then and now for both Jordan and other countries. But it remained an open question even many years after the Arab Spring. Indeed, questions of participation, opportunity, and empowerment have dominated Jordanian politics for decades, and they continue to do so.

Rebooting Reform or Much Ado About Nothing?

In an attempt to revive the reform process, as early as 2004 King Abdullah appointed the kingdom's former foreign minister and prominent reformer, Marwan Muasher, to the post of deputy prime minister for reform. In that capacity, Muasher was tasked to lead a broad-based committee of Jordanians (drawn from government and across society) in creating what was called the "National Agenda" for reform. That effort resulted in calls for broader political reform within the kingdom, including the rights of women, and a deepening of Jordan's nascent civil society specifically. As Muasher noted at the time, even the concept of civil society has sometimes been reduced to include only charitable NGOs and not also political parties, professional associations, and trade unions, effectively depoliticizing the concept. Consequentially he called for a broader conceptualization of civil society, to include all of these types of organizations, independent of the state itself—with goals ranging from social to economic to political. In this way, he surmised, political liberalization in Jordan and elsewhere could finally move forward, but only with a strengthened civil society as its base.[14]

Unveiled in 2005, the National Agenda was met with overt hostility by many antireform hard-liners within the regime, and with considerable indifference on the part of a Jordanian public that seemed to have grown tired of the recurring pattern of new top-down initiatives and slogans emanating from the regime itself. The problem in this case wasn't necessarily the National Agenda itself but rather with reactions to it, which ranged from jaded to wholly reactionary. Muasher and other participants in the National Agenda for Reform were quite serious and committed to real reform and change, but many in society has such low expectations that they reacted with stony silence, while reform opponents made their opposition known at maximum volume.

In the words of one Jordanian writer and activist, "We have many regime slogans: think big, act big; Jordan first; political development; the National Agenda—these are Western-style marketing slogans. They work more for marketing outside the country, but not inside the country."[15] Similarly, another activist argued:

This is the problem, the contradiction between speeches and implementation. We have now had Jordan First, Political Development and the new ministry for it, and now the National Agenda. Continually new programs are launched, but still with little effect. Little actual involvement. The quota for women, for example, or the National Center for Human Rights, these are both okay but very small steps. The National Center for Human Rights, for instance, is not actually fully independent of the government. These are advances in relatively small details. . . . We don't suffer like the people of Syria or Saudi Arabia, but we don't need to compare ourselves to them. We are stable and have a better economic situation. But why do we have to pay a political price for this? This should simply be the norm. We have a mature and educated population. Few listen to the real extremists here. Palestinians for example may have real grievances, but we don't see mobs in the street. We all try to solve things with soft pressure.[16]

It may be, however, that faith in "soft pressure" had faded by 2010 and 2011, as many Jordanians did indeed take to the streets—not as "mobs" but as organized protests—demanding real reform.

While these problems trigger recurrent grassroots responses, they nonetheless remain problems largely within the elite itself. Even when there are proreform constituencies within the regime, within government, and within the palace, they are countered by fierce opposition from conservative and even reactionary elements in the same institutions. In his own assessment, Muasher has argued that Jordan essentially has an elite problem: "The problem is that the political system doesn't want it (reform)— the political elite, the intelligence services, and the status quo in Jordan and the Arab world in general. Opening the system to them boils down to reducing their privileges. The excuses are endless. But the bottom line is that they don't want their privileges to go."[17]

In the years immediately following the accession of King Abdullah in 1999, both conservative and reform constituencies seemed to think that a young and active king was on their side. Yet more than a decade later, in the Arab Spring era, it was more common to hear both sides say that they had been abandoned—and that the king was on the *other* side.

Reform activists from civil society organizations and political parties argued that the monarchy by 2011 had retrenched and become more authoritarian than it had been in 1999. Right-wing "old-guard" elites, in contrast, seemed to feel that the regime had gone too far, selling the country out in its quest for neoliberal economic development. As noted in chapter 2, this debate has also taken on a steadily more nationalist tone, as ethnic identity politics has risen sharply in response to domestic and regional crises. Conservative East Jordanian nationalists, for example, increasingly question "reform" at all and often argue that it is not about liberalization or democratization but is too often mistaken for being synonymous solely with Palestinian empowerment, which they see coming at the expense of the status quo, and perhaps at the expense of Jordan's very identity as a nation and state.[18] Many Jordanians—both for and against reform—wondered aloud which side the king really was on regarding the issue of reform.

There seemed to be an opposition consensus at least on the issues of seriously tackling corruption, providing more inclusion in the political system, and establishing more responsible governance in the kingdom. But even opposition activists differed on the details. During multiple visits to Jordan during this newer era of reform debates—in 2011 and after—what was most striking was the frequent use of the word *appeasement* by almost all parties in their assessment of assorted reform proposals. Jordanian nationalists argued that the reforms were merely appeasing Palestinians and Western foreign aid donors. Conversely, many Palestinian Jordanian activists felt that the whole system was centered on a core policy of appeasement of tribal East Jordanians. Proreform activists feared that the regime would also engage in appeasement of its more conservative and authoritarian Gulf allies by pulling the plug on nascent reform efforts. As Jordan grew ever closer to Saudi Arabia in the Arab Spring era, these fears only increased.

Meanwhile, antireform elements, who felt that the system should stay as it is, complained that various reform efforts were simply misguided attempts at appeasement—of women, of liberals, of Islamists, of Palestinians, and so on. But their Jordan was a tribal, East Jordanian nationalist and Hashemite state. To them, that was and is the real Jordan. In their view, the other elements threatened to dilute that Jordan, or worse, threatened to overrun it while masked in the guise of reform. As noted in chapter 2, even in the streets, especially in 2011 and after, regime "loyalists" responded to critics and proreform demonstrators with increasing demonstrations of their own. Proreform demonstrations were therefore often accompanied, or perhaps shadowed, by loyalist counterdemonstrations. Jordan's reform struggles, in short, were carried out not only within the halls of governing institutions but also, at times, in the streets.

Even before the region-wide uprisings, a set of Jordanian holidays commemorating the armed forces, the anniversary of the king's coronation, and Jordanian independence all combined for several days of parades and often highly orchestrated pageantry. In the post–Arab Spring period, Jordan has seen a heightened emphasis on nationalist, patriotic, and Hashemite symbolism. During national celebrations, Jordanian flags and red-and-white-checked keffiyehs abound (while the black-and-white versions associated with Palestinian identity seem to momentarily vanish). The displays range from military bands and parades to individuals creating parades of their own—such as those who pound on car horns, blare nationalist music, tote Jordanian flags from their vehicles, or rev the engines of their flag-draped Harley-Davidson motorcycles, slowly maneuvering their way down Amman's posh Rainbow Street or in other West Amman neighborhoods.

But many Jordanians found these displays to be over the top and altogether too fawning or perhaps too contrived. Countless Jordanians, in fact, who are loyal and patriotic citizens, are as uncomfortable with these displays as they are with opposition groups like the Muslim Brotherhood. They often see these polarized positions as equally tone deaf and counterproductive to

Jordan's future. These Jordanians see themselves as both proregime *and* pro-reform. This is not a contradiction. They do not want to see regime change or any kind of explosion of violence or unrest in Jordan, but they do favor reformist change and greater inclusion in the Jordanian system. They too feel that corruption is extensive and needs to be fought, but they do not identify either with the opposition, in the sense of political parties, Hirak movements, and street demonstrators, or with the more virulent loyalist or reactionary elements either.

Following a day of nationalist and royalist pageantry, several Jordanians who see themselves in this more middle position noted that they were distinctly uncomfortable with the events. In multiple different meetings, and in every case without prompting, they used the same term to describe their discomfort even with the patriotic displays. One, leaning forward to whisper her concern, summarized a view shared by many—that it didn't seem Jordanian; rather, she said, it seemed Ba'athist, like something one would see in that type of authoritarian system or ideological regime. That categorization would be decidedly jarring and even offensive to most regime officials in a country that sees itself as almost the polar opposite of its neighbor to the north, Syria. Yet in my own discussions with Jordanians, the term kept coming up. Two Jordanians, coming to the same conclusion at the same time, used the same term "Ba'athi" and then shook their heads in disapproval.[19] These were fiercely patriotic people, and none was arguing that the regime or the state was itself remotely Ba'athist, to be clear, but rather that the ostentatious and state-organized displays seemed like something one would find in one of several other Arab countries, not in Jordan.

Still, these same Jordanian citizens also wanted the regime to be more vocal—not just more vocal than the opposition, but also more vocal than self-described "loyalist" supporters, whose demonstrations so often seemed to include *bultajiyya* or thuggish elements, and hence seemed to carry an aura not of a positive patriotic message but rather of a barely veiled and negative message that suggested danger to any who dared dissent. These more moderate or centrist Jordanians wanted the king to speak out to the nation and to clarify where he was on the issues of reform and change. Government efforts were inconsistent and often incoherent, leaving the field open to wild speculation in the press and social media regarding just what exactly was going on. As one former government official complained, "All our spokespeople are mute. It's like Charlie Chaplin TV."[20]

The Arab Spring and Rebooting Reform . . . Again

During the Arab Spring, with dramatic regime change occurring in other Arab states, Jordan's opposition grew larger and more coordinated in its attempts to push the regime back toward the reform process. As noted in the preceding chapters, most activists still called for reform, not revolution. But opposition activists did call for the curbing of monarchical powers, a shift toward greater democratization, and ultimately more of a constitutional monarchy in Jordan. Jordan's constitution of 1952 provided for a strong executive authority vested in the king, a bicameral legislature, and an independent judiciary. Reformers of almost all stripes tended to argue, however, that since the 1950s the balance of power in state institutions had shifted steadily and ultimately almost entirely toward the monarchy.

Reformers argued for a more balanced system, with a clearer separation of powers, checks and balances between institutions, elected governments, and legislatures with genuine powers. Many called for a restoration of the constitution of 1952, associating the 1950s with multiparty politics, and more of a role for parliament and government in policy making, rather than a monarchical monopoly on power. The constitution from 1952 actually remains in place, however, so what some activists really mean is the original version of the constitution, without the host of amendments and assorted temporary laws that had clogged the Jordanian system in the decades thereafter.[21]

While many reform activists call for a constitutional monarchy, many conservative proregime elites regard this as already accomplished. The Jordanian system includes a monarchy, a parliament, a prime minister and cabinet, and a constitution. This, they argue, marks Jordan as a constitutional monarchy. So Jordanians for and against reform and liberalization argue in terms of constitutional monarchy but with markedly different visions regarding what this actually means. To be clear, a constitutional monarchy is not just the presence of the above institutions but rather a political system in which the powers of the monarchy are more limited, the elected parliament is stronger, the judiciary is truly independent, the government is democratically elected, and branches of government check and balance one another. In the constitutional monarchies of Europe—for example, in the United Kingdom, Denmark, or Spain—power is vested in elected representatives in parliament, not in the monarchy. In that sense, Jordan is not yet a constitutional monarchy as the term is usually understood internationally. Power is concentrated in the palace, with very limited roles for parliament, or for that matter for the prime minister and cabinet ministers.

To what extent this would change, and whether power would devolve to these other institutions, was a central question in the Jordanian version of the Arab Spring, and indeed in reform debates both before and after that period.

While the Jordanian debate over economic reform has centered on the pros and cons of the continuing neoliberal policy agenda, and hence trying to bring issues of fairness and equality to an agenda that is largely about efficiency and growth, the political reform debate is centered most often on issues of institutions, power, and participation in public life. Since the "reform era" of 1989 to 1993, Jordan in many ways appeared to be stuck at a crossroads between more liberalization and democratization, on the one hand, and a more authoritarian path, on the other. While Jordan has oscillated between these two extremes, it has never fully embraced either. Even in its most authoritarian moments, Jordan didn't develop into the full-blown police state that characterized so many other countries in the region; but neither has it allowed full liberalization and democratization, despite the very promising start in 1989, and despite considerable rhetoric over the years regarding liberalization and democratization. Instead, the Jordanian state has alternated between periods of openness and repression over the years, with the intelligence services—the GID, or Mukhabarat—playing a very large role in public life.

The role of the GID in Jordanian politics might be described as "behind the scenes" but barely so. Many Jordanian journalists and political activists alike are familiar with the GID phone call to visit the intelligence headquarters "for a cup of coffee." This is a far cry for the overt repression associated with many other Middle East states but is regarded by many in the Jordanian opposition as "soft repression," the upshot of which is a tendency toward a climate of self-censorship. Many Jordanian dissidents, of course, would not regard GID actions as "soft" at all. But the GID's role is so extensive, at times, that even government officials and highly placed regime elites also complain about it. Some even within the regime, in other words, see the GID as being essentially its own unaccountable fiefdom. One official, for example, was quite blunt in his assessment, arguing that "they should be servants, not masters. This country is ruled by the intelligence services."[22] Another official, also in the upper echelons of the state, argued that the Mukhabarat was the major obstacle to reform in the kingdom and that its antireform efforts were beyond any constitutional or legal role. "Nothing happens," he added, "without their knowledge, or consent, or both."[23]

In the early years of the Arab Spring era, the GID role remained extensive in public life, but the old norms among citizens regarding caution and self-censorship seemed to fade, or at least were significantly challenged. Jordanians were more likely to speak out, in public, in demonstrations, or online, and on far more topics than ever before. So in some respects politically active elements in society were far ahead of the intelligence services, with activists operating in an entirely new milieu, while the intelligence agencies had some catching up to do. As the Arab uprisings expanded, however, and civil wars and insurgencies deepened across Jordan's borders, so too did the state's emphasis on security over political openness or domestic reform.

As noted in chapter 1, Jordan has remained a kind of middle case that is neither fully authoritarian nor fully democratic; the kingdom might therefore be best described as a hybrid regime or liberalizing autocracy, in which the regime has allowed moderate levels of political reform, with the aim of preserving rather than transforming the system.[24] In contrast, and just as consistently, political opposition in Jordan has for decades called on the regime to choose the path of greater democratization, and to move beyond mere cosmetic reforms toward a genuine transformation. Many Jordanians, both those for reform and those who are more conservative and cautious, complain that the security and intelligence services play far too large a role in public life, dampening or even smothering attempts at greater reform, openness, and change. In 2011 and after, the Arab Spring reinvigorated these debates and struggles over the meaning and depth of political reform in the kingdom.

From the protests of 2011 onward, the regime was under considerable pressure, and not all in the same direction. Some pushed for a return to reform and more change, some for less change and for the regime to hold the line against what they viewed as mobs and nothing more. With tensions mounting and street demonstrations showing no sign of abating, the palace did respond, by unveiling a top-down set of reform initiatives that it argued would transform politics in the Hashemite Kingdom. In June 2011

King Abdullah delivered a rare televised address to the nation, announcing a wide range of planned political reforms. Most important, he announced that Jordan was moving toward actual parliamentary governments, rather than the norm of governments serving as royal appointees. He called for reforms regarding elections, parliament, and the strengthening of political parties. In short, he touched on many of the key demands emanating from Jordan's varied opposition movements. But the king also tempered expectations by suggesting that chaos and disorder would prevent matters from moving too quickly. Jordan would proceed along a path to reform but slowly, carefully, and with caution.[25]

In making his speech, the king was responding not only to the extensive levels of street activism but also to demands for reform from almost every direction. He decried disunity and *fitna*—pointedly using an explicitly religious and Islamic term referring to the grave sin of creating social chaos or disorder. He further criticized what he deemed to be irresponsible media reporting. But the king also reiterated his call for strengthening the party system and shifting from royally appointed governments to those drawn from the majority bloc in a democratically elected parliament. This would amount to dramatic change in Jordan's modern politics, echoing not even the reform era of 1989–1993 but rather the 1950s, when the monarchy still held tremendous power but elected parliamentary governments also had some level of real influence on political life.

The king seemed to be going further even than many opposition parties and movements. Yet the public response was decidedly underwhelming. If the king had made this exact speech several years earlier, the response might even have been enthusiastic. It might have been seen as pathbreaking. But the muffled response suggested even more pessimism than usual in Jordanian politics. There seemed to be a pervasive lack of faith that rhetoric would be met with actual implementation. Even immediately after the speech, every Jordanian I met with expected to be disappointed. This was true even among those who strongly supported each of the king's points. Many had a conditional response to the king's suggestion of democratically elected governments. As one activist put it, summarizing the view of many, "It's a good idea . . . if it happens."[26] Many reformers credited the king with good ideas but also immediately noted that the speech omitted any timetable for the various reforms.[27]

In the Arab Spring era, the state initiated a new series of reforms, essentially unveiling a "reform from above" campaign in response to pressures from below. At first these measures seemed to echo the 1989–1993 reform period. In 1990 King Hussein had gathered a broad cross-section of the political elite to craft a new National Charter, allowing for greater political freedoms but within the framework of loyalty to Jordan as a Hashemite Kingdom. In 2011 King Abdullah similarly established a National Dialogue Committee (technically appointed by the government of Prime Minister Ma'rouf al-Bakhit). The fifty-two-member task force represented key leaders from the Islamist movement (at least initially), leftist political parties, professional associations, civil society organizations, as well as members of the business community.

Perhaps from the perspective of some in government, this was quite a diverse cross-section of Jordanians, led by a prominent senator and former prime minister (and one known for his support for reform), Taher al-Masri. But the committee included no members of Jordan's many youth movements, in a country where the clear majority of citizens are under the age of twenty, and it included merely four women. While Islamist representatives were initially included, the Muslim Brotherhood ultimately decided to boycott the proceedings, arguing that it would amount to much ado about nothing, and that the opposition had already made quite clear what its reform demands were. Despite questions about the representative nature of the committee, it was charged with examining comprehensive reforms, from the electoral system to the laws on political parties, public assembly, and media.

In April 2011 the king also appointed a Royal Committee to Review the Constitution. The committee examined the entire constitution, proposing a series of amendments that were later approved by parliament. These included revisions that limited the ability of the king to dissolve parliament indefinitely or to rule by decree in its place. The constitutional amendments also established a constitutional court and the Independent Electoral Commission (discussed in chapter 6). Marwan Muasher, Jordan's former chief official in charge of reform, wrote at the time that the constitutional amendments were "a first step in the right direction." Yet while the set of amendments represented a needed update and revision of the constitution, they essentially left most monarchical power in place. It was a start, however, and as Muasher wrote, collectively the amendments meant that "the constitution will witness its first major en masse overhaul since it was adopted in 1952."[28] The amended constitution, however, led to the usual divergence of views in Jordan regarding continuity and change.

Conservatives often cite this amendment process as complete and as proof of significant and even sweeping change. They note that the king himself urged the committee not to review a few key amendments but to review the entire document. Liberals, progressives, and reformists, however, tend to see more continuity than change. They may see it as a key first step but feel that far more extensive change is needed, especially regarding the concentration of power within the monarchy.

The monarchy itself, meanwhile, continued to emphasize the rhetoric of reform and change, with new committees, new commissions, and new initiatives. In December 2012 the regime established a National Integrity Commission as a first step toward increasing transparency in politics and toward reining in corruption. Even with the revolving door of prime ministers and governments (noted in chapter 2), new reform measures proceeded one after another, as part of a larger package of reforms in governance and political life. Following his June 2011 address to the nation, as noted in chapter 6, King Abdullah continued what he viewed as a national conversation by issuing a series of "Discussion Papers" outlining a succession of reforms.[29] The first of these was issued on December 29, 2012, and was written with the forthcoming January 2013 elections in mind.

The discussion paper cited a new electoral law, soon to produce a new parliament, whose members would be consulted for their input in naming the next prime minister. By September 2014 the king had presented five different discussion papers, arguing that these were to initiate constructive political dialogue across the country regarding comprehensive political reform. Officials at the Royal Hashemite Court also emphasized that no other Arab leader, whether king or president, was engaging the public in such a direct way. The king's discussion papers addressed changes in government and governance and also staked out a vision for engaged citizenship, with emphasis on responsive government but also emphasizing responsibilities of citizens as well as effective political participation, activism, journalism, and media.

In the fifth paper the king listed a series of achievements as well as goals in the reform process as essential "Pillars for Deepening Our Democratic Transition." He cited a revised constitution, new laws on political parties, elections, and public assembly, the creation of the Independent Electoral Commission, and changes to the State Security Court (SSC) laws that would restrict SSC jurisdiction to cases of "treason, espionage, terrorism, drugs and currency counterfeiting."[30] Hereafter, civilians were to stand trial only before a civilian, not a military, court. In actual practice, this last measure has been particularly problematic, as even online political commentary that is deemed subversive has at times led to arrest and conviction under the SSC, despite the changes in the law itself.

In addition to reforms regarding government, political parties, and elections, other reform initiatives were aimed at civil society. The Dimuqrati (Democratic) program, for example, was aimed at Jordan's youth, who could apply within a "Youth Empowerment Window" for grants to support various grassroots or local citizenship initiatives. The Dimuqrati initiative was led by a highly regarded reform advocate, Dr. Omar Razzaz, who saw it as part of a much larger process. As a de facto but unique form of rentier state—that is, one that had been built on an implied social contract regarding public-sector jobs and privileges yet without extensive natural resources to back this up—Jordan's "reform" process would have to include far more than institutional or policy change. It would have to be more comprehensive—political and economic, to be sure, but also social and cultural. Dimuqrati was intended to help develop democratic values and processes at a very local level. "We've tapped into something that the youth have in them, but haven't been able to do," Razzaz noted.[31] A key problem, he added, was not the youth or students but a national educational system that emphasized a conformist structure and rote learning rather than critical thinking. A strong supporter of educational reform, Razzaz later became Jordan's minister of education, tasked with the urgent but also rather overwhelming job of reforming the national educational system.

Just a few years before, Razzaz had also been tapped for another state-driven reform initiative. In 2013 the regime appointed a commission of leading economists to investigate every instance of privatization since 1989. Corruption in the context of the state's neoliberal privatization agenda was, after all, a major complaint across the Jordanian political spectrum, not just from street protestors but even in the top echelons of the elite itself. The privatization commission, led by Razzaz, was charged with examining every privatization deal in an effort to uncover any corruption but also to make the entire process more transparent. The committee was also tasked with evaluating the pros and cons of privatization itself.[32]

King Abdullah II, however, was even more committed to neoliberal economic reforms than his late father, King Hussein, had been. In keeping with the economic reform process, Jordan moved steadily toward a neoliberal model of development, with emphasis on privatizing state-owned industries, lowering barriers to trade, and encouraging extensive foreign investment. Upon ascending the throne in 1999, King Abdullah II pursued these measures with even more energy and enthusiasm. Since Jordan is not blessed with sufficient oil, gas, or even water to be economically influential in the region, or even to supply its own population, the kingdom remains dependent on foreign aid and economic deals with regional and global allies. The king seemed convinced that this development model was Jordan's only viable path, and that it required constant recruiting of foreign investors and frequent pitches in foreign capitals to both public officials and private-sector business people, for investment, aid, and trade. This economic emphasis, in turn, has implications for Jordan's foreign relations, as it requires ensuring that the kingdom always has multiple economically generous allies. And that, in turn, necessitates moderation in foreign policy. Jordan cannot afford, in other words, to alienate any allies, donors, or investors.

But Jordan's neoliberal policies also have domestic political consequences. As privatization has continued, the public-sector enterprises and social safety net have both shrunk. As noted in chapter 5, constituencies that previously relied on work in the public sector, and on generous government payoffs, have found themselves in ever more dire circumstances, even as Jordan's economy remains deeply in debt, dependent on foreign aid, and mired in high rates of unemployment and underemployment. It is for these reasons, then, that traditional bases of regime support—from the April 1989 riots onward—have increasingly questioned the regime's commitment to them as communities. All Jordanians, regardless of region, ethnicity, or other background, had to deal with a rapidly rising cost of living, especially in terms of food and housing. In Jordan, as in other Arab countries in this era, protests challenged these conditions and also challenged previously established "red lines" regarding what topics were acceptable even for protest. Jordanian protests and opposition forces accordingly began to focus not just on institutions, parties, and electoral laws but also on regime priorities and specific concerns with growing corruption in the political and economic systems alike.

Concerns such as these have led to debates about what types of reforms to prioritize. They have also aggravated issues within Jordanian identity politics, not just between communities but also over whether reforms themselves had a genesis that was itself Jordanian, or foreign. As a Transjordanian nationalist put it:

Reform is too often about identity politics, but from outside of Jordan. It is mainly the views of NGOs and civil society organizations about giving Palestinians more rights. Too often "reform" is really a foreign agenda. What is equality though? Rights? What about distribution? The Palestinians are empowered now, to the point that they are getting everything. We should ask first, who or what is Jordan? Jordanian? Then move on to political reform.[33]

Economic reforms, begun long before the Arab Spring, had already resulted in significant political and social changes, even changing the nature of state-society arrangements. As Anne Marie Baylouny has noted, "Economic liberalization led to a radical change in the regime's base of support, marginalizing the previous regime backers—the East Bank population—and replacing them with a strengthened military, formerly only part of the regime's support." The military and other security services, as noted previously, are mainly drawn from the East Bank population, but the key point is that neoliberal economic changes have had a profound political impact, rearranging the social and political structure while also increasing the size and power, even in domestic political life, of the armed forces. Baylouny has referred to this phenomenon as "militarized liberalization" or "militarizing welfare."[34] For those who feel that they have lost out in this transition, dissent is therefore rooted in anger over economic as well as political changes.

Many regime loyalists and policy makers have also noted the importance of economic change and dissent but have drawn very different lessons—not drawing back from neoliberalism but rather pushing it further. For many in the Hashemite regime, economic factors were the key drivers of the Arab Spring, and economic factors would also be the solutions. Jordan would survive the onslaught of the Arab Spring by dealing with economic discontent. This, some officials argued, would help temper social and political demands as well. Jordan needed aid, investment, and job opportunities, and it needed to erase the enormous gap between rich and poor by creating a genuine middle class. On his numerous visits to the United States, for example, King Abdullah met with the U.S. president, powerful members of Congress, and key cabinet and military officials, but he also routinely met with chambers of commerce and private-sector business elites, essentially making the same pitch: Jordan is a loyal ally to the

United States, but it needs help; so commit to the kingdom politically, militarily, and economically.

This was especially important in the Arab Spring era, but even before the era of uprisings and protests the Jordanian regime had long been worried about Jordan's economic vulnerability. Fayez Tarawneh, a former prime minister and later chief of the Royal Hashemite Court for much of the Arab Spring era, noted—referring to Jordan's difficult neighbors—that "our geographic proximity and demographic nature puts us on the hot seat. Looking inward, King Abdullah is convinced that the Jordanian economy is very vulnerable to these regional problems."[35] This has long been the case for the kingdom, given its regional setting, but it seemed especially difficult during the Arab Spring, with conflict across most of Jordan's borders at a time when its economy was already in crisis.

While the king maintained an extensive international travel schedule, including making the economic pitches noted above, domestic opposition also began to criticize that too—arguing that the king spent too much time outside of Jordan. "He is too comfortable at home, and too weak abroad," noted one critic dismissively.[36] But the king also hosted a continual stream of foreign visitors to Jordan itself, including kings, presidents, prime ministers, business leaders, and investors. And he on many occasions made sure that Jordan would host international meetings of wealthy investors and powerful political and economic elites, via the World Economic Forum (WEF). In May 2015, Jordan hosted for the ninth time the Middle East conference of the WEF, underscoring the esteem with which the country is held in some of the wealthiest circles of private business capital and also in some of the most powerful regional and global states.

At the 2015 meeting of the World Economic Forum, Jordanian officials, including the king himself, pulled out all the stops in terms of selling their audience of movers and shakers on the viability of investment in Jordan. In some respects, the regime was trying to turn a set of negatives from the Arab uprisings—regional chaos, disruption, and turmoil—into a positive for Jordan. The region had descended into turmoil as the original Arab Spring took a darker and more violent turn into civil wars, unrest, and terrorism. But comparatively speaking, the Hashemite Kingdom appeared to be an oasis of stability in an otherwise volatile neighborhood. The economic message was clear: that Jordan remained open for business. The meeting at Jordan's Dead Sea resort included slick multimedia presentations on economic opportunities in the kingdom, such as direct foreign invest-ment and especially public-private partnerships in transportation, inter-net and communications technology, energy, infrastructure, and urban development.

But these policy preferences suggested pursuing even more vigorously a neoliberal economic agenda, whereas many Jordanian political protests—not just since 2011 but since 1989—condemned that very process. As noted in previous chapters, protesters especially from traditionally proregime, tribal, and East Jordanian communities tended to decry the loss of the social safety net, of government employment and financial guarantees, and hence often called for a restoration of a larger public sector, turning away from privatization and its economic hardships, and also turning away from the many corruption opportunities that tend to emerge precisely in major eco-nomic shifts such as privatization.

Jordanian analyst Osama al-Sharif argued, however, that much of the political reform agenda was essentially "on hold" as early as the summer of 2012, under severe pressure from the kingdom's own economic crises as well as the worsening situation next door in Syria. There were multiple warning signs, but perhaps the strongest indicator was at the head of government itself, when proreform prime minister 'Awn al-Khasawneh resigned and was replaced by stalwart conservative Fayez Tarawneh. This handover of power in some respects marked the return of "old-guard" ele-ments to the top echelons of the regime, alongside more technocratic and neoliberal elites. "Years of economic policies had sidelined the old guard," Sharif wrote, "but they also failed to produce the economic miracle that Jordanians were promised. Many neoliberals—the so-called 'digital' offi-cials, whom Abdullah had adopted—were tainted by corruption charges."[37] The Jordanian public, meanwhile, seemed increasingly alarmed by devel-opments across the border as the Syrian war worsened, and by basic and everyday economic survival issues. Even as the cost of living remained tre-mendously difficult for most Jordanians, thousands of refugees continued to arrive, and the state's fiscal crisis worsened.

Within government, other political appointments seemed to reinforce the sense of a shift from reformist to antireformist officials. In October 2014 King Abdullah appointed a new Senate, pointedly ousting its former pres-ident, proreform former prime minister Taher al-Masri and replacing him with a hard-core conservative and former prime minister, 'Abd al-Ra'uf al-Rawabdah. The royally appointed Senate tends to include former prime ministers and other top officials, but the new Senate left out the most prominent reformers among former prime ministers: Masri, Khasawneh, and 'Abd al-Karim al-Kabariti.[38] For many Jordanians, these events were not particularly meaningful, marking simply the latest reshuffling of the Senate, cabinet, or other institution. But for Jordanians who had grasped the Arab Spring as having special promise, these measures seemed to mark the turning point from an almost frantic pace of street protests and state reform measures toward something more like business as usual. Many wondered aloud if Jordan had taken two steps forward, only to take two steps back.

Similarly, many activists argue that women's rights have lagged far behind other issues even within reform debates. Aside from long-standing debates over electoral quotas (discussed in chapter 6), for example, activists complained that the committees and commissions associated with various state-driven reform initiatives had scant representation for women.[39] As noted above, the committee to revise the constitution included only four women among its fifty-two members. Women in Jordan received the right to vote and hold elected office in 1974, yet activists often note that reform and representation continue to lag behind. When the constitution was revised amid the Arab Spring, Jordan's long-standing women's rights movement campaigned to change article 6 of the Jordanian constitution to ban discrimination based on gender. Despite extensive debate, the amended article ultimately banned discrimination based on race, language, or religion but not gender.[40] Low levels of female representation in government and in the various reform committees have hindered the efforts of women's rights activists but have not reduced their commitment to activism. Yet women's representation is low not just in politics and government but also within the economy. In a country where more women graduate from colleges and universities than men (usually 55 percent of graduates), women remain underemployed in both the public and private sectors.[41]

Women's rights activism within the kingdom, while concerned with the massive gender gap in representation in government and the official (and paid) parts of the economy, have also focused on more specific issue campaigns. The Arab Spring period, for example, gave renewed energy to a long-standing campaign over citizenship rights. Activists sought to reform laws that prevented children of women who married non-Jordanian men from having Jordanian citizenship. After the 2013 elections the reform-oriented Mubadara (Inititative) bloc of members of parliament seemed finally to have secured a government commitment to support changing these laws, allowing the offspring of Jordanian mothers and non-Jordanian fathers to have full citizenship rights in what was, after all, their own country. Yet the effort stalled, in part amid the usual reactionary efforts that emerge in Jordan regarding any initiative that might affect identity politics in any way. With new elections and a new parliament after 2016, and the electoral loss of leading Mubadara reform MPs such as Mustafa Hamarneh, the measure seemed to have slid backward yet again.

Another long-standing reform campaign, however, secured a major victory in August 2017 when parliament voted to repeal article 308 of the Jordanian penal code, which had allowed rapists to avoid prosecution and punishment if they married their victims. Activists had argued for years that this was an unconscionable practice, and they finally managed to get government and parliamentary support for abolishing the article, drawing on support from Jordanian civil society and women's rights organizations, and also that of activist MPs such as Wafa Bani Mustafa, a deputy from Jerash.[42] Overall, as is true of many issue areas, women's rights has seen some change but perhaps far too much continuity in Jordan.

Debates about media, in contrast, did not so much fall into the continuity versus change dichotomy but rather turned on questions of wholesale regression. Starting in 2012 and 2013, Jordan's media freedoms took several steps backward. Even before the regional Arab Spring, Jordan had a fairly vibrant online media culture. Its print newspapers, in contrast, remained quite conventional, and many were tainted by widespread belief across Jordanian society of GID influence over reporters and editors. But Jordan was far ahead of most Arab countries in online media since it had embraced the possibilities of the internet almost at the outset. In 2011, with the regional Arab uprisings in full swing, Jordan's online media was primed to expand almost overnight. And it did exactly that. But many state officials preferred a more pliant parastatal print media and distrusted the flurry of online activity. This soon became a key point of debate in both reform and antireform circles.

In August 2012 the Jordanian government made its first moves to restrict internet news sites.[43] The idea was to rein in tabloid-style journalism that critics argued was shoddy at best and amounted to chronic character assassination, libel, and outright disinformation at worst. Almost a year later, in June 2013, a new government and a new parliament took further measures to regulate online news sites, shutting down those that did not comply. The new law required all news websites to register with the government and to have an editor that was a certified member of the Jordan Press Association (JPA). But the entire membership of the JPA had been limited to print media journalists, and many websites objected to registering with the state as a matter of democratic principle.[44] The measures had immediate effects, as the government blocked more than three hundred Jordanian news websites.

Many reform activists and journalists assumed, at the time, that the king would overturn the decisions of parliament and the government, but he did not. A year later, many assumed that the government would not really implement what they saw as a fairly draconian, and rather un-Jordanian, approach to online media. Jordan at that time, after all, had a reputation as one of the most open and most advanced countries in the entire Arab world when it came to information technology, the internet, and social media. Much of the Arabic-language content on the internet came from Jordan. And the king himself had strongly supported this. Openness to online media seemed to go hand in hand with the regime's emphasis on economic development via privatization, encouraging businesses, and especially encouraging international investment in the kingdom.

Shutting down hundreds of news sites, and indeed restricting the internet at all, seemed to run counter to this image of a Jordan that was modern, high tech, and open for business. "Is this what was meant by democratic empowerment?" asked an editor of the news website *JO24.net* at a protest rally.[45] Similarly, Daoud Kuttab, editor of the popular *Ammannet*, noted, "They didn't stop us from working, they stopped Jordanians from seeing our work"—at least temporarily.[46] Even Jordan's superb *7iber* site (discussed in chapter 4) found itself blocked repeatedly. Each of these eventually received state authorization to proceed, but only after registering and complying with the various bureaucratic and financial requirements of the new government measures. Hundreds of other sites, however, were blocked seemingly in perpetuity. Even at the height of the website-blocking controversy, however, many sites continued to post articles via Twitter and Facebook and included instructions on how to get around the blocking by using proxy servers. This was a skill known to many in Libya, Tunisia, and Syria, as citizens found ways to navigate around state-run media under the regimes of Qaddafi, Ben Ali, and Asad, but it was new to many Jordanians.

Some journalists and activists wondered whether it was a more deliberate effort to put existing sites on notice, and hence to encourage Jordan's already problematic media culture of self-censorship, and simply to silence others outright. "They are after the chilling effect," suggested one editor.[47] Others cited a very real set of internal and external crises—from the Syrian civil war to unrest in Ma'an (an often restive and in many respects economically marginalized city in the South of Jordan)—suggesting a state desire to tone down coverage of these volatile issues. Still others suggested that the motivation may have been rooted in concerns over sensationalist news coverage and web-based viral videos. Some Jordanians were sympathetic to the blocking of sites they deemed irresponsible in their reporting, but many in the media were deeply concerned that the restrictive regulations were the very opposite of reform and worried that it represented a major retreat in media and internet freedoms in the kingdom.[48]

In 2017, even as debates continued about freedom of speech and freedom of the press, Jordan added another layer to its state-led reform efforts by holding local and municipal elections. The local elections were part of the kingdom's decentralization plan, based on new municipalities and decentralization laws passed by parliament in 2015. As was true in many national elections, the local polls showed a very low voter turnout—roughly 32 percent—ranging from a high of 60 percent in Ajlun to a low of 15 percent in Zarqa. Islamists returned to the polls and scored multiple victories, including a prominent Muslim Brotherhood figure, Ali Abu Sakr, becoming the new mayor of Zarqa. An overwhelming majority of seats went to various tribal-based candidates, while the only organized list to do well was the National Coalition for Reform—an Islamist-led front that also included many tribal candidates.[49] As has been true in elections at the national level, regime supporters argued that this was yet another clear reform step, while many critics pointed to the low turnout and overall lack of public enthusiasm as signs of lack of faith in the reform process more generally.

Overall, regime supporters, and indeed the regime itself, tend to argue that Jordan's reform process has had successes and failures but that Jordan nonetheless had charted a unique path through the Arab uprisings, opting neither for revolution nor for outright repression. One Jordanian analyst credited the regime with a slow and careful approach to reform but also noted that reform remained a work in progress. "There is still much to do," he said. "We need a new political parties law and a new elections law. But not just any laws. We need good ones. And then we can finally move to parliamentary government." He cited initial changes in laws on elections and parties, as well as decentralization efforts, shifting more governance to municipalities themselves, as key reforms. "But the real question is simply good governance, not just parliamentary or nonparliamentary government. Democracy is not just elections, but a package, right down to education, and creating the culture for these institutional changes."[50] A Western diplomat, following the various reforms closely, had a more pithy assessment of reform in Jordan from 2011 onward: "It's not *nothing*," he said.[51]

Regime officials therefore rattle off a long list of changes—amending the constitution, the Constitutional Court, the Independent Electoral Commission, new laws on parties and elections, the various royal commissions, decentralization efforts, and so on. But many reform activists remained skeptical, arguing that Jordan was rearranging deck chairs and making considerable movement without necessarily going forward. One progressive activist put it this way:

I don't think Jordan is ready for a serious shift. There is not enough political will for a breakthrough. The ruling elite is not under really serious pressure for change. So we are going in slow motion, with one step forward, one step backward. The outcome of the National Dialogue Committee for example is a small step. This can't compare to Egypt or to other Arab events. Given that the constitutional committee recommendations may improve parliamentary life and political life, but they do not tackle the power sharing question here. These are just shifts in smaller rules for the speakership, dissolving parliament, and so on; all small steps. I don't expect the king will be asked to select the prime minister from the biggest bloc or party in parliament. There are only 15 seats out of 130 for national party lists [for the 2013 elections]. So we still have a weak party system. These are just changes at the margins, not serious changes.[52]

A government official working specifically on reform issues took a very different view, addressing in particular the question of where the king himself really stood on these matters:

Is the will there? Yes. He (the king) has a deep understanding of the necessity of the transition. Even as a person, he is not a patronage person. He is more comfortable with a meritocracy. . . . He wants his son to inherit a clean slate, with an orderly process toward a constitutional democracy. But there is no button to push to say "there shall be democracy." But the state is not a single man. There are barriers and agencies, each with their own interests. Reform, by its nature, has winners and losers.[53]

As this chapter has made clear, Jordan saw multiple reform initiatives during and long after the Arab Spring. Changes and reforms from above continued, but so too did the debates about whether each of them was meaningful or merely cosmetic.

There is an old joke some Jordanians tell that seems particularly pertinent here. Two Jordanian friends go together to see a movie. As they leave the theater, one appears disappointed.

"Didn't you like the movie?" his friend asks.

"No," the companion replies, "Just like last time."

"What? You already saw the movie? If you didn't like it, why did you go again?"

"I was hoping for a different ending this time."

With Jordan's reform process too, activists and reformers hoped for a different outcome this time, but many of them feel that their general pessimism has been well-earned. Regime officials often find this to be profoundly frustrating, just as reformers are frustrated with what they see as the limits of palace and government reform initiatives. The latter group generally argues that reforms are too little or even merely cosmetic and not meaningful at all. Members of the former group—that is, policy makers within the regime—argue that they get no credit no matter what they do.

Continuity and Change

Government and palace officials are often noticeably frustrated that the regime is not being credited with what they see as a long list of successful reforms. But opposition and democracy activists are similarly frustrated with what they see as considerable movement and noise but with little actual advancement or meaningful change. Regime officials speak in terms of change, while many in the opposition see far too much continuity.

One of many debating points between the two groups is the issue of constitutional monarchy. For the regime, this is all part of a process, lasting many years, of a constitutional monarchy reforming itself. As noted above, many in the Jordanian opposition also speak in terms of a constitutional monarchy, but they see it as something that Jordan has yet to achieve, and as an end goal in a reform process that actually started long ago, but which they argue has yielded few results.

The level of pessimism was striking. But as noted at the beginning of this chapter, Jordan's liberalization process began in 1989, not in 2011. For many prodemocracy activists and reform advocates in Jordan, what is missing is faith in the regime itself. Indeed, they seemed to have very little faith that the regime was really embarking on a path toward more meaningful change. Since 1989, then, Jordanians have seen myriad initiatives but also many retreats from reform, and they are used to seeing new royal committees, new cabinet reshuffles, and new slogans and marketing campaigns. Half of Jordan's population, in fact, was born after 1989, so for them, they have literally been waiting their entire lives for more meaningful change. As one opposition activist put it, at the height of the regional Arab Spring, "the whole region is moving at high speed like a BMW while we are riding donkeys: . . . *donkeys*, not even horses."[54]

There is a constituency for real reform in Jordan, and it cuts across generational, class, ethnic, and gender divides. But it also seems to be continually thwarted by entrenched antireform elites. As former government reform leader Marwan Muasher noted in a Carnegie Endowment report in 2011, in the midst of the Arab Spring: "In view of the recent uprisings in the Arab world, the political elite must recognize that the only way they can retain power is by sharing it, and governments will have to acknowledge that substituting serious implementation with reform rhetoric fools no one."[55] Jordan has one of the most literate and well-educated populations in the entire Arab world, so if old authoritarian tactics seem to work less and less well in other countries across the region, it seems reasonable to expect that they would be even more useless in Jordan. Jordanians, in short, have heard many reform promises. They have heard so many reform slogans over the years that the whole country seems to have slogan fatigue. Many still hoped for something real. Something meaningful.

All these measures came up against other concerns and pressures, however, including Jordan's regional insecurity and the ever-increasing strains on its economy, especially as refugees continued to flow over the border, fleeing the civil war in Syria, and hence arriving in Jordan at a particularly delicate time socially, economically, and politically. Within domestic politics, government and opposition continued to square off over issues of political and economic reform. But these debates were increasingly overshadowed by Jordan's rising security challenges amid the steadily worsening regional political climate. The next chapter turns to the impact of regional insecurity on Jordan's already contentious domestic politics.

CHAPTER VIII

War, Refugees, and Regional Insecurity

The preceding chapters have examined multiple aspects of Jordanian domestic politics, but the kingdom remains deeply affected by external factors as well, and particularly by the politics of its neighbors and of the broader region. The international setting, in short, matters, even for domestic political outcomes. In 2011, the first full year of the Arab Spring, most of Jordan's raging political debates centered on domestic politics and on the kingdom's many internal challenges. Given Jordan's rather difficult neighborhood, however, it didn't take long before regional events began to overshadow the domestic sphere.

In every year of the regional Arab uprisings, external factors seemed to play an ever larger role. Even in 2011, when most of the focus remained on Jordan's own internal politics, protest movements, and demands for greater domestic change, there was already growing concern regarding spillover from the deepening civil war in Syria and the very real issue of refugees already crossing the border into Jordan. Indeed, of the many conflicts that emerged throughout the years of the Arab uprisings, the Syrian civil war had the most profound impact on Jordan, in many ways regionalizing its domestic politics. As one Jordanian activist noted, "It would be impossible to overemphasize the impact of Syria on Jordanian politics."[1]

Jordanian domestic politics is never exclusively domestic. As a small country with a weak economy and volatile neighbors, the kingdom is at all times vulnerable to external crises and security threats. And there are always external crises and security threats. Always. In a sense, that chronic regional vulnerability represents an unfortunate continuity for Jordan. But the degree of regional insecurity and instability also represented significant changes—changes that would have profound impacts on Jordan and its politics. As noted at the very beginning of this book, even for Jordan—a country that has managed to survive countless regional crises in its more than seventy-year history—the era that followed the Arab uprisings seemed especially dire.

For these reasons, there is really no way to write coherently about Jordan's Arab Spring experience, or its politics afterward, without also writing about its external setting. And during the era of the Arab uprisings, that setting included regional wars and their concomitant refugee flows, as people fled the violence in search of safety. The story of Jordan's modern politics is therefore partly a story of reform and resistance to reform, of liberalization and deliberalization, and of struggles over reform, elections, and even national identity. But it is also a story of a country deeply affected by external events, by a region in turmoil, and by the influx of yet another wave of refugees, joining many waves before them. The Syrian civil war in particular had an enormous impact on Jordanian domestic politics, as did the increasing threat of militant jihadist movements—such as ISIS—in both Syria and Iraq. This chapter examines the impact on Jordanian politics of key external events, each of which had deep domestic impacts: the Syrian civil war, the massive influx of Syrian refugees to Jordan, and the rise of ISIS and jihadist threats across the region.

A Region Ablaze

After the Arab uprisings began, the Jordanian regime was deeply concerned when a popular protest movement brought down a key ally—President Husni Mubarak in Egypt—and worse, led to the (temporary) rise to power of the Muslim Brotherhood in Cairo. But it was the revolution in Syria that would affect Jordan and its politics even more. Even as Jordan remained concerned with politics across its other borders, attention was now focused northward as well, as the Syrian revolution turned into an endemic civil war, while ever larger flows of refugees streamed south across the Syrian border into the Hashemite Kingdom. Jordan's domestic political debates and struggles about reform and change, in short, also took place in this broader regional setting that was anything but secure.

As the Syrian civil war worsened in 2012 and 2013, Jordanian forces reinforced and fortified the northern border of Jordan, at that time worrying over the Bishar al-Asad regime's own forces and especially its stockpile of chemical weapons. But the external and regional environment continued to change rapidly as the Arab uprisings unfolded, forcing the Jordanian state to react and, just as continually, to adjust its policies and priorities. By 2013 the Hashemite regime was looking with alarm at Islamist movements on the rise across the region and new Islamist regimes (Egypt, Tunisia) joining already-established Islamist governments such as that of President Recep Tayyip Erdogan in Turkey. Jordan had problematic relations with all these and correspondingly eyed its own large Muslim Brotherhood movement with some trepidation. But by midsummer 2013 even that fear had changed dramatically. The Muslim Brotherhood was overthrown in a coup d'état in Egypt, while the Syrian civil war raged to the north of Jordan, and to the northeast Iraq remained mired in insurgency and (at least since 2003) seemingly endemic terrorism.

But 2014 also saw the rise of a militant Jihadist movement with pretentions to statehood—the Islamic State in Iraq and Syria (ISIS), sometimes known simply as the "Islamic State." Within Jordan, however, the group was better known by its Arabic acronym as "Da'esh." ISIS established itself in parts of both Syria and Iraq, but it had Jordan in its sights too. Jordan increased its military forces on both the Syrian and Iraqi borders, in response not only to the rising levels of conflict in Syria and Iraq but also to the competing declarations of Salafi jihadist "states"—as ISIS declared itself to be a new "caliphate," while its rival, Jabhat al-Nusra (a division of an older enemy of the Jordanian state, al-Qa'ida), declared the caliphate null and void, instead announcing its own "emirate." These calls resonated with some Salafi militants within Jordan itself, and over time as many as two thousand Jordanian jihadists crossed the border to fight in Syria, some with ISIS, some with Jabhat al-Nusra. As Jordan fortified its Syrian and Iraqi borders, it also made clear that Jordanians who joined jihadist movements were unwelcome to return. Those who attempted to do so were met with gunfire at the border.

The year 2014 was a turning point for the region and therefore affected Jordanian domestic politics as well, specifically by underscoring the decidedly old-school politics of securitization outweighing domestic reform.

The same year saw the territorial expansion of ISIS, shaking the very region around it, but also a resurgence of violence to the west of Jordan, between Israel and Hamas over Gaza. Israel's bombing campaign this time, as in previous wars against Hamas or for that matter Hizbullah in southern Lebanon, had a large civilian death toll. Jordanians may have been divided over the Syrian war, and they were indeed also deeply divided over Hamas, but the bombings of Gaza were an altogether different matter. The Syrian civil war remained a divisive force in Jordan's opposition, while Israel's policies provided an unintended unifying point.

The Israeli bombing campaign against Gaza in 2014 even helped revive a then-moribund street protest movement, as Jordanians of all backgrounds followed the events in Gaza, and in the West Bank as well, closely and with empathy. Government, regime, and opposition all decried the use of "collective punishment" and massive bombardments of Gaza by Israeli forces. While Israel argued that it was simply striking back at Hamas's terrorism, and particularly against waves of Hamas rocket attacks, most Jordanians emphasized the fundamental structural inequality of the conflict and intense level of human suffering. Their main concern, to be clear, was certainly not about Hamas but rather about Gaza and its people—and Jordanians were not as likely to conflate the two as many in the West tended to do. Most Jordanians were focused simply on the loss of civilian lives. And this was true whether they themselves had roots in historic Palestine or in East Bank tribes or, for that matter, whether they were Muslim or Christian, Arab or Circassian. Ironically, the 2014 bombings of Gaza also marked the twentieth anniversary of the Israeli-Jordanian peace treaty. Decades after its signing, the treaty remained in force, but it also remained a cold peace—that is, one between states and regimes but not necessarily between peoples. In 2014, at least, the latest war in Israel and Palestine temporarily unified Jordan's opposition and also diverted attention from the other serious security issues across Jordan's borders.

By the summer of 2014, however, ISIS had surprised Iraq, Jordan, and much of the world by overrunning and capturing the city of Mosul and declaring its new caliphate. For a Jordanian regime already prioritizing regional and domestic security issues, this only galvanized the kingdom's security focus. For Jordan's national security establishment—its armed forces, police, gendarmerie, and intelligence services—mobilizing over regional security threats was a clearer mission, and one that they were more used to. It wasn't as nebulous as domestic concerns over protests and demonstrations. At least for many in the Jordanian security services, there was almost a comfort level in mobilizing in full security mode, and more of a familiar mission in engaging in counterterrorism rather than countering demonstrators in domestic politics. While many in the Hashemite regime regarded the Muslim Brotherhood as a familiar and manageable domestic opponent, ISIS and other Salafi jihadists appeared to be a newer and decidedly more deadly threat. And even as these various regional security threats increased, refugees continued to flow over Jordan's borders, adding another challenge for the Jordanian state, for Jordanian society, and for the Jordanian economy.

Jordan has, without question, been deeply affected by external events and regional insecurity, in its domestic politics, in resurgent identity politics across society, and also in one of its weakest points: its economy. As the destabilization of the region continued, with civil war in Syria and insurgency and terrorism abounding in Iraq, Jordan's already weak and dependent economy was constrained still further by the stifling of its main trade routes. In 2014 and 2015 Jordan's border with Iraq closed often, once ISIS had taken control of much of western Iraq and had even seized the border posts. Similarly, to the north, Jordan's borders with Syria were frequently closed, as the Asad regime, rebels, and jihadists struggled to control the border posts on the Syrian side. This also brought much of the violence of the Syrian civil war to Jordan's northern border. During the various times when the border posts to both Syria and Iraq were closed, this effectively strangled much of Jordan's regional trade.

Jordan's borders seemed to be ablaze in three out of four directions, creating a host of new threats to the Hashemite Kingdom. But of these, the war in Syria, the massive influx of refugees, and the rise of ISIS and militant Jihadism in Syria and Iraq were now the dominant concerns.[2] All others seemed to fade in comparison, as did many prospects for deeper reform or for democratization. The next sections examine each of these three topics in turn.

Jordan and the Syrian Civil War

The Syrian uprising began with peaceful protests, but these were met with violent state responses, and the uprising soon descended into years of brutal and bloody civil war.[3] The Jordanians tried to urge a negotiated settlement, suggesting that Asad should leave power and that a gradual negotiated transition would be best for Syrians and their neighbors. A lengthy civil war, they warned, risked turning Syria into another Afghanistan, or Iraq, or even Somalia—with years of unrest, instability, and terrorism following war. The entire situation was a cause of intense worry in Jordan, since Damascus was so close to the Jordanian capital, Amman, and thousands of Syrian refugees poured across the Jordanian border to flee the violence in their home country, especially from 2011 to 2015.

Jordan's relations with Syria had shifted many times over the years, but much of the history of Jordanian-Syrian relations was characterized by mutual hostility. Under their previous regimes (that is, King Hussein in Jordan and President Hafiz al-Asad in Syria), Jordan and Syria had engaged in a decades-long "cold war." That period came to an end after the passing of both leaders. King Abdullah ascended the Jordanian throne in 1999, while Bishar al-Asad—somewhat surprisingly—succeeded his father in 2000, in a "radical" authoritarian republic that had previously been overtly scornful of hereditary succession. After the regime change in Damascus in 2000, King Abdullah led an attempt to achieve rapprochement with Syria and perhaps even more than that. But while the Jordanian-Syrian cold war was successfully brought to an end, no alliance followed, and the two countries once again pursued very different directions in their regional and domestic policies.[4]

But even in the period of warming relations, some aspects of old cold war politics persisted. U.S. ambassador to Jordan (2001–2004) Edward Gnehm noted how this cast a shadow over Jordan's approach even to the Syrian civil war many years later.

Even in the early years after Assad became President, cross border infiltration into Jordan continued. The Jordanians apprehended persons they identified as Syrian intelligence agents carrying arms and cash. Exchanges of gunfire resulting in deaths and injuries, though never admitted publicly, were all too common. The assassins of a top U.S. diplomat in 2002 came from Syria, and Jordanian-born al-Qaeda leader Abu Musab al-Zarqawi and his group were known to have contacts with Syrian intelligence.[5]

Retribution, in short, remained a real fear for Jordanian policy makers even years later, when confronted with the Syrian civil war, and they had no doubts about the sheer ruthlessness of the Syrian regime. They were worried about what Asad's regime would do (and later, what various jihadist groups fighting in Syria would do), but they were also especially concerned with what would happen in Syria if or when the Asad regime did fall. What would follow? And might it be even worse for Jordan, in terms of both the kingdom's security and another surge in refugees to Jordan?

The regime worried specifically about some form of Islamist ascendancy in Damascus after the war, even suggesting in 2012 that an Islamist axis might be emerging, stretching from Tunisia to Libya to Egypt, including even Turkey, and threatening to emerge in Syria as well. The same regime that had earlier spoken of a Shi'a axis (referring to Lebanon, Syria, Iraq, and Iran) was now seeing potentially a Sunni Islamist axis that seemed to threaten the domestic regime security of Jordan and its Gulf allies alike. Until the overthrow of the Muslim Brotherhood in Egypt in 2013, Islamists did seem to have risen to power in Tunisia and Egypt, appeared to be on the rise in Libya, and were already in power (in the form of the ruling Justice and Development Party, or AKP) in Turkey. Jordanian officials were already concerned Shi'a Islamists ruled in Iran and held too much power in the otherwise weak governments in Iraq and Lebanon. So even aside from the rising sectarian tensions in the region, the Hashemite regime mainly wanted to avoid yet another Islamist regime—of whatever stripe—in a post Asad Syria.[6]

But Islamism in Syria was also alarming in a different way. As armed Islamist movements expanded across Syria, the Jordanians feared the return of Jordanian Salafi jihadists once the war was over. The Jordanian regime worried that unrest would in effect be imported into the kingdom either via Islamist militancy or via Ba'athist sleeper agents, activated by a Damascus regime angered at Jordan's alleged support for the rebel forces. They feared, in short, terrorism coming to Jordan from Syria, as it had from Iraq.[7] As the jihadist presence grew in Syria, so too did this fear regarding what it might ultimately mean for Jordan.

Journalist Tony Karon suggested that Jordan was "living dangerously as Syria burns." He wrote that "security officials in Amman fear that the return home of this cohort of battle-hardened and radicalized Islamists will result in a recurrence of the domestic security nightmare faced by Arab regimes when volunteers who'd fought the Soviets in Afghanistan in the 1980s returned home a decade later." Or, if the war dragged on and on, as indeed it did, it would turn Syria into a "long-term jihadi breeding ground right on Jordan's border."[8] And unlike even the terrorism that had arrived in Jordan from turmoil in Iraq, the distances were markedly different. Syria and Iraq both border Jordan, but conflict in Iraq tended to be hundreds of miles from the border, whereas part of the Syrian civil war involved battles between the Syrian army and rebels or even jihadists over the border posts themselves, as well as endemic clashes in the city of Dera'a, just north of its Jordanian counterpart, Ramtha.

Every possible scenario for Syria seemed horrid for Jordan—the survival of a vengeful and brutal dictatorship? A new Islamist regime? The expansion of a jihadist "state" like that of ISIS? Or even simply continued war and turmoil? These scenarios varied only by degree. But the kingdom had little choice but to engage in its usual foreign policy and alliances tightrope walk, between a vengeful Syria and its own allies, knowing that ultimately it could do little to affect the outcome. As former U.S. ambassador Gnehm put it, "Jordan has very little influence on events in Syria, but enormous stakes in its outcome." Jordanian foreign policy would therefore seek "to avoid antagonizing the Syrian regime and provoking retribution," while simultaneously, Jordan's King Abdullah would have to "continue to monitor the positions of the U.S. and regional states, especially Saudi Arabia, in order to maintain the relationships that he has worked so hard to cultivate."[9]

Even if their Syria policies failed miserably, which seemed likely, Jordan's Western and Gulf allies all had this in common: none of them shared a border with Syria. But Jordan did. Jordan's massive refugee population was a clear reminder of this, as if one was needed. But Jordanian officials therefore remained careful to strike neutral notes, even as they were pulled in a more interventionist direction. Official Jordanian policy oscillated, as Yezid Sayigh has noted, between periods of neutrality and "positive engagement," including Jordanian offers to mediate between the regime and opposition, in order to bring the war to an end.[10]

Jordan retained diplomatic ties with Syria, even after it ousted a particularly undiplomatic Syrian diplomat. The Syrian ambassador was sent home, in short, but the embassy and relations remained open.[11] This was true even when high-level Syrian regime defectors fled to Amman. Jordanian officials tended to draw sharp lines between secular and Islamist opponents of Asad. The regime in Damascus made no such distinction. For Asad's regime, all rebels were terrorists, and the Jordanian regime was therefore backing terrorists, including al-Qa'ida (in the form of the Nusra

Front) and Da'esh or ISIS. Individual Jordanians had indeed joined these organizations, but despite Syrian regime accusations, the Jordanian state was adamantly against them and even joined the coalitions against ISIS, led by the United States and Saudi Arabia.

Even as the Jordanian government insisted that it remained neutral in the Syrian civil war, media reports surfaced suggesting that Gulf Cooperation Council countries—especially Saudi Arabia and Qatar—were purchasing arms for the Syrian rebels and funneling them into Syria via both Turkey and Jordan.[12] Media reports in the West continually discussed CIA training in Jordan of Syrian rebel fighters, and Jordanian government spokespeople just as routinely denied that any such training was occurring within Jordan's borders.[13] Syrian president Asad commented that Jordan was meddling in Syrian affairs, and that this risked bringing the fire soon to burn Jordan too. The comment followed joint military exercises conducted in Jordan, near the border with Syria, that included Jordanian troops and the armed forces of eighteen other countries, including the United States. Jordan noted, correctly, that these were the third annual "Eager Lion" exercises, and that they were planned before Syria's war. Yet they nonetheless drew notice, and anger, in Damascus.

When the 2013 exercises ended, however, the United States pointedly left behind Patriot Missile Defense batteries and F-16 Jet fighters to bolster the Jordanian-Syrian border. It left several hundred troops as well, nominally to maintain the missile batteries and jet fighters. These were sensitive matters within Jordanian domestic politics, however, and both proregime and opposition figures condemned any continued U.S. or other foreign deployment on Jordanian soil. And indeed, the Jordanian regime found itself continually denying that Jordan would serve as the "launchpad" for any U.S. or Western attack on Syria. This cycle of charges and counter-charges repeated itself in successive years, as the annual Eager Lion exercises brought not only the Jordanian and U.S. militaries close to the Syrian border but also forces from dozens of other countries participating in the annual military maneuvers. For Jordan, however, the political risk of provoking the Syrian regime was heavily outweighed by improving its own military readiness and, just as important, signaling to Asad and indeed to any other potential adversary that Jordan had many allies, and their mere presence in the kingdom further signaled their support for Jordanian security.

The Syrian war, and the regional destabilization that it had triggered, remained Jordan's most urgent fear, specifically concerning "spillover" from

Syria to Jordan, undermining Jordanian security and stability. As fighting raged in and near Dera'a, just across the Jordanian border with Syrian, Syrian missiles and artillery shells hit the Jordanian side of the border several times. Yet Jordan's defensive moves, intended to shore up that border, also increased the kingdom's external security dilemma: how to increase Jordanian defenses without unintentionally provoking Syria? Similarly, Jordan's military buildup also exacerbated the regime's internal security dilemma: how to protect its security without raising the ire of domestic political opposition?[14]

As shown in chapter 5, conservative nationalists were sensitive to any slights against Jordanian sovereignty and national identity and were increasingly concerned over the kingdom's fragile demographics. They were already obsessively concerned with preventing Israel from turning Jordan into the "alternative homeland" for the Palestinian people. They had also worried that Iraqi refugees (after the U.S. invasion of Iraq in 2003) might become the new Palestinians, or that Syrian refugees might become the new Iraqis—in short, that Jordan was becoming less Jordanian by the day.[15] So even the presence of foreign allies within Jordan to bolster its border defenses turned out to be a politically sensitive subject. Many left-wing and pan-Arab nationalist activists were just as critical of the regime's policy choices and argued especially that Jordan's alliance choices had carried it too close to Western imperial powers, to reactionary and authoritarian Arab states, and especially to Israel.[16]

As it tried to deal with the internal and external pressures generated in part by the Syrian civil war and the Arab uprisings, the Jordanian regime therefore attempted, as usual, simply to weather the storm. But the regime faced intense pressure from Assad to stay out, and from its own allies (especially Saudi Arabia and the United States) to do more. But even here, regional and global powers alike were at times unclear regarding which fight they were focused on—versus the Asad regime or versus ISIS? Especially since the rapid expansion of ISIS in 2014, the Asad regime had pitched itself as the only alternative to jihadist chaos, even though the regime was itself one of the leading causes of that chaos. Jordan supported the anti-ISIS coalition and maintained its alliances with the United States, Saudi Arabia, and other key powers, but the regime and indeed its various security institutions remained deeply worried not only about the Syrian civil war and the rise of terrorist movements but also about whether even worse security threats would follow.

The regime seemed frustrated, in fact, that its allies were not more effective. In 2013, when the United States threatened military action against the Asad regime after the latter used chemical weapons on its own people, the Jordanians appeared to brace themselves for war. But the Barack Obama administration in the United States then agreed to a negotiated deal that would remove most of Asad's chemical weapons arsenal from Syria, to avoid U.S. military strikes. The war thereafter only intensified, with Russia launching a more decisive military intervention to back up the Asad regime, not only against ISIS and the Nusra Front but especially against rebel forces of the Free Syrian Army.

By saving the Asad regime at perhaps its most precarious moment, the Russian intervention didn't bring an end to the fighting but instead initiated a whole new war and a whole new stalemate, but endemic violence nonetheless. Some Jordanian officials questioned whether Jordan was on the wrong side, and whether the Russians had the right idea all along.[17] Perhaps oddly, Jordan tried to maintain a working relationship with Russia regarding Syria, even as the U.S. military presence in Jordan steadily rose. U.S.-Jordanian military connections have been strong for decades. But now, Jordan was acting as a forward staging area for the U.S.-led military coalition. More and more U.S. advisors and military personnel flowed into the Hashemite Kingdom, focusing mainly on the threat of ISIS, not the threat of Asad. Military transport planes flew low and slow across the airspace of the capital, even as the regime kept the details and extent of these security and military relations as vague as possible within domestic politics. But privately, at least, many foreign policy figures seemed to feel that Jordan's best bet was total opposition to ISIS and the Nusra Front, while also quietly hoping that the Asad regime survived, or at least that some sort of non-Islamist post-Asad regime emerged. Hoping for an Asad victory was contrary to official policy, but many seemed to feel that this might be the most stable possible outcome, out of a range of terrible options.

Jordan, meanwhile, continued to be dependent on the good will of its key regional and global allies in ensuring its own security but also risked being torn in multiple directions by these same allies. In many ways, the Saudi-Jordanian relationship was at once vital (in the eyes of the regime) and also perhaps the most delicate of Jordan's alliances. Jordan had thrown its lot in with both Saudi Arabia and the United Arab Emirates (UAE) as they grew more activist in their own foreign policies, especially in 2013 when it seemed that the Asad regime was sure to fall. At that time,

"Jordan aligned its foreign policy with that of Saudi Arabia and the United Arab Emirates, thus joining what the Jordanian officials who support the move called a frank 'coalition' rather than remaining an implicit 'axis,'" wrote Yezid Sayigh. "They think that Assad's departure is inevitable, and therefore Jordan will gain if it joins the team that is devoting its resources to reach that objective."[18] But Asad held on, and Russian intervention propped up his regime still more. If Jordan had been hoping for more decisive or at least effective policies from its U.S. or Saudi allies, it was disappointed on both counts.

The United States, at least, seemed to share the view of King Abdullah and his regime that the main war was against ISIS, not Asad. Yet Jordan was determined to maintain its alliance with Saudi Arabia and even expected massive infusions of Saudi aid and investment money. The Saudis, however, had cut off another small and aid-dependent country— Lebanon—when it didn't tow the Saudi line. So while the Jordanians attempted to avoid a similar fate from their sometimes vengeful ally (they had not, after all, forgotten the disastrous impact on Jordan of the 1991 Gulf war), they nonetheless found themselves with divergent priorities.

Jordan's focus was and remained the Syrian war. Within that conflict, the regime was concerned mainly with ISIS as the number one threat, with Asad a distant second. By this point, in fact, they were as worried about Asad falling as they were about Asad staying. In fact it was not even Asad but his local allies who appeared to be the greatest worry. The Jordanians were deeply concerned that Hizbullah fighters and forces from Iran's Islamic Revolutionary Guard Corps (IRGC) were operating too close to Jordanian borders. They could perhaps live with Asad, but not with Iranian or Hizbullah forces near their borders. The multiple appearances of Iran's General Qassem Solemani, head of the Quds Force, in Syria itself only added to these concerns. In this, at least, they were partially on the same page as the Saudis, who seemed focused not at all on ISIS but on Iran. The Jordanians were so concerned about Iran's rising profile in Syria, and in the region in general, that they sent Foreign Minister Nasser Judeh to Tehran on March 7, 2015, to achieve some clarity regarding Iranian intentions.[19]

Even as Arab states finally banded together to actually deal with a regional security issue, largely with Saudi leadership, the Jordanians were nonplussed when the direction of intervention just as abruptly changed. By working within the Arab League—an organization not known for its effectiveness—Arab states appeared to be on the verge of establishing an actual military coalition against "extremism," which the Jordanians under-stood to be aimed at the scourge of the region—ISIS and other jihadists. Yet the Saudis turned the coalition on what they viewed as the main source of extremism and destabilization in the Middle East—Iran—not directly, of course, but in the form of a "cold war"-style proxy conflict. Jordan was determined to remain part of the coalition and to cooperate with the Saudis. But Saudi Arabia turned it sights on Yemen, launching an ill-fated military intervention. Like other Saudi attempts at intervention in the region, the Yemen campaign too turned out to be anything but decisive or short and instead dragged on, creating another war of attrition in a region now mired in wars, with an extensive civilian death toll.

This seemingly unrelenting turmoil led to a shift in Jordanian public-sphere debates, introducing a new question: would their Saudi ally push Jordan into joining or even leading a ground offensive in Syria against ISIS?[20] Most in these discussions were strongly against any such move, fear-ing that Jordan, which had already born the brunt of the war and refugee crisis, whereas its Gulf allies had not, might be used as cannon fodder for the latest Saudi intervention plan. Many in Jordan's military and security establishment had long felt that the Saudis and other GCC states would be willing to fight "to the last Jordanian" to further their own ends, and many suspected and resented that they were perhaps viewed as expendable or as de facto mercenaries by their own allies. In some parts of the Jordanian state, the Saudi alliance was seen as vital to the kingdom's economic future, but for others, it seemed to be dragging Jordan ever closer to conflicts—in Syria, Yemen, and potentially Iran or elsewhere—that the kingdom sought to avoid.[21] But even as multiple wars destabilized the entire region, Syrian refugees continued to cross the border into Jordan, presenting the king-dom with an almost overwhelming humanitarian crisis.

Jordan and the Refugee Crisis

The refugee crisis was perhaps the single most tangible challenge to the Hashemite Kingdom resulting from the Syrian war. It represented both a domestic and an international dilemma, and the strains on Jordan's econ-omy, social services, water resources, and political stability were severe, especially in the context of an economic recession in a deeply indebted country.[22] The refugee crisis also affected many of the other themes discussed throughout this book—reform, identity, security; it challenged, in short, almost every other theme in Jordanian politics.

In the first six years of the Syrian war—from 2011 to 2017—hundreds of thousands of Syrian refugees crossed to Jordan to escape the horrors of the Syrian conflict. But in doing so, they joined many previous waves of refugees who had fled their homes and found refuge in the kingdom. Since independence in 1946, Jordan has been swept by wave upon wave of refugees: Palestinians from the west, Iraqis from the east, and now Syrians crossing from the north. Not all Jordan's refugees came from bordering states, although it is hard to find a country that has seen an influx of refugees from so many different directions over time. Jordan even took in Bosnian refugees in the wars that followed the collapse of Yugoslavia in the 1990s. Furthermore, even some of Jordan's key minority groups, such as the Chechens and Circassians, are descendants of earlier waves of refugees (to prestate Jordan, fleeing repression in Russia for refuge in what was then the Ottoman Empire). Refugee flows, in short, are not new to Jordan. The scale of the Syrian influx, however, was a dramatic change and challenge to the kingdom.[23] But Jordan's economy remained unable to cope with these latest refugee flows without extensive daily international support.

By June 2015 the United Nations High Commissioner for Refugees (UNHCR) had registered more than 628,000 Syrian refugees in Jordan. But the Jordanian government routinely doubled this number, arguing that more than 750,000 other Syrians were also in the kingdom—they just weren't registered as refugees. The numbers were also not precise because, while there was clearly a massive inflow of refugees, there were intermittent outflows as well. Even during some of most violent periods in the Syrian civil war, some refugees would risk leaving the camps or cities and making their way back into Syria.[24] Jordanian government officials therefore routinely cited the number of Syrians in Jordan (whether registered as refugees or not) as 1.4 million people. Part of this was instrumental: the greater the refugee burden appeared, the stronger was Jordan's case for more international aid and support. But whether the numbers were exaggerated or not, they were staggering. There was no need for exaggeration, in short, because the burden by any estimate was still overwhelming. Even as the numbers steadily increased from 2011 onward, the clear majority were children, underscoring the human catastrophe that had resulted from the Syrian war.

The influx of Syrian refugees to Jordan amounted to something like a 10 percent increase in the kingdom's population in only a few years, and most Syrians were arriving not just homeless but also destitute. This is at least partially in contrast to other recent refugee flows into Jordan. Iraqis fleeing the U.S invasion and the violence and terrorism that followed came in vastly different circumstances. Some did arrive without any finances, but some managed to get out of Iraq with their savings and some of their worldly goods. While many Iraqi refugees were Sunni Muslims, some were Shi'a and some were Christians. The flow of Syrian refugees in 2011 and after varied considerably depending on what region of the country they were fleeing from, and what border was closest. The Syrian refugee population streaming north into Turkey, for example, was more diverse ethnically and religiously. But those heading south into Jordan were generally more homogeneous. Almost all were Sunni Muslim Arabs from southern Syria. Many were from the city and villages of Dera'a in particular. And most arrived with almost nothing.

Jordan, with the help of the UNHCR, quickly assembled a refugee camp to accommodate an initial influx of perhaps 8,000 people. The Za'atari camp was rapidly overwhelmed, however, and a few years later housed anywhere from 80,000 to 100,000 Syrians. Jordan later added another camp near Azraq. Yet 84 percent of the Syrian refugee population lived outside the refugee camps—in Jordanian host communities, villages, and cities, especially in the northern areas such as Mafraq and Irbid but also in the capital, Amman.[25] Jordan's foreign minister, Nasser Judeh, often explained to Western audiences the impact on Jordan by comparing it to if the United States had to suddenly absorb the entire population of Canada. In 2011 Jordanian officials and local host communities were mostly welcoming, proudly stressing Jordan's traditions of hospitality. As the years wore on, however, and the burden and impact increased, patience began to wear thin.

Absorbing so many refugees would be difficult at any time. But Jordan at the onset of the Arab uprisings was also already in the midst of an economic crisis. The regime has, however, historically cooperated with the International Monetary Fund and had done so for decades. IMF austerity measures had, in the past, led to massive unrest in the country, including riots and protests in 1989, 1996, 1998, and (in the midst of the Arab Spring era) November 2012.[26] Even as the kingdom struggled to stabilize its own economy, it found itself dealing with the additional economic, social, and political costs of hosting hundreds of thousands of desperate Syrian refugees. As they crossed the border into Jordan, even those who found refuge in Jordanian host communities were arriving in some of the poorest towns and cities in the Jordanian North. Many, especially in the initial waves of refugees, were able to draw on familial or even mercantile ties between the sister cities of Dera'a in Syria and al-Ramtha in Jordan. Some received support from tribes with connections across the border. The Bani Khalid tribe, for example, has roots on both sides of the border (since their presence predates the border).

The Za'atari refugee camp, meanwhile, was established in northern Jordan, close to the border and to the city of Mafraq. But it was also built close to the town of Za'atari, whose population of eight thousand more than doubled with the influx of Syrians. Local schools and hospitals were not sufficient to accommodate these new demands. The economic strains on the region's underdeveloped infrastructure were also severe. The refugee influx put still more stress on the area's limited water supply. The local water basin already served Irbid, Mafraq, Ajlun, and the eastern Badia regions, and it was now expected to serve twice the population or more. Local officials complained that even the roads were inadequate—they were not built for heavy trucking of aid and relief supplies and some were already a half century old and in desperate need of update and repair.

The Za'atari camp for Syrian refugees was originally envisioned as a temporary refuge, but before long it had become the second largest refugee camp on Earth.[27] Za'atari grew so large, and so quickly, that it was often referred to as the fourth largest city in Jordan (after Amman, Irbid, and Zarqa). Despite the dire circumstances, individuals and families in the camp attempted to re-create some semblance of their former lives or forge new ones, creating something like a community in Za'atari.[28] Legitimate criticism can be leveled at the global donor community and especially at regional and global powers for promising much but often failing to deliver fully on their pledges, but the efforts on the ground—by UNHCR, the Jordanian government, NGOs, international aid workers, and Jordanian volunteers—were extensive and impressive. In the midst of a sprawling refugee camp, aid workers were doing everything they could to make the lives of others better.

Za'atari opened in northern Jordan in July 2012. What started as a scattering of tents soon became a mixture of both tents and prefabricated housing (usually called "caravans" or trailers). Some families linked two caravans together, with aluminum or other ad hoc paneling used to create a kind of courtyard, sitting room, or storage space between them. As the camp expanded, it became a clearer grid, broken into twelve districts for the purposes of distribution of food and supplies. Much of the initial expansion was the result of trial and error, but UNHCR and the Jordanian authorities made gradual adjustments, including serious attempts at urban planning, as the camp steadily grew.

After a series of problems with food distribution, protests, and riots, Jordanian military forces changed their strategy in order to have less of a visible presence within the camp. They established themselves instead on the outskirts of the ring road surrounding the camp, creating a security cordon on the perimeter of Za'atari. Within the camp, Jordanian authorities allowed various forms of commerce to emerge largely without interference. This, in turn, led to the development of a market street, originally dubbed (sarcastically) the "Champs Elysees." The name stuck. More than five hundred businesses emerged in Za'atari, most of which are stalls and small shops selling goods and services. These include salons, fruit and vegetable markets, small restaurants (generally falafel and hummus stands), and shops for perfumes, cellular phones, sweets, and wedding dresses. There was even a small jewelry store and a pet shop, with parakeets prominently displayed.

Periodic distribution of basic foodstuffs and supplies occurred at centralized distribution centers, while more extensive supplies could be found at the Safeway that opened at one end of the camp. Coupons were available for key staple foods, while other items were sold for cash but at wholesale prices. The Jordanian manager of the Za'atari Safeway had a team of Syrian employees as part of the camp's cash for work program. UNHCR developed an iris-scanning system to register refugees but also to use—in cooperation with the World Food Program and Jordanian banks—for authorizing electronic purchases of food, rather than relying on coupons or food vouchers.

In addition to the commercial life within the camp, schools were built, with UNICEF support. Not all children attended, however, as many families encouraged young sons to work instead to earn some money for the family, often using wheelbarrows to haul just about anything for cash. For many daughters, the challenge was very different, as a clear problem developed regarding early marriage of young Syrian girls to local or foreign men. This problem was well recognized by UNHCR and the Jordanian authorities, but while they strongly discouraged the practice, it seemed to persist nonetheless.

Still, international donors and local aid workers tried to add elements to the camp that were specifically geared toward children so that they don't have to be young laborers or child brides but simply children. There are now some playgrounds, children's activity centers, and dirt and gravel soccer pitches. The latter elements were part of the efforts of the Asian Football Development Project (AFDP) and the Norwegian Refugee Council (NRC) to engage both boys and girls in soccer, in the interests of their health and well-being, and to try to build a semblance of community even for children who have lost their homes and communities back in Syria. The youth program may be the most inspiring feature of life in an otherwise very uninspiring and difficult set of circumstances.[29]

The soccer initiative was led by Prince Ali bin Hussein, then FIFA vice president for Asia and head of the AFDP. Other NGOs provided schools, clinics, and field hospitals and distributed foodstuffs and supplies. AFDP augmented these important efforts with a project of its own, meant to bring soccer even to refugee camps. "Food, water, and housing are all priorities," noted Prince Ali, "but kids also have to have something to do. And sport can build a community spirit. It's a test case of how you can use sport for good." Prince Ali is a member of the ruling Hashemite family and half-brother to King Abdullah II. As FIFA vice president for Asia, he was already known for expanding soccer programs, especially for women and girls, across Asia. When the Syrian war and refugee crisis began, the prince and the AFDP urged FIFA to ensure that refugee children would not be forgotten. "Football is not an elitist sport, it's a game for everyone," Prince Ali said, "and it can help promote the health and well-being of girls and boys."[30]

AFDP partnered with UNHCR and PepsiCo to sponsor a series of programs called "Kick for Hope." In addition to bringing soccer to the camp, the related "Spirit of Soccer" campaign actually used football as a teaching tool to educate children about the risks of land mines, while training them in soccer fundamentals. Importantly, all the AFDP efforts address both boys and girls. As a further example of just how international these types of efforts tend to be, the AFDP also worked with the Football Association of Norway to construct eight soccer fields for both Syrian refugees and Jordanian host communities—one in Ramtha, two in Mafraq, one in the small village of Sareeh, two in Za'atari, and two more in the newer Azraq refugee camp. The results of these efforts were clear on the football fields themselves. By the thousands, boys and girls played, learned skills, and developed at least some semblance of community despite the loss of their homes and communities in Syria. These efforts for children and sports wouldn't end the war or the refugee crisis, but organizers and activists hoped that they might at the least play a role in building community and values, and perhaps even—in some way—trying to save Syrian refugee children from becoming a lost generation.

Local officials, NGOs, international organizations (IOs), and the government alike all complained that international grants and donations remained routinely at less than 20 percent of what was actually needed to support Syrian refugees in Jordan. Resources rose and fell with international attention and donations but were never sufficient to meet overall demand. Jordan, like other countries dealing with refugee crises, also faced the increasing problem of donor fatigue. But despite previous donations, the refugee problem wasn't going to evaporate. So fatigue or not, the kingdom had to find continual sources of support for refugees and for host communities alike. The latter communities often feel neglected relative to the refugees themselves. So despite the difficulties of living in the Za'atari refugee camp, for example, there were some Jordanians in the surrounding area who complained that refugee life was actually easier than their own lives, and that the regime and the world community should pay attention to them too.

The refugee crisis affected Jordan in countless ways, including infrastructure, housing, food, water, education, and even social norms. "We are famous for our hospitality," noted one official in 2015, "but look as us now in the fifth year."[31] To its credit, Jordan allowed Syrian children to attend school. With limited resources in terms of capital, number of teachers, and facilities, most schools began operating double shifts, but with the same teachers working both. Teachers themselves acknowledged that this led to a drop-off in quality of education, while families complained that their own costs increased as many felt compelled to employ tutors to make up for the decline in the quality of education. The teachers themselves, of course, were working horrendous hours, with each of their double shifts featuring overcrowded classrooms and insufficient school supplies.[32]

Food and housing prices, already problematic, increased with the rapid rise in demand. Local Jordanians often blamed Syrians for this, and also for taking their jobs. Jordanian officials, especially those from small villages in the North, argued that the influx of Syrians had led to a plethora of social ills, including rising crime, drug-dealing, drug addiction, robberies and break-ins, beggars, vagrancy, and even an alleged rise in stray dogs. "We want to be hospitable," said one official. "We want to keep people safe, but we are overwhelmed."[33] It is possible that some of these social problems did increase with the rise in local population numbers, but there is also a tendency to blame the Syrians for a variety of social and economic problems.

One social problem that was clearer was the change in marriage norms for both Syrian and Jordanian communities, neither of which were known for polygyny or child marriage. But as the crisis wore on, and despite efforts by the Jordanian government and international aid workers against these practices, there was a trend of Syrian families, in exchange for a cash dowry, allowing a young daughter to wed a Jordanian man. Some of the Jordanian men were already married and were thus adding a young Syrian wife to the household. Both of these practices preyed on children and women, and both were opposed by every form of authority or organization in Jordan—the government, civil society organizations, NGOs, and UNHCR—yet the rise in child brides and polygyny continued, in a radical social change for the Syrian and Jordanian communities alike.[34]

The economic impact is actually harder to measure. As noted above, the strain on infrastructure was clearly severe, and the refugee influx also triggered increasing costs for housing and food. But the impact on employment is more complicated. For public opinion, there is no question that the effect has been decidedly negative, with Syrians willing to work for less and taking Jordanian wage jobs. But in the first five years of war and refugee crisis, Syrian weren't actually allowed to work. Those who did were therefore working in the informal economy or black market. In most cases they seemed more likely to take jobs from foreign guest workers rather than Jordanians. But there was also an increase in the number of jobs in the refugee areas, specifically, working with the international donor and relief communities—from UNHCR to UNICEF to Save the Children. Civil society organizations, sometimes connected to these larger international organizations, also proliferated. Employment in the relief-work sector therefore went up, but not all the employees were locals. Many made the short drive from Amman for work. This again underscored the need to focus not only on the plight of refugees but also on that of already impoverished—and now heavily strained—Jordanian host communities.[35]

While resentments seemed to increase over time and patience began to wear thin, there was actually very little intercommunal conflict. But many

Syrians and Jordanians alike worried about the prospects for conflict down the line. When asked what Mafraq would be like five years hence, one official muttered under his breath, "It will be Syrian." Another, with more volume, stated simply, "It is a bomb waiting to go off."[36] While most Syrians were very willing to work to support their families and therefore wanted access to the legal and formal economy, most Jordanians remained supportive of their Syrian counterparts. Most people, regardless of community, simply wanted the war to end, security to return to Syria, and for Syrians to be able to go home.

Yet there were negative signs as well. Veteran journalist Daoud Kuttab noted that there seemed to be a rise in hate speech, not on the part of most people but of a vocal minority that blamed most things on the influx of Syrians. Part of the problem, he argued, was that there were few counters to this. It was basically a one-sided conversation. "All we hear are Jordanians," he said. "Syrians have no real way to be heard, to have their voices reach Jordanians." Kuttab's Amman-net radio station responded with an innovative radio program called "Syrians Among Us" with Jordanian and Syrian co-anchors.[37] This, at least, allowed Syrians a voice in Jordan and let Jordanians and Syrians hear, discuss, and debate key issues in what was increasingly looking like a common future.

By 2013 Jordan's representative to the United Nations, Prince Zayd Bin Raad, described the refugee issue to the U.N. Security Council as a "crushing weight" on Jordan. Demands increased within Jordan that the government shut down the border entirely. Many Jordanians felt that the kingdom had done its part, that it had reached full capacity and more, and that enough was enough. When President Obama visited Jordan in April 2013, deliberately to underscore U.S. support for the kingdom, he and King Abdullah held a joint press conference, which naturally touched on the refugee crisis. The king was asked about closing the border to shut down the influx of refugees. "How are you going to turn back women, children, and the wounded?" he asked in response. "This is something that we just can't do. It's not the Jordanian way." He continued:

We have historically opened our arms to many of our neighbors through many decades of Jordan's history. So that means a challenge that we just can't turn our backs on. So that's the reality that we are facing on the ground. So Jordan has always been a safe haven to people around us through many, many decades. So, unfortunately, from our point of view, refugees will continue to come to Jordan, and we will continue, within our means, to look after them as best as we can.[38]

Yet as the years wore on, pressure continued to build—socially, economically, and politically—and, as the war continued and the refugee crisis continued to expand, Jordanian policy eventually began to shift.

The Jordanian state felt cash-strapped in dealing with what now seemed to be not a crisis but a long-term problem. But so too did Syrians in Jordan. Even those who had managed to find safety in Jordan while bringing some personal funds with them had, five years later, tapped out their finances. Many, of course, had exhausted their finances within the first year or even within months, while others arrived in penury from the first moment. These increasingly severe economic circumstances have very real political implications, and not just in the North. As Doris Carrion notes in a Chatham House study of the refugee crisis, "If the economic situation fails to improve across the country, and resentment of refugees continues to fuel other national grievances, protests against government policies could escalate in the coming five to 10 years. Unrest in Jordan has tended to come from the southern tribal areas, but the ingredients are now in place for the north also to become a centre of discontent."[39]

The refugees, of course, were powerless to do anything about this. The shift would have to come from the Jordanian government. In 2015 and 2016 in particular, most officials—whether local or in the capital—seemed to realize that the initial crisis period was over, but now the longer-term problem remained. That is, the state needed to move beyond short-term crisis mode and toward long-term planning. The war showed no sign of ending. And many came to realize that the Syrians were not going home anytime soon, forcing a rethinking of the entire situation. The prospect of Syrians in Jordan for the long term naturally added to the already hypersensitive concerns of Jordanian nationalists that the Jordan they knew was steadily slipping away. As discussed in chapter 5, identity politics was already a complicated and difficult issue, but the influx of yet another wave of refugees seemed to make it still more volatile as a social and political concern. Any discussion of Syrian rights, therefore—even the right to work—had to be handled delicately by policy makers with these social and political sensitivities in mind.

By 2015 the regional refugee crisis had become a global one, with refugees now fleeing for a third or fourth time—this time to Europe. The refugee surge started among increasingly desperate Syrian refugees, many so desperate that they risked a dangerous and often deadly overseas journey on flimsy rafts or barely functioning boats to cross the Mediterranean Sea. As the death toll in the Syrian war continued, so too did the death toll of refugees on roads and on the high seas. It was in this context that the European Union and Jordan agreed to the "Jordan Compact." The deal was designed to encourage refugees not to risk the journey to Europe but to stay in Jordan. For a Jordan already overwhelmed by the refugee crisis, and spending perhaps 25 percent of its state budget on refugee issues alone, the incentive was this: the European Union agreed to open its markets to select Jordanian manufactured goods, while Jordan agreed to allow Syrian refugees to work in its Special Economic Zones (SEZs) that produced these same goods. Most employees in the SEZs are not Jordanians, so the measure also avoided the issue of competition with Jordanians. The Jordan Compact was reached at the 2015 London international donor conference and included pledges of increased international support.[40]

This also made manifestly clear the links between international relations and domestic politics, not only in Jordan but also in Europe. But for Jordan, at least, the international pressure to change its domestic approach to refugees was extensive. Expecting significant increases in Western financial support for the kingdom, the Hashemite regime complied and began to change policy. In 2016 Jordan began experimenting with various policies to address labor issues, including a program to grant 200,000 Syrians permits to enter select parts of the workforce. Part of the idea was based on targeted employment; that is, on letting Syrians compete for jobs that Jordanians were, for the most part, not doing. There were ample opportunities and needs for workers in manufacturing, construction, and agriculture, for example. Economically, the idea was to shift Syrians from the informal to the formal economy and to boost the Jordanian economy via Syrian labor. In short, the plan was meant to turn a burden into a boon for Jordan. But politically, the state was careful to note that Jordanians would not be losing jobs to Syrians. Other guest workers, from Egypt or South Asia, for example, would. Syrians could be used to bolster Jordan's manufacturing base.

As the regional situation worsened, Jordan continued to market itself as an oasis of stability. By encouraging rather than blocking Syrian employment, Jordan might then be able to lure more businesses to relocate to, or invest in, the country. To do so it would need to deal with its own cumbersome bureaucracy and regulations, in all likelihood, but the key was to sell Jordan's location and situation as an asset rather than a liability. As Andrew Harper, head of the UNHCR in Jordan, put it, "If it's an oasis, let's try to grow things on it."[41]

There were many other steps that might be taken, but which the state seemed reluctant to undertake. The International Labor Organization (ILO) urged Jordan to, in effect, formalize the informal economy—and therefore to increase legal employment, collect taxes, and ensure labor rights.[42] Targeting specific employment opportunities for Syrians was one way of allowing Syrians in while also avoiding competition with Jordanian workers. This the Jordanian government had indeed decided to experiment with. Other policies, such as a minimum wage, remained more controversial. Advocates for a minimum wage argued that it would support both the Jordanian and Syrian communities by reducing the exploitation of Syrian laborers, on the one hand, while eliminating the undercutting of wages (and employment) of Jordanian workers, on the other. In addition, since citizenship did not seem to be on the table, the state would nonetheless have to address the question of basic civil rights. Was there another status here, short of citizenship, that needed to be clarified and rights protected? If so, then another possibility might be to open employment permits not connected to a particular nationality, but more broadly (and therefore to include Syrians, Iraqis, and Palestinians from Gaza) to allow access to the labor force with concomitant rights. But these were more extensive steps, and it had taken the state five years to even experiment with limited numbers of worker permits.

By making its gradual shift in labor policy, however, Jordan was also making a shift of a broader kind: moving from short-term crisis management toward longer-term and perhaps even sustainable policy. Political resistance would be extensive. As noted in chapter 5, countless issues in Jordanian politics find their way back to identity politics at some point. And allowing Syrians into the economy on a legal basis would be stiffly resisted by hard-core nationalists as yet another threat to Jordanian identity. But the regime was not even considering extending political rights or citizenship. These were, to be sure, even more volatile issues than labor and employment. But most Syrians at that point weren't actually pushing in any way for political rights or citizenship; rather, they were looking for economic inclusion and really for more basic needs: the right to work, the right of their children to get an education, and access to healthcare.

This chapter has already chronicled two enormous regional challenges to Jordan—the Syrian civil war and the resultant refugee crisis—but unfortunately for all concerned, there was also a third challenge: the rise of a new jihadist movement in both Syria and Iraq, and one that had Jordan in its sights.

Jordan and the Challenge of ISIS

Even as Jordan had been affected by the regional politics of the Arab uprisings, the summer of 2014 was something of an insecurity overload. Jordan's economy remained mired in a seemingly endemic crisis while regional conflicts seemed to increase in almost every direction. ISIS—the self-declared "Islamic State"—had established itself across both the Syrian and Iraqi borders. For many Jordanian officials, ISIS was more than just another jihadist or terrorist group because it was also a territorial threat. This one had aspirations to statehood. This one, in fact, had pretensions toward a new caliphate. An independent and sovereign Jordanian state did not fit into any of these plans. Jordan was clearly in the sights of ISIS as part of what it saw as its natural territory, and also as an enemy regime—one that maintained a peace treaty and full relations with Israel, while also allowing American and British and other Western troops to deploy on its soil.

More alarming perhaps to the Jordanian state was the fact that the threat didn't just emanate from across its borders but also from within. Salafis—not of the quietist but rather of the more militant and jihadist persuasion—had already staged rallies in Zarqa, even clashing with police. But now rallies were also taking place in the seemingly always restive Ma'an, with some activists raising the ISIS flag, while others supported Jabhat al-Nusra. Both organizations claimed to include large numbers of volunteers, and some estimates suggested that perhaps two thousand Jordanians had crossed into Syria to join one or the other group.[43]

In September 2014 a U.S.-led coalition began launching airstrikes on ISIS in Syria and Iraq and, to the surprise of many, Jordan declared itself part of that coalition. As the Royal Jordanian Air Force joined in the air strikes launched against ISIS, many Jordanians feared that retribution would follow in the form of terrorism within Jordan itself. That fear was rooted in real experience. On November 9, 2005—in what Jordanians sometimes call "Jordan's 9/11"—a precursor to ISIS, al-Qa'ida in Iraq, carried out three simultaneous bombings of hotels in Amman, killing sixty and injuring hundreds. The bombings had been masterminded by former Jordanian national, and then head of al-Qa'ida in Iraq, Abu Musab al-Zarqawi. That memory haunts many Jordanians in government and opposition alike. It was one of those moments of national crisis and tragedy in which all who were old enough to remember the event can tell you exactly where they were at the time, who they were with, and how they felt. Like so many discussions of security threats in Jordan, in short, the idea of jihadist terrorism isn't hypothetical. And that moment in Jordanian history has been forgotten by no one in Jordanian society, and certainly by no one in the security and intelligence services.

In the United States, the Obama administration had predicated its foreign policy on not reproducing the unilateral recklessness of its predecessor, the George W. Bush administration, which had launched the disastrous invasion of Iraq in 2003. In 2014, following the execution of U.S. hostages by ISIS, the Obama administration prepared to act against the terrorist group. But the administration also seemed aware of the dangers of yet another U.S.-led coalition attacking Arab and Muslim territories, even against a fairly notorious terrorist organization. After the years of Bush administration unilateralism, the Obama administration was adamant that any military moves in the region should be more multilateral and that they should include Arab and Muslim states. Five Arab countries agreed to join the U.S.-led anti-ISIS coalition: Bahrain, Kuwait, Saudi Arabia, the United Arab Emirates, and Jordan.

For the United States, the idea was to add to the legitimacy of military strikes by receiving local backing and even active support. For the five Arab states in question, however, the threat was more direct, as each saw ISIS as a major threat not just externally but also potentially internally and hence to their own regime security as well. This particular constellation of states, however, certainly didn't represent the democratic and reformist spirit of the Arab spring but, if anything, seemed to represent a coalition of Sunni Arab monarchies against ISIS, and perhaps also against revolutionary or even reformist change of any kind. Unlike most of the GCC states in the coalition, however, Jordan had pursued a series of reforms during the Arab Spring. And Jordan was certainly more directly threatened by ISIS, given its long borders with both Syria and Iraq and the presence of a large Salafi jihadi movement within its borders. So the regime felt that it had little choice and had to play an active role in confronting ISIS. But by being linked so closely to reactionary GCC states, it also risked being seen, especially in its own domestic politics, as not significantly different from its authoritarian, antireform, and antidemocratic Arab allies.

King Abdullah made his case for joining the anti-ISIS coalition—forcefully and often—to venues varying from Western capitals to meetings with key stakeholders and power brokers in Jordan itself. Meeting with the top brass of the Jordanian Armed Forces, with parliamentary MPs, or with journalists, the king delivered a fairly strident message that neutrality or avoiding the ISIS conflict were not options. In a speech at the United Nations in 2015, he made his case yet again: "All should realize that we must take a side in the confrontation between the moderate and extremist approaches. There is no grey area." Speaking to MPs in Jordan's House of Representatives, the king said that "all world countries are in a state of war between moderation or extremism." Muslims, he argued, were vital parts of that fight, which he described as "a civil war within Islam." This was a war against terrorism, he said, that "would not take one or two years. If the military battle takes a brief time, the security and ideological war might extend to 10 or 15 years."[44] In many settings, the king pointedly referred to Da'esh and other jihadists as "*khawarej*, the outlaws of Islam," and repeatedly called the fight a "Third World War."[45]

As the air campaign against ISIS intensified, the Jordanian state stepped up its efforts against any signs of the group within Jordan itself. Islamist activists in possession of ISIS flags were arrested in Irbid. In October 2014 four imams in Jordan were banned for life from preaching in mosques after they advocated "coming to the aid" of ISIS. "The minbar [pulpit] is a sacred right and privilege, and we will not tolerate its use for political agendas, inciting violence, and particularly the support of extremist groups," Hayel Daoud, the minister of Awqaf, told the Jordanian press.[46]

By the summer of 2014, the ISIS threat seemed ever more imminent, both at the borders and within the kingdom itself. Protestors raised ISIS flags in Ma'an, in southern Jordan. Jordan's growing Salafi community had sent thousands of recruits to fight for either ISIS or Jabhat al-Nusra in Syria. The Jordanian regime may not have minded the departure of thousands of jihadis, but now it worried that they eventually intended to come back. Responding to incidents of "attempted infiltration" along both its Syrian and Iraqi borders, Jordan increased its border security with troops and armored units and opened fire on any armed groups or individuals approaching its borders.

For some Jordanian security officials, there were almost too many security threats to sort through. Some saw the main threat as already within Jordan's borders, in the form either of pro-Asad sleeper agents or of jihadis perhaps among the vast refugee population in the kingdom, or even of the homegrown variety from within Jordanian society itself. Others saw ISIS still as a cross-border and hence more distant threat and remained focused on the traditional Islamist opposition within the kingdom—the Muslim Brotherhood—perhaps hoping that Jordan would follow the lead of its allies Egypt, Saudi Arabia, and UAE in banning the group outright.[47] But these perceived threats seemed to pale in comparison to ISIS and other jihadi groups.

As the regime's security concerns steadily grew, they had important effects on the kingdom's domestic politics. The Jordanian parliament in June 2014 passed a controversial new counterterrorism law that gave the state vague and elastic license to move against citizens deemed to support terrorist groups in any way (including in online commentary). In August 2014 another palace initiative was passed by parliament with lightning speed. This time, MPs gave the king full authority to appoint top security and defense officials, including the heads of the Mukhabarat and the Jordanian Armed Forces.[48] Previously these were royal appointments, but with the often pro forma prerequisite of consultation with the prime minister and his government. In Jordan's 150-member lower house of parliament (at the time), 108 voted for the amendments, 8 voted against, and 3 abstained.[49] The amendment removed the role of government, and for that matter parliament, in royal oversight, just as the regime's rhetoric referred to a Jordanian future with democratically elected parliamentary governments.

Supporters of these measures argued that they were in keeping with the reform process, and that they improved the separation of powers and therefore allegedly removed both the military and intelligence services from politics. There were some who supported the moves, however, simply because they didn't trust any future parliamentary government with key security or defense appointments. They especially didn't trust any future government that might include any variation of the Muslim Brotherhood. But most reformers and democracy activists opposed the measures, arguing that they concentrated still more power in the monarchy, away from the government, the parliament, and—very important—from public accountability. Opponents, in short, saw the new amendments as an alarming reversal in the reform program, and as part of a series of moves that seemed to tilt power almost entirely toward the monarchy, precisely the opposite of what the reform process was supposed to be about.[50] Many Jordanians also ridiculed the parliament for its rare act of legislative efficiency, since the parliament was not known for its ability to be speedy on any other issue.[51]

Still, the regime and its many supporters saw all this as evidence of a steady and methodical "reform march." Most activists seem unconvinced, however. "It's a different system," noted one activist, "but nothing new. Just repackaged. I'm not optimistic. The constitutional amendments, for example, don't call for optimism. Jordan is no longer a constitutional monarchy." Another was even blunter: "The Constitution says Jordan is a constitutional monarchy," he said, "but it is an autocracy."[52] In a legal analysis of the controversial amendments, Jordanian attorney Sufian Obeidat echoed the assessment that the changes marked a moment of regression rather than reform. "Constitutionalizing the monopolization of power," he wrote, "opens wide the door for oppression and corruption. The constitutional amendments complicate matters more and delay any hope for democratic reform in Jordan." He concluded that the amendments represented "a significant retreat from the token progress towards constitutional democracy and limited government initiated in the aftermath of the Arab Spring."[53]

The timing of Jordan's various moves to consolidate monarchical power, and also to shore up state security, coincided with similar moves across much of the region. The Arab Spring was now routinely referred to as having shifted to an Arab Winter, characterized by an "Arab Thermidor" or the return of security states across the region. In the Jordanian case, however, the issue was not so much a return of the Mukhabarat but mainly that they had never left.[54] Yet Jordanians themselves remained divided on the implications of this point. Democracy activists and reformers, even those in the upper echelons of the state itself, often regard the GID as the single largest obstacle to liberalization, democratization, or change. But many Jordanians are willing to accept a fairly large and even intrusive role for the GID in public life, if that is the cost of national security. The latter group just as routinely points across Jordan's borders to the many security disasters of the kingdom's regional neighborhood. Critics, in contrast, see this as the timeless excuse for counterreform and for reactionary politics.

Unfortunately for both sides of this debate, regional insecurity seemed to be in overdrive, with Jordanian media on a minute-to-minute basis showing the disasters of civil wars, conflicts, and violence in Syria, Iraq, Libya, Yemen, and Palestine, as well as the militancy and even brutal executions of hostages by terrorist groups like ISIS.

In August 2014, after seeming to allow various pro-ISIS demonstrations to take place without state interference, the regime suddenly began to move against people the security services had identified, not just as Salafis or even Salafi jihadists, but specifically those alleged to have declared support for ISIS. Security forces arrested dozens of pro-ISIS Jordanians, basing this crackdown on the recently revised laws. Legally, they were also able to do so under the strengthened counterterrorism laws, allowing those arrested to be referred to the State Security Court (rather than civilian courts) for membership in an illegal organization and on suspicion of intent to engage in or support terrorism.[55]

Even as the state rounded up alleged jihadis, it also released from prison one of the movement's most prominent Salafi leaders and thinkers, Abu Muhammad al-Maqdisi.[56] This was the second such surprising move regarding a key jihadi leader. After years of controversial efforts to arrange for the extradition from the United Kingdom of another Salafi jihadi leader, Abu Qatada, Jordanian courts dropped charges against him on the basis of insufficient evidence. In a previous trial, Abu Qatada had been convicted in absentia of planning millennial bombings in Amman and had been sentenced to death. Now, both Abu Qatada and Maqdisi were freed from Jordanian prisons. Some Jordanian analysts speculated that perhaps Jordan's Mukhabarat was deliberately trying to divide the Salafi jihadi movement in the kingdom. Many believed that the Mukhabarat had had a hand in similar efforts to divide the Muslim Brotherhood, so why not the Salafi movement as well?[57] Abu Qatada and Maqdisi each issued statements condemning ISIS, but each also continued to support al-Qa'ida and Jabhat al-Nusra. Yet both also condemned the Jordanian state itself after the kingdom joined the coalition against ISIS. Maqdisi, in fact, found himself rearrested after he suggested that the divided jihadi movements should unite in the face of this Western-led coalition and bombing campaign—a campaign that Jordan was now a part of.[58]

Within the kingdom, the intelligence services closely monitored any signs of ISIS or al-Qa'ida support. This included physical participation in demonstrations or protests but also online activism and commentary. The new counterterrorism law included online "incitement" under its definition of terrorism, and it was under this law that the state began arresting ISIS sympathizers. Jordan's campaign against militancy and extremism would therefore include countering threats at the borders, in internal protests, online, and also within mosques. The new campaign saw the minister of Islamic affairs touring the country, meeting with imams and preachers, and explaining new state guidelines for sermons. The guidelines demanded that imams refrain from speaking out against the king, the royal family, allied Arab states, or key Western allies, including the United States. Imams were also to steer clear from anything that seemed sectarian and under no conditions were to speak in favor of jihad. The minister of Islamic affairs even suggested that sermons should be brief. "Fifteen minutes is okay," he told an audience in Zarqa, even suggesting that the Prophet Muhammad himself "was short and to the point—often 10 minutes, no more."[59] The role of the state in "guiding" sermons, or for that matter in monitoring them, is not actually new in Jordan or elsewhere in the region; but the regime did make this a key part of its overall campaign against ISIS and jihadist extremism. For the Hashemite regime, these moves were in keeping with Jordan's already established role in global interfaith cooperation efforts and in spreading a counterextremism message of moderate Islam, or what the Hashemite regime has often called "real Islam."[60]

For most Jordanians, however, it was the capture of a Jordanian pilot—a participant in the anti-ISIS coalition—that riveted the attention of a nation. Lieutenant Muath al-Kassasbeh was captured by ISIS after his plane went down near Raqqa, then the ISIS "capital" in Syria. A pilot in the Royal Jordanian Air Force, Kassasbeh was a member of a large and influential tribe in Jordan's southern city of Kerak. After his capture, Jordanians followed the news closely as the government attempted to get him released. Online campaigns as well as demonstrations in his support occurred throughout the country. The hashtag and phrase *Kulina Muath*—"We are all Muath"—covered social media. It was also featured on signs at demonstrations, and Muath's picture appeared on large billboards and banners across the country. Every Jordanian knew what he looked like. Every Jordanian followed the leaked bits of news, and an entire nation waited anxiously, hoping for the safe return of a "son of Jordan" to his homeland. But the already tragic story grew more tragic still as ISIS released a carefully choreographed video of Muath's brutal execution. The video showed Muath in a large steel cage, surrounded by his jihadist captors, who then murder him by setting him on fire. The public reaction ranged from rage at the murder to horror at the nature of the killing.

ISIS timed the release of the execution video to coincide with King Abdullah's high-profile visit to the United States. In Washington, D.C., Foreign Minister Nasser Judeh and Secretary of State John Kerry had just signed a memorandum of understanding between Jordan and the United States, increasing U.S. aid from $660 million to $1 billion annually. Within half an hour of the press conference, ISIS released the video for maximum propaganda effect. Reports afterward suggested that Muath was likely killed weeks before the video was released, meaning that ISIS was negotiating his release even after the group had murdered him. It had allegedly offered to exchange the captured pilot for an al-Qa'ida terrorist, Sajida al-Rishawi, an Iraqi national who was the lone surviving terrorist from the suicide bombings in Amman in 2005 (Rishawi's suicide vest had failed to detonate). One day after the ISIS video release, Jordanian security officials responded by executing, at dawn, Sajida al-Rishawi and another Iraqi jihadist, Ziyad Karbuli.

In Washington, King Abdullah told the U.S. Congress that the "gloves are off" and that Jordan would wage a "relentless" war on ISIS.[61] Speaking to the Jordanian public on state television, he said, "We are waging this war to protect our faith, our values and human principles and our war for their sake will be relentless and will hit them in their own ground."[62] The king made the point often that this was Jordan's war, and that Jordan had no choice but to be directly involved. At home, some Jordanians agreed. And certainly most were opposed to ISIS. But some, even near the Kassabeh home in Karak, blamed not just ISIS but also the international coalition, and the regime for joining it.[63] Other Jordanians questioned Jordan's role.[64] Was it enabling the Asad dictatorship by striking at one of its fiercest enemies? Was it unintentionally enabling Iran in Syria but striking at Sunni Muslim jihadists? Should Jordan be striking at fellow Arabs and Muslims at all, regardless of the Islamic State, and for that matter, should it be part of what many Jordanians regarded as a Western imperial coalition? In the immediate aftermath of Kassasbeh's execution, many asked these questions more quietly. But the tone grew louder as time passed. And indeed, while most Jordanians opposed ISIS, al-Qa'ida, and Asad as well, they weren't necessarily convinced that it was "their war."[65]

The Jordanian Armed Forces issued a statement describing Muath al-Kassasbeh as a martyr and pointedly stating the date of the murder as January 3, 2015—one month before the release of the ISIS video. On February 5, 2015, the military released another statement, this time announcing "Operation Martyr Muath" as it launched air strikes on jihadist forces in ISIS-controlled territory. After the initial drama of that response, however, Jordan, like other Arab states in the coalition, seemed to tone down its participation, perhaps unwilling to risk another such incident. But Jordan also played a large role as the de facto forward staging area for the entire anti-ISIS coalition. In this context, the U.S. military presence steadily grew in Jordan. British forces also worked with their Jordanian counterparts in training and support. France sent a squadron of Mirage jet fighters to bolster Jordan's northern borders. German military personnel later also arrived in Jordan, redeploying air power and support personnel to the kingdom from an increasingly inhospitable Turkey in the midst of a row in Turkish-German relations.

Jordan was now on a war footing, in short, and these military preparations underscored the kingdom's extensive military and intelligence connections to the dominant Western powers, and especially to the United States. But as Pete Moore has noted, Jordan has also had a "war economy," perhaps varying only by degrees, for much of its existence.[66] The military played a key role in the foundation of the state and, since independence in 1946, Jordan has been connected to regional wars, whether it participated in them or not—from the Arab-Israeli wars, to the various Gulf wars, to the multiple iterations of the U.S.-led "War on Terrorism." The kingdom, its domestic politics, and its economy have all been intimately tied to these events for decades. But given the unpopularity of U.S. policy in the region, and especially of U.S. military interventions, Jordan's strong Western alliances were at once military assets but also domestic political liabilities. The details of Jordan's connections to foreign military powers were, of course, kept vague by Western governments and the Jordanian regime alike. Many Jordanians routinely added an extra zero to any number they came across estimating the size of the Western military presence in the kingdom. But at times, unexpected incidents underscored the connections anyway.

In November 2015 a Jordanian officer opened fire without warning on his own colleagues at a police training center in Muwaqqar, east of Amman. Five people were killed: two Jordanian officers, one South African officer, and two American trainers. The shooter himself, Anwar Abu Zayd, was killed in the shootout that followed. The precise motives remained unclear, but the attack occurred precisely on the ten-year anniversary of the worst terror attack in Jordanian history—the Amman bombings by al-Qa'ida in Iraq that killed sixty people. The attack also highlighted Jordan's extensive but controversial international security connections and the kingdom's role in various Western coalitions. The shootings occurred at the U.S.-funded Jordan International Police Training Center (JIPTC), which was established in 2003, after the U.S. invasion of Iraq. Jordan had warned against that war but in the aftermath had supported U.S. efforts to train a new Iraqi police force. Since then, more than 75,000 officers had been trained at the facility, including Iraqi, Palestinian, and Libyan personnel.[67] The United States also supported the King Abdullah Special Operations Training Centre (KASOTC), which trained allied personnel in special forces and counterterrorism operations.

In November 2016, one year after the Muwaqqar incident, another shooting brought still more unwanted public attention to Jordan's extensive international security connections and to the presence on its soil of Western military personnel. A Jordanian soldier guarding the gate to the Prince Faysal air base (near al-Jafr in the South) opened fire on approaching U.S. soldiers who were working in Jordan as military trainers, ultimately killing three. Local authorities initially treated the incident as a tragic accident based on miscommunication at the base gate but later changed to murder charges—although it was still not treated as an act of terrorism. The assailant, a Jordanian soldier, was later convicted by a military court and sentenced to life in prison. The soldier's tribe, the Huwaytat, rejected the sentence, releasing a statement that said: "We condemn this ruling against this nation's son, who was defending himself and his country and was shot by the Americans who refused to stop at the base. . . . Is Arab blood cheap and American blood more worthy? This is an unjust ruling."[68] Protests soon erupted in the town of al-Jafr. Local tribal activists believed that the soldier, who had pled not guilty, was defending the base, not launching an attack, while both the U.S. and Jordanian government's and militaries seemed to think otherwise (and video evidence seemed to confirm this view). While some questions remained, so too did a broader concern: these incidents uncomfortably echoed the types of "Green on Blue" attacks that plagued U.S. operations with counterparts in Iraq and

Afghanistan. Yet while they were alarming for U.S. and Jordanian officials alike, they remained rare occurrences in the Hashemite Kingdom.

For most Jordanians, however, relations with any foreign country, ally or otherwise, were of secondary importance to the kingdom's own internal security. Many wondered when or how regional turmoil would affect domestic stability, or if it would lead to threats not just from without but also from within. By March 2016 these questions were no longer hypothetical, as special operations forces, police units, and intelligence officers raided an apartment building in Irbid in northern Jordan, converging on a jihadist cell inside the kingdom itself. The operation turned into an eleven-hour gun battle between Jordanian security forces and ISIS militants. At least seven jihadists were killed, as was a Jordanian officer.[69] The domestic dimensions of Jordan's security fears had shifted from potential to vividly real.

The Irbid clash was exactly the type of event that many Jordanians had feared would eventually occur within the kingdom. Even though Irbid is in the far North, only ten miles from the Syrian border, this militant cell wasn't from across the border but from Jordan itself. This wasn't, in short, one of the many ISIS attempts at cross-border infiltration but was instead "homegrown."[70] State officials praised the operation as a successful act of counterterrorism that had foiled ISIS plots in Jordan and potentially therefore saved many lives. But while many Jordanians were pleased that terrorist attacks may have been thwarted, they were also alarmed that what many had feared—ever since the deadly attacks in 2005—had finally come to pass: that jihadist terrorism had once again come to Jordan.

Abu Musab al-Zarqawi, the architect of the 2005 attacks (who was later killed in a U.S. missile strike with the assistance of Jordanian intelligence in tracking him down), was himself a Jordanian from Zarqa. Jordan's Salafi movement, as noted earlier, had been steadily growing, particularly in the poorest parts of cities such as Zarqa, Irbid, Mafraq, and Ma'an. Kirk Sowell, an analyst with particular expertise in the Jordanian Salafi movement, noted that "Irbid is, and has been for years, an area where IS—and not the Nusra Front—has been strong. The key leaders in Zarqa and Mafraq have gone over to the Nusra wing of Salafi jihadist thought, but in Irbid, the dominant ideology is IS, not al-Qaeda."[71]

Attacks occurred in other parts of the country too, including on the borders and even in makeshift refugee camps. After allowing refugees to cross the border for several years, Jordan began imposing more restrictions, sometimes amounting to almost full border closure, in order to ensure domestic security and also stem the tide of refugees. But this resulted in a massive number of Syrian refugees stranded in a kind of "no man's land" between Jordan and Syria. Known as the "Berm" because of the large dirt mounds marking the border, the area held, by some estimates, as many as 85,000 Syrian refugees by 2017.[72] ISIS attacked the camps several times, usually aiming for Jordanian security forces there. Unlike Za'atari, the refugees of the Berm area had no electricity, no plumbing, and no sanitation. Humanitarian efforts varied, depending on the security situation. But the attacks themselves, in addition to making the lives of the refugees more difficult, also reinforced the resistance of security officials to allowing more refugees in the kingdom.

In December 2016 four militants affiliated with ISIS engaged in yet another gun battle with security forces, this time in the southern city of Kerak. The clash began outside the city, during a raid on the militants' apartment, but they soon fled to Kerak and tried to make a stand at the Crusader castle there, a popular tourist site. The ISIS militants ultimately killed ten people, including seven Jordanian security officers, two local civilians, and a Canadian tourist, before they were themselves killed. Based on the weaponry and explosives found at the apartment, Jordanian security officials were convinced that the group had intended to carry out larger-scale terrorist attacks.[73]

One final example, however, was even more home grown. It was not carried out by ISIS militants, but it was just as tragic. Nahed Hattar, a controversial opposition figure and well-known writer, was arrested for reposting a political cartoon on Facebook. The cartoon mocked an ISIS fighter for being irreverent and morally depraved, but the ensuing social media firestorm suggested that Hattar himself—an Arab Christian known for strong nationalist views—had insulted Islam and religion in general and had somehow incited sectarianism. The government, in fact, brought charges against him along these lines. But in broad daylight, on a September morning in 2016, a lone gunman assassinated Hattar on the steps of Jordan's Supreme Court. For many Jordanians this was a bracing moment, regardless of their attitudes toward Hattar. It seemed consummately un-Jordanian, like something that would happen in many other countries in the region but not Jordan. Some, at least, hoped that it was a tragic isolated incident but feared that perhaps it represented something bigger, suggesting that regional violence, intolerance, and sectarianism were now cropping up within the

Jordanian body politic itself. The act spurred condemnation from the monarchy, the government, and opposition forces alike. It even led some to tie the tragedy back to reform efforts, especially efforts to update Jordan's education system so that its domestic messages matched its extensive international campaigns for interfaith tolerance and pluralism.

Even though the incidents were relatively few and far between, they were nonetheless alarming, as they seemed almost out of character for a Jordan that had known—if not economic prosperity—at least domestic security.[74] The country has, after all, consistently marketed itself both at home and abroad as a kind of oasis in an otherwise volatile region.[75] Despite the rarity of terrorist attacks within Jordan, they nonetheless seemed to confirm to Jordan's security forces that counterterrorism needed to be the top priority. This very calculus, of course, is also precisely what many reform advocates fear. While they too value security and stability, they quite legitimately fear that these priorities would prove to be a barrier against reform and change. Reform versus security is, of course, a false dichotomy. But it is an all too common one worldwide. Yet incidents such as these—in Irbid, in Kerak, and on the borders—are also precisely why many affiliated with Jordan's police, military, security forces, and intelligence agencies believed that security efforts should outweigh reform.

Continuity and Change

Whether the issue is reform, security, identity politics, or the precarious state of the economy, Jordanian domestic political debates are never entirely domestic. The kingdom's small size and its weak and even dependent economy make Jordan especially vulnerable to regional crises. When the regional Arab Spring began, Jordan was already embroiled in its own economic crisis, which was then compounded by regional turmoil, not only in terms of regional violence but also in the forms of rising jihadist threats and massive refugee flows into the kingdom. As the cross-border violence rose and fell, whether from the Syrian civil war, the ISIS conflict, or conflicts in Israel and Palestine, the two constants of this era for Jordan's regional context were rising insecurity and rising refugee flows. There is no way to overstate the depth of the refugee crisis. The burden was greatest, of course, on the refugees themselves, especially the majority who are children and who many fear may ultimately constitute a "lost generation" for Syria. But for host countries—especially Jordan, Lebanon, Turkey and Iraq—the burden was also overwhelming, with international donor pledges rarely matching actual funds needed for services, food, water, and lodging.

This chapter has attempted to show the profound impact of external factors, regional turmoil, and especially the Syrian civil war on the politics of the Hashemite Kingdom of Jordan. The Arab uprisings had indeed shaken Jordan, as they had the entire region, with no two outcomes quite alike across the various Arab states. In the case of Jordan, the kingdom already had its hands full with its own struggles over domestic political reform and its own economic crisis. But the arrival of the regional Arab Spring exacerbated both dilemmas, while also adding intensely to the external security constraints on the kingdom. The Syrian war especially piled still more burdens on Jordan's politics, economy, and society. Many regime officials insist that reform in Jordan has advanced despite regional turmoil and insecurity. They argue that activists and critics need to understand this, and to give credit where it is due. "We need to talk not just of rights but also of duties," noted one official. "His Majesty is sincere and he is patient, and that is why we are safe now."[76] An activist, responding to the standard list of state-driven reforms, and the argument that security needed to take priority over reform, had a shorter and blunter response: "Don't insult our intelligence," she said.[77]

Indeed, even though it would be difficult to exaggerate the security challenges to Jordan today, many liberal and progressive reform activists across the kingdom feared that the regime's security efforts were serving to derail Jordan's already limited and incomplete political reform process.[78] As noted in chapter 7, many democracy and reform advocates felt that media too had become a casualty of Jordan's resurgent securitization policies. In an analysis of the overall reform question, Ziad Abu Rish has argued that media restrictions were but one of multiple regime moves that amounted to "doubling down," not on reform but on deliberalization and, in effect, counterrevolution. He cites, specifically, restrictions on media, on speech, and on public assembly, and extensive use of government gag orders on Jordanian media in response to various internal crises (including many of the incidents documented in this chapter).[79]

Regional politics, as this chapter has shown, has had profound effects on Jordanian domestic politics—not just during the era of the Arab uprisings but indeed before, during, and after the Arab Spring. Correspondingly, Jordan attempts to use its foreign policy to navigate the mine fields of regional politics, often playing an outsized role in regional politics. During the Arab uprisings, Jordanian foreign policy was an essential part of the state's attempt to maneuver through yet another period of regional challenges for the Hashemite Kingdom. It is a measure of Jordan's economic dependency, however, and of the impact on the kingdom of regional war and refugee flows, that the king and other regime officials spent so much of their time lobbying donors for more funds. Given Jordan's heightened economic, political, and even military insecurity in the context of the regional Arab uprisings and wars, the kingdom doubled down on its traditional emphasis on the importance of external aid and allies. Regional and global allies might indeed be vital to the economic and military dimensions of Jordanian security, but they remain more controversial in terms of their impact on domestic politics, especially the politics of reform and change.

While supporters of the Hashemite regime lauded the regime-led reform process and heralded its various achievements, many activists feared that the kingdom's own allies were a major source of concern for domestic reform. Many democracy activists argued that the United States and the European Union were satisfied with procedural and cosmetic reforms rather than meaningful democratization, while local allies—such as Egypt, Saudi Arabia, and the GCC monarchies—were actually far worse influences, in the sense of creating decidedly reactionary influences on Jordan's reform program.[80] In short, even as activists pushed for far greater levels of change, Jordan's Arab allies in particular seemed to favor far less change. None of the GCC states could be seen as a model of pluralism, moderation, or liberalization, while Egypt under General Abdel Fattah el-Sissi had become even more authoritarian than the earlier Mubarak regime. Some Jordanian activists even worried that antidemocratic elements had already penetrated Jordanian society, regardless of the intentions of the state, especially in the form of Saudi influences on Jordan's growing Salafi and other Islamist movements. Jordan's neighbors and allies, they argued, were an anchor dragging down domestic reform efforts, just as the state's tendency to view almost all matters via a security prism also undermined domestic reform.

Even aside from the influences of allies—whether positive or negative— many Jordanians also worried that Jordan's fears of terrorism, and its attempts to ensure regime and national security, would be the undoing of the already-limited reform process. Activists and reformers feared that the severity of internal and external jihadist threats would lead the state to clamp down still further on media, public assembly, and dissent in the name of counterterrorism and regime security. For many democracy activists, this had become a matter not of change but rather of continuity. To them, it seemed to be an old and predictable story, with constant talk at the highest levels of a clear reform path, various achievements cited, goals noted, and all with much fanfare. Many reformers argue that there is much noise but little progress. Some argue that post–Arab Spring reform efforts are not even as far along as those of the earlier 1989 reform era. The regime, however, argues that the present differs profoundly from the past, and that the reform agenda has even reached the intelligence services themselves. Former Mukhabarat chief Muhammad al-Dhahabi, for example, was arrested and convicted of corruption. His replacement, Faisal al-Shobaki, was tasked with modernizing and bringing reform to the General Intelligence Directorate itself.

During the Arab uprisings, and long after, Jordan confronted security threats from without and within. Yet that is not a particularly unusual situation in Jordanian history; what was different was the depth and intensity of these concerns. While Jordanians hotly debated questions regarding the depth or necessity of reform in the kingdom, it was nonetheless clear that the intelligence and security apparatus of the state remained strong and even pervasive in public life. Securitization, in short, seemed once again to have outweighed reform.

CHAPTER IX

Jordanian Politics Beyond the Arab Uprisings

The Arab uprisings toppled regimes in Tunisia, Egypt, Libya, and Yemen, met counterrevolution in Bahrain, and descended into a brutal civil war in Syria that soon affected the entire region. Throughout the years of the Arab Spring, Jordan remained stable and at least to some extent secure. But it was also a tense and fragile stability. While Jordan did not see revolution or civil war, its politics were nonetheless characterized by both continuity and change. Relative quiet after the initial 2011–2012 protests has sometimes been misread as acquiescence rather than a temporary respite. The Arab Spring may have ended, but political activism in Jordan certainly has not. As this book has shown, Jordan's protest and opposition movements are diverse and extensive. They differed on many things, but in general they all touched on three dominant themes and demands: the revival of a long-dormant political liberalization process; the restoration of the fuller economic and social safety net and, even more important, of more equitable economic opportunity, all of which seemed to have eroded in an era of privatization and other neoliberal economic reforms; and finally, a serious effort to stamp out corruption in public life.

Unlike many other states in the region, Jordan's regime survived the initial waves of the Arab Spring, at least in the sense of avoiding its more violent and revolutionary manifestations. The Hashemite regime argues that this is due to its emphasis on soft security, a revived reform drive, and its own efforts in responding to public demands. King Abdullah II noted on many occasions that the Arab Spring was not a constraint but an opportunity. The Arab Spring was a necessary wake-up call to Arab regimes for reform and change. Yet in the years that followed, regime and opposition in Jordan retained markedly different images of what exactly transpired during this period. The Hashemite regime argues that Jordan once again demonstrated its exceptionalism and durability, as a regime willing to reform itself. Opposition forces argue that power remains concentrated in the monarchy, and that the goal of a truly constitutional monarchy and parliamentary government remains far off to say the least.

In 2011 young activists in Jordan were inspired and hopeful about democratic reform. But many have since come to believe that Jordan remains almost unchangeable, with much fanfare over reforms but little depth or actual change. The regime and its supporters argue that Jordan has done all that reasonably can be done in the current volatile regional climate. But reformers and democracy activists argue that they have heard this story line before, and they know how it ends. Democratization or liberalization efforts in countless times and places throughout the world have been abandoned in the name of national security. Regime critics argue that this has already happened in Jordan, with fears of ISIS and other jihadist terrorist groups providing the final nail in the coffin of the reform process. Jordan does indeed live in a difficult regional setting, but that is always the case. It varies only by degree. The state's emphasis on securitization, however, has often had a dampening and sometimes even smothering effect on hopes for change.

Lack of overt revolution, however, should never be read as acquiescence. Relative quiet does not necessarily translate to acceptance of the status quo. And even though the Arab Spring took a dark turn toward violence and instability in so many parts of the Middle East, it is in the many other locations—those without revolutions or civil wars—that regimes themselves would do well to remember that lack of full-scale revolution does not mean that any of the motivating factors behind the Arab uprisings have gone away. In most places across the region they remain entirely unresolved. In Jordan, even though authoritarian resilience remains a key force, so too is individual and social mobilization. Political scientists speak in terms of upgrading authoritarianism, which is an important dynamic, but we might also consider the upgrading of activism, as both state and social forces adjust, maneuver, change, and attempt to counter and influence one another.[1] For

Jordan as well as most Arab states in the region, the social, economic, and political grievances of the Arab uprisings remain, even if protests have (in relative terms) declined.

So can we see a return to the streets on the scale of 2011 and 2012, or perhaps well beyond those numbers? And if so, under what circumstances? The most likely incentive would be an economic austerity jolt like those that triggered the riots of November 2012 (and April 1989 for that matter). In 1989 some activists referred to the riots as an uprising or "Jordanian Intifada." If austerity measures can trigger a return to street protests, these might still be confined to policy; that is, calling for a repeal of particularly galling austerity measures may or may not morph into calls for more widespread change, including regime change. In the current security environment, when most Jordanians worry about regional instability spilling over the borders, especially in the form of terrorism arriving in Jordan, it is not likely that street protests would quickly escalate beyond their trigger issue, unless the response itself was draconian. In the several years following the start of the Arab Spring, Jordan essentially managed to avoid the violence of its neighbors. There were countless protests and demonstrations, but for the most part the state continued its policy of "soft security." But the danger remained of something simply going wrong. Demonstrators are so used to this script between government and opposition that it would take very little to be seen as a government violation of that script.

Jordan's protest movement never rallied around a symbolic figure. There was no Jordanian martyr along the lines of Egypt's Khalid Sa'id or Tunisia's Muhammad Boazizi. But what if there were? If security forces overreact, including in the sometimes confusing and competitive struggles over jurisdiction between the police and the gendarmerie, protests could quickly escalate out of control. If the victim were a young, tribal "son or daughter of Jordan," one would expect nationalist activist groups ranging from the Hirak to the military veterans or other groups to share in their outrage. But even this type of scenario would likely remain something that could be managed without triggering a social explosion.

Still, it may not be likely, but the potential is nonetheless there for a social upheaval in Jordan. The anger and discontent do indeed simmer just below the surface of public life for many people in society. Certainly economic factors and overly severe austerity measures are most likely to trigger the next round of riots or unrest. But these would not be likely to destabilize the entire country unless other factors were also present. Many factors would have to come together simultaneously to create a perfect storm for this kind of massive unrest—specifically: if a perceived regime transgression were read as an outrage across Jordanian groups and factions (and hence across identity fault lines); if an overzealous and overly violent response by state security forces moved beyond "soft security" with deadly consequences; and, very important, if the opposition managed to pull together for a unified response. This analysis has shown why the latter is sometimes so difficult to achieve with disparate and diverse forms of opposition. But if the outrage in question were something that tapped into grievances across ideological and even identity lines, such as if a clear and egregious case of corruption were traced directly to top of the regime itself, then the opposition might indeed form a national coalition for change, whether in a reformist or even a more revolutionary direction.

The regime wants to avoid this type of scenario almost at all costs. And that is precisely the point of the recurring and even cyclical reform process. Opening the system in small doses, especially through elections to a largely weak and ineffective parliament, serves to rekindle at least the motions of reform and does in fact engage many citizens, even as others dismiss the process as cosmetic. Even many opposition elites, at one point or another, engage in the electoral process, with some occasionally winning. This mere act of participation changes opposition-regime dynamics. It is an act of participation but also of cooptation. That doesn't mean, however, that change must remain ephemeral. Some reform advocates choose to participate, and even accept government positions, not because they are willing to be bought off, or because they can't see what is really happening, but because they are willing to try to push for change anyway. This too changes the dynamics, removing incentives, at least for some, to be protesting in the streets.

Similar tactics are used even within the regime itself. Every election cycle brings new opportunities for proregime figures to find themselves in parliament, in the royally appointed Senate, or in cabinet posts, all with the lifetime pensions to go with the job, no matter how short-lived. One Jordanian official, who had served in multiple cabinet posts, once joked that at some point every Jordanian would be an official and therefore on the pension payroll, and hence stability would be assured.[2] Joking aside, however, there is in effect a kind of elite recycling in the corridors of power—both among elites who see themselves as supporters and sometimes among those who see themselves as critics of the regime. This does not apply, of course, to Jordan's grassroots movements. But not all can be co-opted. From the perspective of some in the regime, there is always soft security to simply contain the demonstrations, and coercion for those deemed to have gone too far.

In addition to this de facto elite recycling, Jordan has also engaged extensively in reform initiatives that can also have a familiar ring to them. Even before the era of the Arab uprisings, the regime had periodically provided small elements of reform and change to keep those reformers (and foreign critics) at bay, often with new slogans and marketing campaigns having more prominence than the actual reforms. The process in many ways matters more than an ultimate outcome. Put another way: the wheels of reform seem constantly to be spinning, but reformers complain that the country doesn't necessarily move forward. There is considerable movement without actually changing locations. More meaningful reform would actually take Jordan to places yet unexplored, but more often than not, reforms involve much movement but not necessarily forward movement—the policy equivalent of running in place. As one disappointed reform activist noted, even before the outbreak of the Arab uprisings, the monarchy's "words are with the reformers, but its actions are for the status quo."[3] Another put the matter more bluntly, even while making the argument that activists need to push for change anyway, regardless of resistance from the state: "Jordan is a tribal society," he said. "It is a deep state society. And the deep state is deeper here than in Egypt."[4]

None of the various state strategies—cooptation, containment, coercion, or recycling reform—are unique to monarchies or to Jordan. As I suggested in chapter 1, Jordan's survival is not a case of Jordanian cultural exceptionalism or of monarchical exceptionalism. Rather, the state offers various waves of reform, while also pursuing strategies and tactics meant to divide and rule the opposition, and to coopt and contain its opponents. Coercion is used too, but compared to the rest of the region, it is (usually) used sparingly. And beyond its domestic strategies, the regime relies strongly on outside allies for its own security and survival, and also for economic injections to get the state through another crisis, effectively paying off the ruling coalition, and then always seeking the next aid source to keep the kingdom afloat.

Regime supporters argue that Jordan—as both state and society—survived the Arab Spring because of smart decisions, reform programs, and social support. The regime does indeed have a strong base of domestic support, and it has wisely chosen a softer approach to its own security. It is, in effect, maintaining a liberalizing autocracy and a hybrid regime, and it also has many critics. But the promises of meaningful reform now date to 1989—before most Jordanians were born. Many Jordanians have grown weary of reform promises, billboard slogans, and marketing campaigns. Many are also tired of "change" amounting to a reshuffling of the Jordanian oligarchy rather than more genuine pluralism and inclusion. But regional insecurity has not helped their cause either, providing an ever-present set of security threats to undermine hopes for greater change.

The regime has, paradoxically, been both harmed and helped by the chaos around it. Clearly the violence of Syria and Iraq and the rise of ISIS all threaten Jordan too. But on the other hand, it has bought the regime more time, as even critics and opposition forces toned down their rhetoric and demands (aside from the Salafi jihadists, of course). The country has suffered under the strain of hundreds of thousands of refugees, with Syrians joining the previous waves of Iraqis, Palestinians, and others. But the regime has also seen its aid increase from the United States, the European Union, and Gulf allies, all to help get the regime and the country through yet another period of crisis. Jordan and its regime have proven adept at the fine art of muddling through and of managing to survive against the odds. But at some point the odds will change, the strain will become too much, or something will go very wrong. That is why the regime's best defense is to engage the opposition, in a more genuine reform process that includes these groups and gives them something to fight for, rather than something to struggle against. It would also shift the political emphasis from subjects to citizens.

King Abdullah has made clear that he expects his son one day to rule over a very different Jordan and even to play a very different kind of role, with the monarchy itself changing in its relations with the rest of the state and society. But the king also moved to quell any thoughts of alternative succession, by elevating his son, Prince Hussein, to an almost omnipresent role in meetings with national and foreign dignitaries. The crown prince is, after all, nothing less than a king in training. In doing so, the king appeared to be mindful of the questioning in some circles in Jordanian politics regarding the succession at all (especially among Jordanians for whom identity politics is *the* key factor in Jordanian political life).

But most Jordanians seem to be loyal to the monarchy, to a Jordan that is not only Jordanian but also Hashemite. Even Jordan's opposition forces are, most of the time, careful to couch their complaints or demands in the context of a loyal opposition. They call for a more constitutional monarchy, but few call for ending the monarchy itself. There are, however, more than two sides to this issue. More radical republican demands may be rare indeed (although they do exist), but there are also those who see themselves as loyalist and royalist and hence supportive of the monarchy but not necessarily of the monarch. And here we have certainly seen rampant personal criticism, directed at both the king and the queen, that has crossed lines as perhaps never before in modern Jordanian politics. Some of the most virulent criticism of the royal couple was harsh indeed, but even these critics still support the regime. Their intense and personal attacks were meant to save the monarchy from itself, from its perceived detour away from more traditional and nationalist Jordanian agendas. The retired officer's movement, for example, felt that their years of service made their loyalty to the state beyond question, and therefore empowered them to tell their own monarch some things that they felt were simply harsh truths.

Still, for most Jordanians, monarchical succession is not a significant concern. Many want to see significant changes in the political system, but more are concerned about the sheer cost of living, high unemployment rates, and the prospects for themselves and their families. It may not be likely, but Jordan does have the potential to unravel or explode. The level of pent-up anger and frustration is extensive. To assume that "it can't happen in Jordan" would be hopelessly naïve. But similarly, to assume such an explosion is certainly just as faulty. Since its independence in 1946, rumors of Jordan's impending death have always turned out to be exaggerated, to paraphrase Mark Twain's original quip. That doesn't mean that it won't at some point be true. But to this point, at least, Jordan has managed to maneuver its way through countless internal and regional crises.

The late King Hussein had a well-established reputation as the great survivor of Middle East politics, fending off myriad challenges to his rule. But in many ways the great survivor of Middle East politics was not just the late monarch but rather Jordan itself. It is Jordan the country, Jordan the state, and Jordan the society that has been the great survivor. Most Jordanians—conservatives, liberals, reactionaries, reformers, and advocates of radical change alike—share a deep love of country. They too want it to continue to survive and to prosper. They have vastly different visions for what that Jordan will look like down the road, but the kingdom may finally have reached the point where muddling through is no longer enough.

The kingdom operates with a chronic fiscal crisis, a massive budget deficit, high rates of unemployment (especially among youth), and few natural resources on which to rely. These economic factors may ultimately be more destabilizing than any other social or political factors. Indeed, Jordan's extensive economic liabilities and its dependency on other states, coupled with its internal political and social strains, amid wave after wave of regional turmoil, is ultimately not a sustainable model. "It's not sustainable," quipped one former government official, "it's just sustained anyway."[5] The kingdom's economic situation is so routinely dire that foreign policy and alliances are essential tools for regime and state survival. The kingdom is dependent on foreign aid and therefore vulnerable to the preferences of its main financial benefactors—the United States, the European Union, Saudi Arabia, and other Gulf states. Jordan's combination of fiscal crisis and regional insecurity have together served to deepen not just these key alliances but also specifically the military dimension especially of Jordan's relations with Western powers. This, in turn, has only added to the state's already-existing propensity for reliance on securitization as key to its domestic and regional survival.

Paradoxically perhaps, the combination of economic and regional insecurity suggests the necessity to open the system still further, rather than clamping down and turning Jordanian society (also suffering from these same constraints) into a pressure cooker. Yet economic crisis and regional insecurity tend to be used in precisely the opposite fashion—as the main drivers or even excuses for being unable to do more. Meanwhile, the refugee crisis has added still further to Jordan's already profound social, economic, and political pressures. The country does, indeed, need to engage in more extensive change, in deeper, and more meaningful reform, inclusion, and pluralism, not just to survive but also to thrive and prosper. The risks will be great, but so is the country, and they are therefore risks worth taking, with the hope that Jordanians many years from now can still point to the Mark Twain quote—"the reports of my death have been greatly exaggerated"—and make it their own.

Notes

1. Continuity and Change Amid the Arab Uprisings

1. This was the title, for example, of the collection of essays (which I contributed to) about Jordan during the Arab Spring compiled by the Project on Middle East Political Science (POMEPS), *Jordan, Forever on the Brink*, POMEPS Briefings no. 11, May 9, 2012.
2. Marwan Muasher, *The Second Arab Awakening: And the Battle for Pluralism* (New Haven, Conn.: Yale University Press, 2014).
3. On the uprisings of the Arab Spring, see, for example, Jason Brownlee, Tarek E. Masoud, and Andrew Reynolds, *The Arab Spring: Pathways of Repression and Reform* (Oxford: Oxford University Press, 2015); Marc Lynch, *The Arab Uprising: The Unfinished Revolutions of the New Middle East* (New York: Public Affairs, 2012); Marc Lynch, ed., *The Arab Uprisings Explained: New Contentious Politics in the Middle East* (New York: Columbia University Press, 2014); and Rex Brynen et al., *Beyond the Arab Spring: Authoritarianism and Democratization in the Arab World* (Boulder: Lynne Rienner, 2012).
4. On the many economic dimensions of the uprisings, see Pete Moore, "Fiscal Politics of Enduring Authoritarianism," *The Arab Thermidor: The Resurgence of the Security State*, Project on Middle East Political Science, December 2014; Pete Moore, "Before and After Uprising: Political Economies of the 2011 Uprisings," *Taiwan Journal of Democracy* 10, no. 1 (July 2014); and Pete Moore, "The Bread Revolutions of 2011: Teaching Political Economies of the Middle East," *PS: Political Science and Politics* 46, no. 2 (April 2013).

5. Some analyses that stress the longer-term context and patterns of resistance and repression in the region include John Chalcraft, *Popular Politics in the Making of the Modern Middle East* (Cambridge: Cambridge University Press, 2016); Adam Hanieh, *Lineages of Revolt: Issues of Contemporary Capitalism in the Middle East* (Chicago: Haymarket Books, 2013); and Charles Tripp, *The Power and the People: Paths to Resistance in the Middle East* (Cambridge: Cambridge University Press, 2013).

6. See, for example, the essays collected in *Arab Uprisings: New Opportunities for Political Science*, POMEPS Briefings no. 12, 2012.

7. In his book *The Arab Uprising*, Marc Lynch has referred to this as "The Empire Strikes Back."

8. For an important critique of the field of Middle East studies in this regard, see F. Gregory Gause III, "Why Middle East Studies Missed the Arab Spring: The Myth of Authoritarian Stability," *Foreign Affairs* 90, no. 4 (July/August 2011): 81–90.

9. See, for example, Jason Brownlee, "And Yet They Persist: Explaining Survival and Transition in Neo-patrimonial Regimes," *Studies in Comparative International Development* 37, no. 3 (2002): 35–63.

10. For some of the important essays that *did* focus on the Middle East, see, for example, Rex Brynen, Bahgat Korany, and Paul Noble, eds., *Political Liberalization and Democratization in the Arab World*, vol. 1 (Boulder, Colo.: Lynne Rienner, 1995).

11. See, for example, the four-volume set on transitions by Guillermo O'Donnell, Phillipe Schmitter, and Lawrence Whitehead, *Transitions from Authoritarian Rule* (Baltimore: Johns Hopkins University Press, 1986).

12. Raymond Hinnebusch, "Authoritarian Persistence, Democratization Theory and the Middle East: An Overview and a Critique," *Democratization* 13, no. 3 (2006): 373–95. See also Steven Heydemann and Renauld Leenders, "Authoritarian Learning and Authoritarian Resilience: Regime Responses to the Arab Awakening," *Globalizations* 8, no. 5 (2011): 647–53.

13. Thomas Carothers, "The End of the Transition Paradigm," *Journal of Democracy* 12, no. 1 (2002): 5–21.

14. Morten Valbjorn, "Reflections on Self-Reflections: On Framing the Analytical Implications of the Arab Uprisings for the Study of Arab Politics," *Democratization* 22, no. 2 (2015): 218–38.

15. Steven Heydemann, "Upgrading Authoritarianism in the Arab World," Brookings Institution, Saban Center Analysis Paper no. 13 (2007).

16. Joshua Stacher, *Adaptable Autocrats: Regime Power in Egypt and Syria* (Stanford, Calif.: Stanford University Press, 2012).

17. Curtis R. Ryan, "Political Strategies and Regime Survival: The Case of Egypt," *Journal of Third World Studies* 18, no. 2 (2001): 25–46.

18. Jason Brownlee, *Democracy Prevention: The Politics of the U.S.-Egyptian Alliance* (Cambridge: Cambridge University Press, 2012).

19. I develop an approach to the regime security dynamic more thoroughly in a previous work: Curtis R. Ryan, *Inter-Arab Alliances: Regime Security and Jordanian Foreign Policy* (Gainesville: University of Florida Press, 2009).

20. See, for example, Augustus Richard Norton, "The Future of Civil Society in the Middle East," *Middle East Journal* 47, no. 2 (1993): 205–16; and Augustus Richard Norton, *Civil Society in the Middle East* (Leiden: E. J. Brill, 1995).

21. Lisa Anderson, "Searching Where the Light Shines: Studying Democratization in the Middle East," *Annual Review of Political Science* 9, no. 1 (2006): 189–214.

22. Marc Lynch, ed., *The Arab Uprisings Explained: New Contentious Politics in the Middle East* (New York: Columbia University Press, 2014), 316.

23. Lina Khatib and Ellen Lust, eds., *Taking to the Streets: The Transformation of Arab Activism* (Baltimore: Johns Hopkins University Press, 2014).

24. Asef Bayat, *Life as Politics: How Ordinary People Change the Middle East* (Stanford, Calif.: Stanford University Press, 2010).

25. Lisa Wedeen, *Ambiguities of Domination: Politics, Rhetoric, and Symbols in Contemporary Syria* (Chicago: University of Chicago Press 1999).

26. Marc Lynch, *Voices of the New Arab Public: Iraq, al-Jazeera, and Middle East Politics Today* (New York: Columbia University Press, 2006).

27. For example: Jeanne A. K. Hey, ed., *Small States in World Politics: Explaining Foreign Policy Behavior* (Boulder, Colo.: Lynne Rienner, 2003).

28. Especially on the economic underpinnings of Jordanian politics, see Anne Mariel Peters and Pete Moore, "Beyond Boom and Bust: External Rents, Durable Authoritarianism, and Institutional Adaptation in the Hashemite Kingdom of Jordan," *Studies in Comparative International Development* 44, no. 2 (2009): 256–85.

29. Sean L. Yom, *From Resilience to Revolution: How Foreign Interventions Destabilize the Middle East* (New York: Columbia University Press, 2016).

30. See "Security Dilemmas in Arab Politics," chap. 2 in Ryan, *Inter-Arab Alliances*.

31. Larry Diamond, "Hybrid Regimes," *Journal of Democracy* 13, no. 2 (2002): 21–35; Frederic Volpi, "Pseudo-democracy in the Muslim World," *Third World Quarterly* 25, no. 6 (2004): 1061–78; Daniel Brumberg, "The Trap of Liberalized Autocracy," *Journal of Democracy* 13, no. 4 (2002): 56–68. Jillian Schwedler and I discuss the notion of Jordan as hybrid regime in Curtis R. Ryan and Jillian Schwedler, "Return to Democratization or a New Hybrid Regime?: The 2003 Elections in Jordan," *Middle East Policy* 11, no. 2 (Summer 2004): 138–51.

32. See the collection of essays *The Arab Monarchy Debate*, POMEPS Briefings no. 16, December 19, 2012, http://pomeps.org/wp-content/uploads/2012/12/POMEPS_BriefBooklet16_Monarchies_web.pdf.

33. F. Gregory Gause, III, "Kings for All Seasons: How the Middle East Monarchies Survived the Arab Spring," Brookings Doha Center Analysis Paper no. 8, September 2013, https://www.brookings.edu/wp-content/uploads/2016/06/Resilience-Arab-Monarchies_English.pdf.

2. The Arab Spring Protests in Jordan

1. I am drawing here on earlier takes on these issues: Curtis R. Ryan, "Jordan and the Arab Spring," in *The Arab Spring: Change and Resistance in the Middle East*, ed. Mark L. Haas and David W. Lesch, 116–30 (Boulder, Colo.: Westview Press, 2013); and Curtis R. Ryan, "Oasis or Mirage? Jordan's Unlikely Stability in a Changing Middle East," *World Politics Review*, January 15, 2015.
2. Jillian Schwedler has done the most extensive research on the politics of protest in Jordan. See Jillian Schwedler, "Spatial Dynamics of the Arab Uprisings," *PS: Political Science & Politics* 46, no. 2 (April 2013): 230–34; Jillian Schwedler, "The Political Geography of Protest in Neoliberal Jordan," *Middle East Critique* 21, no. 3 (December 2012): 259–70; Jillian Schwedler, "Cop Rock: Protest, Identity, and Dancing Riot Police in Jordan," *Social Movement Studies* 4, no. 2 (September 2005): 155–75; and Jillian Schwedler, "More than a Mob: The Dynamics of Political Demonstrations in Jordan," *Middle East Report* 226 (Spring 2003): 18–23.
3. Mohammed Yaghi and Janine A. Clark, "Jordan: Evolving Activism in a Divided Society," in *Taking to the Streets: The Transformation of Arab Activism*, ed. Lina Khatib and Ellen Lust, 236–67 (Baltimore: Johns Hopkins University Press, 2014).
4. Author interviews with prodemocracy activists and with self-described regime loyalists, Amman, Jordan, June 2013.
5. For several different takes on Jordan's Arab Spring experience, see, for example, Sarah A. Tobin, "Jordan's Arab Spring: The Middle Class and Anti-Revolution," *Middle East Policy* 19, no. 1 (2012): 96–109; Nur Koprulu, "Consolidated Monarchies in the Post-Arab Spring Era," *Israel Affairs* 20, no. 3 (2014): 318–27; Nuri Yesilyurt, "Jordan and the Arab Spring: Challenges and Opportunities." *Perceptions* 19, no. 4 (Winter 2014): 169–94; and Sean L. Yom, "The New Landscape of Jordanian Politics: Social Opposition, Fiscal Crisis, and the Arab Spring," *British Journal of Middle Eastern Studies* 42, no. 3 (2015): 284–300.
6. Author interview with King Abdullah II, Amman, May 21, 2012.
7. Author interview with King Abdullah II, Amman, May 21, 2012.
8. Samuel Helfont and Tally Helfont, "Jordan's Protests: Arab Spring Lite?" *Foreign Policy Research Institute E-Notes*, July 2011.
9. "Jordan and Its King: Caught in the Middle as Usual," *Economist*, October 22, 2011; "Jordan and Its King: As Beleaguered as Ever," *Economist*, October 13,

2012; "Jordan: Surprisingly Stable for the Moment," *Economist*, November 9, 2013.

10. "Jordan: Surprisingly Stable for the Moment."

11. Mona Christophersen, *Protest and Reform in Jordan: Popular Demand and Government Response* (Oslo: Fafo Report, 2013).

12. Malika Bouziane and Katharina Lenner, "Protests in Jordan: Rumblings in the Kingdom of Dialogue," in *Protests, Revolutions, and Transformations—The Arab World in Upheaval*, Working Paper no. 1, Center for Middle Eastern & North African Studies (Berlin: Freie Universitat Berlin, July 2011), 148–65.

13. Mohammed Yaghi and Janine A. Clark, "Jordan: Evolving Activism in a Divided Society," in *Taking to the Streets: The Transformation of Arab Activism*, ed. Lina Khatib and Ellen Lust, 236–67 (Baltimore: Johns Hopkins University Press, 2014).

14. Nicolas Pelham, "Jordan Starts to Shake," *New York Review of Books*, December 8, 2011.

15. Marwan Muasher, *The Second Arab Awakening: And the Battle for Pluralism* (New Haven, Conn.: Yale University Press, 2014), 114.

16. See Schwedler, "Spatial Dynamics of the Arab Uprisings" and "The Political Geography of Protest in Neoliberal Jordan."

17. See the account by democracy activist and blogger Naseem Tarawneh, "The Quick Death of Shabab March 24 and What It Means for Jordan," *Black Iris* (blog), March 26, 2011, http://www.black-iris.com/2011/03/26/the-quick-death-of-shabab-march-24-and-what-it-means-for-jordan/.

18. David Fox and Katrina Sammour, "Disquiet on the Jordanian Front," Carnegie Endowment for International Peace, September 27, 2012.

19. Assaf David, "The Revolt of Jordan's Military Veterans," *Foreign Policy, Middle East Channel*, June 16, 2010.

20. BBC News, "Jordan Tribes Criticize Queen Rania's 'Political Role,'" February 8, 2011.

21. Author interview, Amman, June 2011.

22. Tariq Tell, "Early Spring in Jordan: Revolt of the Military Veterans," Carnegie Middle East Center, November 4, 2015.

23. Author interview, Amman, June 2011.

24. Author interview, Amman, June 2011.

25. Author interview with Jordanian government officials, June 2011.

26. Curtis R. Ryan, "What's (Maybe) New in Jordan," *Foreign Policy, Middle East Channel*, October 11, 2012.

27. Zaki Bani Rashid, "The Jordanian Spring Has Begun," *Guardian*, October 19, 2012.

28. Joby Warrick and Taylor Luck, "Jordan Calm for Now, but New Storms Loom," *Washington Post*, November 21, 2012.

29. Author interview, Amman, May 2012.

30. "Jordan and Its King: Caught in the Middle as Usual."

31. International Crisis Group, "Popular Protest in North Africa and the Middle East (IX): Dallying with Reform in a Divided Jordan," *ICJ Middle East/North Africa Report* no. 118, March 12, 2012.

32. Author interview with 'Awn al-Khasawneh, Amman, May 2012.

33. Khasawneh quoted in the *Jordan Times*, October 20, 2011.

34. Author interview, Amman, December 2012.

35. Ryan, "What's (Maybe) New in Jordan."

3. Political Parties and the "Traditional" Opposition

1. This chapter expands on an earlier analysis in Curtis R. Ryan, "Political Opposition and Reform Coalitions in Jordan," *British Journal of Middle East Studies* 38, no. 3 (2011): 367–90.

2. See Joas Wagemakers, *Salafism in Jordan: Political Islam in a Quietist Community* (Cambridge: Cambridge University Press, 2016); and Quintan Wiktorowicz, *The Management of Islamic Activism: Salafis, the Muslim Brotherhood, and State Power in Jordan* (Albany: State University of New York Press, 2000).

3. See Kirk H. Sowell, "Jordanian Salafism and the Jihad in Syria," Hudson Institute, March 12, 2015, http://www.hudson.org/research/11131-jordanian-salafism -and-the-jihad-in-syria.

4. See also Ellen Lust, "Elections Under Authoritarianism: Preliminary Lessons from Jordan," *Democratization* 13, no. 3 (2006): 456–71; and Jennifer Gandhi and Ellen Lust, "Elections Under Authoritarianism," *Annual Review of Political Science* 12, no. 1 (2009): 403–22.

5. The Hashemite monarchy banned political parties in 1957, following a failed military coup attempt against the regime by Nasserist and leftist officers. The overthrow of the neighboring Hashemite monarchy in Iraq in 1958, and the killing of the entire Hashemite royal family there, served to underscore the regime's conviction that the greatest threat to its survival—in the 1950s— came from Nasserist, leftist, and Pan-Arab parties and movements. On this period, see Uriel Dann, *King Hussein and the Challenge of Arab Radicalism, 1955–1967* (New York: Oxford University Press, 1989); and Kamal Salibi, *The Modern History of Jordan* (London: I. B. Tauris, 1998), 197–221.

6. Jordanians were so ready for the resumption of multiparty elections, in fact, that a series of studies had already been published on Jordanian political parties in anticipation of the return of party life. See, for example, Ahmad Abu Khusa, *al-Dimuqratiyya wa al-Ahzab al-Siyasiyya al-Urduniyya* (Democracy and

Jordanian political parties) (Amman: Middle East Publishing Company, 1991); M.A.S al-Abdalat, *Kharita al-Ahzab al-Siyasiyya al-Urduniyya* (Map of Jordanian political parties) (Amman: Dar al-Ubra, 1992); Suleiman Sways, "Kharita al-Ahzab al-Siyasiyya fi al-Urdun" (A map of political parties in Jordan), *al-Urdun al-Jadid*, 1990, 122–41; and Riad al-Khatib Iyad, *al-Tayarat al-Siyasiyya fi al-Urdun wa Nas al-Mithaq al-Watani al-Urduni* (Political tendencies in Jordan and text of the Jordanian National Charter) (Amman, 1991).

7. Ellen M. Lust-Okar, "The Decline of Jordanian Political Parties: Myth or Reality?" *International Journal of Middle East Studies* 33, no. 4 (2001): 545–69.

8. Jillian Schwedler, *Faith in Moderation: Islamist Parties in Jordan and Yemen* (Cambridge: Cambridge University Press, 2006); Janine A. Clark, "The Conditions of Islamist Moderation: Unpacking Cross-Ideological Cooperation in Jordan," *International Journal of Middle East Studies* 38, no. 4 (2006): 539–60; and Jillian Schwedler and Janine A. Clark, "Islamist-Leftist Cooperation in the Arab World," *ISIM Review* 18 (2006): 10–11.

9. Michaelle Browers, *Political Ideology in the Arab World: Accommodation and Transformation* (Cambridge: Cambridge University Press, 2009), 176.

10. Malcolm Kerr, *The Arab Cold War: Gamal 'Abd al-Nasir and His Rivals, 1958–1970* (London: Oxford University Press, 1970).

11. On Jordanian parties and the party system, see *al-Dimuqratiyya fi al-Hayat al-Dakhiliyya li al-Ahzab al-Siyasiyya al-'Arabiyya* (Democracy in the practice of Arab political parties) (Amman: al-Quds Center for Political Studies, 2010); and *al-Qu'anin al-Nazimat li al-'Amal al-Hizbi fi al-Urdun* (Revisiting political party legislation in Jordan) (Amman: al-Quds Center for Political Studies, 2010).

12. Jillian Schwedler, *Faith in Moderation: Islamist Parties in Jordan and Yemen* (Cambridge: Cambridge University Press, 2006); see also Wiktorowicz, *The Management of Islamic Activism*.

13. Curtis R. Ryan, "Islamist Political Activism in Jordan: Moderation, Militancy, and Democracy," *Middle East Review of International Affairs* 12, no. 2 (2008): 1–13.

14. In the elections of 1989, all candidates technically ran as independents since parties remained illegal. From 1993 onward, however, candidates have been able to run with legal party affiliations. Underscoring the weakness of the Jordanian party system, however, most candidates in any election have been nonpartisan or independent rather than from Islamist, leftist, or nationalist parties. On the 1989 elections, see Kamel S. Abu Jaber and Shirin H. Fathi, "The 1989 Jordanian Parliamentary Elections," *Orient* 31 (1990): 67–86.

15. Author interviews with opposition activists, journalists, and government officials, Amman, Jordan, June 2010, December 2010, and June 2011.

16. Mary C. Wilson. "Jordan: Bread, Freedom, or Both?" *Current History* (February 1994): 87–90. For details on the elections in 1993, see also Glenn E. Robinson,

"Defensive Democratization in Jordan,'" *International Journal of Middle East Studies* 30, no. 3 (1998): 387–410; and Curtis R. Ryan, "Elections and Parliamentary Democratization in Jordan," *Democratization* 5, no. 4 (1998): 194–214.

17. For further details on the 1989, 1993, and 1997 elections, see Curtis R. Ryan, *Jordan in Transition: From Hussein to Abdullah* (Boulder, Colo.: Lynne Rienner, 2002), 15–45.

18. On the 2003 elections, see Curtis R. Ryan and Jillian Schwedler, "Return to Democratization or New Hybrid Regime?" *Middle East Policy* 11, no. 2 (2004): 138–51.

19. Asher Susser, "Jordan: Preserving Domestic Order in a Setting of Regional Turmoil," *Middle East Brief* no. 27, Crown Center for Middle East Studies, Brandeis University, March 2008, 4–5.

20. The electoral law of 2010 kept the uneven districts but added four new seats for Amman, Irbid, and Zarqa (cities with large Palestinian populations) and doubled the women's quota from six to twelve seats in parliament. For an analysis of the details and reactions, see Curtis R. Ryan, "Jordan's New Electoral Law: Reform, Reaction, or Status Quo?" *Foreign Policy, Middle East Channel*, May 24, 2010, http://mideast.foreignpolicy.com/posts/2010/05/24/jordan_s_new_electoral_law_reform_reaction_or_status_quo.

21. On the 2010 elections and their aftermath, see Curtis R. Ryan, "Déjà Vu All Over Again? Jordan's 2010 Elections," *Foreign Policy, Middle East Channel*, November 15, 2010, http://mideast.foreignpolicy.com/posts/2010/11/15/jordanians_go_to_the_polls.

22. Author interview with democracy activist, Amman, June 2001.

23. On the state and the Islamist movement, see *al-Dawla wa al-Ikhwan, 1999–2008* (The state and the Brotherhood, 1999–2008) (Amman: al-Quds Center for Political Studies, 2008); and *al-Din wa al-Dawla: al-Urdun* (Religion and the state: Jordan) (Amman: al-Quds Center for Political Studies, 2010).

24. Browers, *Political Ideology in the Arab World*; Francesco Cavatorta, "Divided They Stand, Divided They Fail: Opposition Politics in Morocco," *Democratization* 16, no. 2 (2009): 137–56; and Francesco Cavatorta, "More than Repression; Strategies of Regime Survival: The Significance of Divide et Impera in Morocco," *Journal of Contemporary African Studies* 25, no. 2 (2007): 187–203.

25. Jillian Schwedler, "Islamists in Power? Inclusion, Moderation, and the Arab Uprisings," *Middle East Development Journal* 5, no. 1 (April 2013); and Jillian Schwedler, "Can Islamists Become Moderates? Rethinking the Inclusion-Moderation Hypothesis," *World Politics* 63, no. 2 (April 2011): 347–76.

26. Opposition to the 1994 Jordanian-Israeli peace treaty led leftist and Islamist activists to organize, through the political parties and the professional associations, an "antinormalization" campaign from 1994 onward, so that the

peace remains a cold one between the two governments but with limited links between the two societies. Paul L. Scham and Russell E. Lucas, " 'Normalization' and 'Anti-Normalization' in Jordan: The Public Debate," *Israel Affairs* 9, no. 3 (2003): 141–64.

27. For extensive analysis of cross-ideological cooperation and its limits in Jordan, see Janine A. Clark, "Threats, Structures and Resources: Cross-Ideological Coalition Building in Jordan," *Comparative Politics* 43, no. 3 (2010): 101–20; Clark, "The Conditions of Islamist Moderation"; and Schwedler and Clark, "Islamist-Leftist Cooperation in the Arab World."

28. Francesca Sawalha, "Opposites Attract on Petition to Declare War on Iraq 'Illegal,' " *Jordan Times*, April 1, 2003.

29. Author interview, Amman, December 2012.

30. Ellen Lust-Okar, "Divided They Rule: The Management and Manipulation of Political Opposition," *Comparative Politics* 36, no. 2 (2004): 169; and Ellen Lust-Okar, *Structuring Conflict in the Arab World: Incumbents, Opponents, and Institutions* (New York: Cambridge University Press, 2005).

31. Jillian Schwedler, *Faith in Moderation: Islamist Parties in Jordan and Yemen* (Cambridge: Cambridge University Press, 2006).

32. See Scham and Lucas, " 'Normalization' and 'Anti-Normalization' in Jordan."

33. Curtis R. Ryan, "Peace, Bread, and Riots: Jordan and the International Monetary Fund," *Middle East Policy* 6, no. 2 (1998): 54–66.

34. Lust-Okar, "Divided They Rule," 172.

35. Clark, "The Conditions of Islamist Moderation," 555–56.

36. Oraib al-Rantawi, "Coalition Presses for Electoral Reform in Jordan," *Arab Reform Bulletin*, April 14, 2010.

37. Similarly, even when groups do overlap considerably, most activists do not seem to view one group as subsuming another, or one as being above another. They simply overlap, and individuals therefore are often participants in multiple organizations, groups, or coalitions. Author's interviews with democracy activists, Amman, June 2010, December 2010, and June 2011.

38. Author interview with a youth and social media activist, Amman, June 2011.

39. Ryan, "Jordan's New Electoral Law."

40. This point was made to me consistently in interviews with democracy activists, journalists, and government officials, especially in June 2010, December 2010, and June 2011.

41. Author interview, Amman, August 2016.

42. Author interview, Amman, June 2011.

43. Hisham Bustani, "The Alternative Opposition in Jordan and the Failure to Understand the Lessons of the Tunisian and Egyptian Revolutions," *Jadaliyya*, March 20, 2011, http://www.jadaliyya.com/pages/index/959.

44. Bustani, "The Alternative Opposition in Jordan"; and author interview with Hisham Bustani, Amman, June 12, 2001.

45. Oraib Rantawi, director of the prodemocracy al-Quds Center for Political Studies, estimated that the number of coalitions and youth movements had already reached more than thirty in only a matter of months and was continuing to grow. Author interview with Oraib Rintawi, Amman, June 12, 2011.

46. Author interview, Amman, June 2011.

47. Taylor Luck, "Southern Protests Continue," *Jordan Times*, July 8, 2011.

48. While many Jordanian youth movements were inspired to reform activism by the Tunisian and Egyptian revolutions, the first of these movements actually emerged on January 7, 2011 (before the January 25, 2011, Egyptian revolution) in the form of the Dhiban Popular Movement for Change in Dhiban, Jordan, calling for an end to corruption and the ouster of the government of then–prime minister Samir al-Rifa'i. For a discussion of the dynamics of organization of many of the movements, see Taylor Luck, "Despite Differences, Youth Movements Still Depend on Traditional Parties to Materialise," *Jordan Times*, July 29, 2011.

49. Nicolas Pelham, "Jordan's Balancing Act," *Middle East Report Online*, February 22, 2011, http://www.merip.org/mero/mero022211.

50. See, for example, Muhammad Abu Rumman's analysis of state-opposition relations and divisions within the Islamist movement in "Jordan's Parliamentary Elections and Islamist Boycott," *Arab Reform Bulletin*, October 20, 2010.

51. Author interview in Amman, June 2011.

52. Author interview in Amman, June 2011.

53. Luck, "Despite Differences."

54. Some movements, such as the Kerak Popular Youth Movement, went further organizationally by creating a steering committee to include representatives from parties and professional associations as well as independent activists. Luck, "Despite Differences."

55. Lamis Andoni, "Jordanians Demand Change," *Al-Jazeera*, February 21, 2011, http://english.aljazeera.net.

56. *Ammon News*, February 4, 2011, http://www.ammonnews.net.

57. A. T. Homoud, "Reform Gets a Heavyweight," *JO Magazine*, July 3, 2011.

4. The Hirak and Changes in Political Activism

1. Fida Adely, "The Emergence of a New Labor Movement in Jordan," *Middle East Report* no. 264 (Fall 2012), http://www.merip.org/mer/mer264/emergence-new-labor-movement-jordan.

2. Nicholas Seeley, "The Battle Over Nuclear Jordan," *Middle East Report* no. 271 (Summer 2014), http://www.merip.org/mer/mer271/battle-over-nuclear-jordan.

3. The discussion in this chapter owes much to meetings and discussions with activists well beyond the capital but throughout the governorates, over the course of ten visits to Jordan between 2010 and 2016. I am also indebted to several Jordanian scholars and journalists who have covered the Hirak movement from the beginning.

4. See the excellent analysis by Sara Ababneh, "Troubling the Political: Women and the Jordanian Day-Waged Labor Movement," *International Journal of Middle East Studies* 48 (2016): 87–112.

5. Sean L. Yom, "Tribal Politics in Contemporary Jordan: The Case of the Hirak Movement," *Middle East Journal* 68, no. 2 (Spring 2014): 229–47.

6. Yom, "Tribal Politics in Contemporary Jordan."

7. Sean L. Yom and Wael al-Khatib, "Jordan's New Politics of Tribal Dissent," *Foreign Policy, Middle East Channel*, August 7, 2012, http://foreignpolicy.com/2012/08/07/jordans-new-politics-of-tribal-dissent/.

8. Tariq Tell, *Early Spring in Jordan: Revolt of the Military Veterans*, Carnegie Middle East Center, November 4, 2015.

9. See Sara Ababneh, "Troubling the Political: Women and the Jordanian Day-Waged Labor Movement," *International Journal of Middle East Studies* 48 (2016): 87–112; and Adely, "The Emergence of a New Labor Movement in Jordan."

10. Author interviews, Jordan, June 2014.

11. Bessma Momani, *Arab Dawn: Arab Youth and the Demographic Dividend They Will Bring* (Toronto: University of Toronto Press, 2015).

12. Ezra Karmel, "How Revolutionary Was Jordan's Hirak?," Identity Center, Amman, Jordan, June 2014.

13. Yom, "Tribal Politics in Contemporary Jordan."

14. Jillian Schwedler, "Jordan's Islamists Lose Faith in Moderation," *Foreign Policy, Middle East Channel*, June 30, 2010.

15. Curtis R. Ryan, "One Society of Muslim Brothers in Jordan or Two?" *Middle East Report Online*, March 5, 2015, http://www.merip.org/one-society-muslim-brothers-jordan-or-two.

16. Schwedler, "Jordan's Islamists Lose Faith in Moderation."

17. Author interview, Amman, June 2015.

18. Tamer al-Samadi, "Jordan Steps Up Campaign Against Opposition Groups," *al-Monitor*, October 22, 2013.

19. "Jordan: End Trials of Protesters for 'Undermining Regime,'" Human Rights Watch, October 29, 2013.

20. Author interview, Amman, December 2011.

21. Author interview, Amman, June 2013.

22. Danya Greenfield, "Jordan's Youth: Avenues for Activism," *Atlantic Council Issue Brief*, August 2013; Evie Browne, "Community Activism in Jordan," *GSDRC Helpdesk Research Report* 957, 2013; and Marty Harris, *Jordan's Youth After the Arab Spring*, Lowy Institute for International Policy, February 2015.

23. See, for example, the hashtag debate with Marwan Muasher, http://www.makanhouse.net/event/hashtag-debates.

24. Maqha Amman or Le Café Politique is a Facebook group with closed membership in order to allow for open discussion among members without worrying about internet "trolls."

25. Author interview with Taqaddam activist, Amman, December 2012.

26. Author interview with Taqaddam activist, Amman, August 2016.

27. I am expanding here on earlier investigations of this topic in Curtis R. Ryan, "Not Running on Empty: Democratic Activism Against Israeli Gas in Jordan," *Middle East Report Online*, April 16, 2015, http://www.merip.org/not-running -empty-democratic-activism-against-israeli-gas-jordan; and Curtis R. Ryan, "Reviving Activism in Jordan," *Middle East Report* no. 281 (Winter 2016), http:// www.merip.org/mer/mer281/reviving-activism-jordan.

28. "Jordan BDS Statement on Gas Deal with Israel," *Jadaliyya*, October 2, 2016, http://www.jadaliyya.com/pages/index/25219/jordan-bds-statement-on -gas-deal-with-israel.

29. Author interview. See also Hisham Bustani, "Importing Israeli Gas: Jordan's Self-Harming Energy Choice," *Middle East Eye*, September 30, 2016, http:// www.middleeasteye.net/columns/importing-israeli-gas-jordan-s-self-harming -energy-choice-1839478241.

30. Author e-mail correspondence with Jordanian activists, April 2015.

31. Author Skype interview, August 2016.

32. The website for the public tribunal over the gas deal is https://gastribunaljo .wordpress.com/.

33. Multiple articles on all aspects of the gas deal and the campaign against it have been assembled by the 7iber group, https://www.7iber.com/politics-economics /what-we-know-about-the-israeli-gas-deal/.

34. Seeley, "The Battle Over Nuclear Jordan."

35. Osama al-Sharif, "Jordanians Fuming Over Gas Deal with Israel," *al-Monitor*, October 5, 2016, http://www.al-monitor.com/pulse/originals/2016/10/jordan -israel-gas-deal-popular-protest.html.

36. Beverly Milton-Edwards, "Protests in Jordan Over Gas deal with Israel Expose Wider Rifts," Brookings Doha, October 26, 2016, https://www .brookings.edu/blog/markaz/2016/10/26/protests-in-jordan-over-gas-deal -with-israel-expose-wider-rifts/; Mel Plant, "Amman Hit by Protests Over Secret Jordan-Israel Gas Deal," *Middle East Eye*, September 30, 2016, http:// www.middleeasteye.net/news/jordan-israel-gas-deal-protests-1735311523;

and Zena Tahhan, "Jordanians Reject 'Stolen Gas' in Israel-Jordan Deal," *al-Jazeera*, October 3, 2016, http://www.aljazeera.com/news/2016/10/jorda nians-reject-stolen-gas-israel-jordan-deal-161002131442112.html.

37. For an insightful and critical analysis of cycles of mobilization, demobiliza tion, and protest in Jordan, see Naseem Tarawneh, "The Jordan-Israeli Gas Deal and Our Perpetual Déjà Vu: A Reminder of the Bigger Battles We're Not Fighting," *Black Iris*, October 6, 2016, http://black-iris.com/2016/10/06/the -jordan-israeli-gas-deal-and-our-perpetual-deja-vu/.

38. Author correspondence with activists in the movement, August 2016.

39. Marwan Muasher, *A Decade of Struggling Reform Efforts in Jordan: The Resilience of the Rentier System* (Washington, D.C.: Carnegie Endowment for International Peace, 2011), 4, 23.

40. Hisham Bustani notes that the latter group tends to be seen as "neoliberal" but that both groups actually tend to subscribe to this ideology. See Bustani, "The Alternative Opposition in Jordan and the Failure to Understand Lessons of Tunisian and Egyptian Revolutions," *Jadaliyya*, March 22, 2011, http://www .jadaliyya.com/pages/index/959.

5. Identity Politics, Real and Imagined

1. This chapter expands beyond an earlier first cut at the topic in Curtis R. Ryan, "Identity Politics, Reform, and Protest in Jordan," *Studies in Ethnicity and Nationalism* 11, no. 3 (2011): 564–78. Similar issues are also explored in Curtis R. Ryan, "Governance, Reform, and Resurgent Ethnic Identity Politics in Jor dan," in *Governance and Politics in the Middle East*, ed. Abbas Khadim, 342–56 (London: Routledge, 2013).

2. Ned Parker, "Jordan Democracy Activists Enjoy Camaraderie, Freedom to Protest," *Los Angeles Times*, January 24, 2013, http://articles.latimes.com/2013 /jan/24/world/la-fg-jordan-herak-20130125.

3. Suleiman al-Khalidi, "Divisions, Fear of Turmoil Dampen Jordanian Dissent," *Reuters*, January 24, 2014, http://www.reuters.com/article/2014/01/24/us -jordan-stability-idUSBREA0N0AK20140124.

4. Jordanian population statistics do nothing to clarify the matter since any cen sus in the kingdom simply records the growing ethnically Arab population and does not distinguish between Palestinian Jordanians and East Jordanians. In its statistics, the United Nations Relief Works Agency (UNRWA) put the total number of Palestinian refugees in Jordan in 2011 at 1,999,466. But many Pal estinian Jordanians were not actually refugees and do not live in camps. While some Palestinians became Jordanian citizens as refugees of the 1948 and 1967

wars with Israel, others became Jordanian citizens through peacetime migration following the Jordanian annexation of the West Bank in 1950.

5. Key studies of Jordanian and Palestinian identity issues include Adnan Abu Odeh, *Jordanians, Palestinians, and the Hashemite Kingdom in the Middle East Peace Process* (Washington, D.C.: United States Institute of Peace, 1999); Laurie A. Brand, "Palestinians and Jordanians: A Crisis of Identity," *Journal of Palestine Studies* 24, no. 4 (1995): 46–61; Mustafa Hamarneh, Rosemary Hollis, and Khalil Shikaki, *Jordanian-Palestinian Relations: Where To? Four Scenarios for the Future* (London: Royal Institute of International Affairs, 1997); Marc Lynch, *State Interests and Public Spheres: The International Politics of Jordan's Identity* (New York: Columbia University Press, 1999); and Joseph A. Massad, *Colonial Effects: The Making of National Identity in Jordan* (New York: Columbia University Press, 2001).

6. See, for example, Yoav Alon, *The Making of Jordan: Tribes, Colonialism, and the Modern State* (London: I. B. Tauris, 2007); Yoav Alon, *The Shaykh of Shaykhs: Mithqal al-Fayiz and Tribal Leadership in Modern Jordan* (Stanford: Stanford University Press, 2016); Schirin H. Fathi, *Jordan—An Invented Nation? Tribe-State Dynamics and the Formation of National Identity* (Hamburg: Deutches Orient-Institut, 1994); Linda Layne, *Home and Homeland: The Dialogics of Tribal and National Identities in Jordan* (Princeton, N.J.: Princeton University Press, 1994); Massad, *Colonial Effects*; and Andrew Shryock, *Nationalism and the Geneological Imagination* (Berkeley: University of California Press, 1997).

7. Naseem Tarawneh, "Troubling Tribalism," *Jordan Business* (June 2010): 69.

8. Sean Yom and Wael al-Khatib, "Jordan's New Politics of Tribal Dissent," *Foreign Policy, Middle East Channel*, August 7, 2012.

9. Luisa Gandolfo, *Palestinians in Jordan: The Politics of Identity* (London: I. B. Tauris, 2012), 267.

10. Asher Susser, "The Palestinians in Jordan: Demographic Majority, Political Minority," in *Minorities and the State in the Arab World*, ed. Ofra Bengio and Gabriel Ben-Dor (Boulder, Colo.: Lynne Rienner, 1999).

11. Hisham Bustani, "Jordan's New Opposition and the Traps of Identity and Ambiguity," *Jadaliyya*, April 20, 2011, http://www.jadaliyya.com/pages/index /1303.

12. Marianne Marar, "I Know There Is No Justice: Palestinian Perceptions of Higher Education in Jordan," *Intercultural Education* 22, no. 2 (2011): 177–90; Marianne Marar, "Dual/Duel Identities: Jordanian Perceptions of Academic Equity," *Intercultural Education* 20, no. 4 (2009): 371–78; and Riad Nasser, "Exclusion and the Making of Jordanian National Identity: An Analysis of School Textbooks," *Nationalism and Ethnic Politics* 10 (2004): 221–49.

13. Fathi, *Jordan—An Invented Nation?*; Layne, *Home and Homeland*; and Massad, *Colonial Effects*.

14. Hassan A. Barari, "Four Decades After Black September: A Jordanian Perspective," *Civil Wars* 10, no. 3 (2008): 231–43.

15. Mohammed Ali al-Oudat and Ayman Alshboul, Ayman, "'Jordan First': Tribalism, Nationalism and Legitimacy of Power in Jordan," *Intellectual Discourse* 18, no. 1 (2010): 65–96; and Andrew Shryock, "Dynastic Modernism and Its Contradictions: Testing the Limits of Pluralism, Tribalism, and King Hussein's Example in Hashemite Jordan," *Arab Studies Quarterly* 22, no. 3 (2000): 57–79.

16. Nawaf Tell, *Jordanian Security Sector Governance Between Theory and Practice*, Working Paper no. 145 (Geneva: Geneva Centre for the Democratic Control of Armed Forces, 2004).

17. Yitzhak Reiter, "The Palestinian-Transjordanian Rift: Economic Might and Political Power in Jordan," *Middle East Journal* 58, no. 1 (2004): 72–92.

18. Adnan Abu Odeh, *Jordanians, Palestinians, and the Hashemite Kingdom in the Middle East Peace Process* (Washington, D.C.: United States Institute of Peace Press, 1999), 198.

19. Author interview, Amman, June 2005.

20. Author interview, Amman, May 2006.

21. *Wasta* refers to the use of family and clan influence and connections to get ahead in public life. The quote is from an author interview, Amman, May 2006.

22. Author interview, Amman, June 2010.

23. Author interview, Amman, June 2011.

24. Author interview, Amman, June 2011.

25. See detailed accounts of these debates in Lynch, *State Interests and Public Spheres.*

26. Curtis R. Ryan, "'We Are All Jordan' . . . But Who Is We?" *Middle East Report Online*, July 13, 2010, http://www.merip.org/mero/mero071310.

27. Hisham Bustani, "Jordan: A Failed Uprising and a Regime in Renewal," *Your Middle East*, May 6, 2013.

28. The discussion in this and the next several paragraphs is based on author interviews in Amman, June 2010.

29. Nicolas Pelham, "Jordan's Balancing Act," *Middle East Report Online*, February 22, 2011, http://www.merip.org/mero/mero022211.

30. Author interview, Amman, June 2012.

31. Author discussions with state and security officials, Amman, June 2011.

32. Author interview, Amman, June 2011.

33. See, for example, Shryock, "Dynastic Modernism and Its Contradictions," 66–70.

34. Author interview, Amman, June 12, 2011.

35. Asaf David, "The Revolt of Jordan's Military Veterans," *Foreign Policy, Middle East Channel*, June 16, 2010, http://mideast.foreignpolicy.com/articles/2010/06/15; Robert Fisk, "Why Jordan Is Occupied by Palestinians," *Independent*, July 22, 2010: 26.

36. Author interview, Amman, December 2011.

37. Pelham, "Jordan's Balancing Act."

38. In interviews in Jordan in June 2010, December 2010, and June 2011, I heard variations of these complaints from countless Jordanians, even though I never once asked about attitudes regarding the queen.

39. Laurie A. Brand, Rym Kaki, and Joshua Stacher, "First Ladies as Focal Points for Discontent," *Foreign Policy, Middle East Channel*, February 16, 2011, http://mideast.foreignpolicy.com/posts/2011/02/16.

40. "Alf shakhsiyya Urduniyya tarfad al-tadakhul bi Surriya wa al-kunfadral iyya" (A thousand Jordanian figures reject intervention in Syria and confederation), *Saraya News*, April 30, 2013, http://www.sarayanews.com/index.php?page=article&id=196518#.UX-fw1fvjaY.facebook.

41. Curtis R. Ryan, "Jordan's Security Dilemmas," *Foreign Policy, Middle East Channel*, May 1, 2013, http://foreignpolicy.com/2013/05/01/jordans-security-dilemmas/.

42. "Alf shakhsiyya Urduniyya tarfad al-tadakhul bi Surriya wa al-kunfadraliyya."

43. "Senate President Taher al-Masri Discusses Syria," *Jordan Vista*, April 30, 2013, http://vista.sahafi.jo/art.php?id=46dc335c6491f985305d82db3690b1b1b1aa5ef8.

44. The Facebook group can be found at http://www.facebook.com/shabab24march.

45. Author interview, Amman, June 2011.

46. Author interview, Amman, June 2011.

47. Author interview, Amman, June 2011.

48. Author interview, Amman, July 2001.

49. The Faisali and Wahdat soccer teams have tended to dominate Jordan's Premier League of football, with Faisali known for a strong, nationalist, East Banker fan base, versus a strongly Palestinian nationalist fan base for Wahdat. Fans of both clubs have been known to taunt one another with chants that police and security forces sometimes find to be subversive, and at times this has erupted into violence. At other times, the drama remains on the football pitch rather than in the stands. See, for example, the discussion by James Montague, "Football's Greatest Rivalries: al-Faisaly v al-Wehdat, *World Soccer*, December 26, 2015, http://www.worldsoccer.com/features/footballs-greatest-rivalries-al-faisaly-v-al-wehdat-366655.

6. Struggles Over Elections and Electoral Systems

1. In this chapter I draw on initial online thoughts and blog posts regarding the various twists and turns of Jordanian electoral law debates. These changed so many times in such a short time that the online posts turned into something

of a running tally of changes. I have not simply reproduced those commentaries for this chapter, but I have drawn on them to get the details correct. The first of these was Curtis R. Ryan, "Déjà Vu All Over Again? Jordan's 2010 Elections," *Foreign Policy, Middle East Channel*, November 15, 2010, http://foreignpolicy.com/2010/11/15/deja-vu-all-over-again-jordans-2010-elections/.

2. On these debates and the elections of 1989, 1993, and 1997, see Curtis R. Ryan, *Jordan in Transition: From Hussein to Abdullah* (Boulder: Lynne Rienner, 2002), chap. 2.

3. Author interviews, Amman, Jordan, December 2010.

4. Ryan, "Déjà Vu All Over Again?"

5. Author interviews with Jordanian reform activists and with Jordanian conservatives opposed to opening the political system, Amman, June 2011.

6. Author interviews with activists, Amman, June 2011 and May 2012.

7. Curtis R. Ryan, "The Implications of Jordan's New Electoral Law," *Foreign Policy, Middle East Channel*, April 12, 2012, http://foreignpolicy.com/2012/04/13/the-implications-of-jordans-new-electoral-law/.

8. Curtis R. Ryan, "Jordan's High Stakes Electoral Reform," *Foreign Policy, Middle East Channel*, June 29, 2012, http://foreignpolicy.com/2012/06/29/jordans-high-stakes-electoral-reform/.

9. Author interview with King Abdullah II, Amman, December 2012.

10. Curtis R. Ryan, "What's New (Maybe) in Jordan," *Foreign Policy, Middle East Channel*, October 11, 2012, http://foreignpolicy.com/2012/10/11/whats-maybe-new-in-jordan/.

11. Author interview with 'Abd al-Ilah al-Khatib, Amman, May 2012.

12. Author interview with 'Abd al-Ilah al-Khatib, Amman, May 2012.

13. Curtis R. Ryan, "What to Expect from Jordan's Elections," *Foreign Policy, Middle East Channel*, January 18, 2013, http://foreignpolicy.com/2013/01/18/what-to-expect-from-jordans-elections/.

14. King Abdullah II, Discussion Paper no. 4: "Toward Democratic Empowerment and 'Active Citizenship,'" June 2, 2013, http://www.kingabdullah.jo/index.php/en_US/pages/view/id/253.html.

15. Author interview with King Abdullah II, Amman, May 21, 2012.

16. King Abdullah II, Discussion Paper no. 5: "Goals, Achievements, and Conventions: Pillars for Deepening Our Democratic Transition," September 12, 2014, http://kingabdullah.jo/index.php/en_US/pages/view/id/254.html.

17. This eyewitness description is based on my participation as an international election observer in 2013 for the polls with the National Democratic Institute (NDI) electoral observation team.

18. Curtis R. Ryan, "Jordan's Unfinished Journey: Parliamentary Elections and the State of Reform," Policy Brief, Project on Middle East Democracy

(POMED), March 2013, http://pomed.org/wp-content/uploads/2013/03
/POMED-Policy-Brief-Ryan-March-2013.pdf.

19. "Jordanian Islamists Step Up Anti-election Threats," *National*, January 16, 2013.
Hamza Mansour made similar comments to me when I asked him about this
in the context of my role as an election observer with the NDI in 2013.

20. Curtis R. Ryan, "Elections, Parliament, and a 'New' Prime Minister
in Jordan," *Foreign Policy, Middle East Channel*, March 11, 2013, http://for
eignpolicy.com/2013/03/11/elections-parliament-and-a-new-prime-minister
-in-jordan/.

21. Author interviews with regime officials, Amman, June 2014.

22. Raed Omari, "New Electoral Law Sheds One Vote System," *Jordan Times*, September 1, 2015, http://www.jordantimes.com/news/local/new-elections-bill
-sheds-one-vote-system.

23. "Tanshur muswada qanun al-intikhab" (Draft electoral law published),
Ammon News, August 31, 2015, http://www.ammonnews.net/article.aspx
?articleno=241404.

24. Bethan Staton, "Jordan's Women Fight for Political Representation," *al-Jazeera*,
March 8, 2016, http://www.aljazeera.com/news/2016/03/jordan-women
-fight-political-representation-160306101829565.html.

25. Staton, "Jordan's Women Fight for Political Representation."

26. "Less than 40 Percent of Voters Will Go to Polls," *Jordan Times*, August 21,
2016, http://www.jordantimes.com/news/local/less-40-eligible-voters-will-go
-polls-19-undecided-%E2%80%94-study.

27. Aaron Magid, "Why Many Jordanians Have Little Stomach for Upcoming
Elections," *Al-Monitor*, July 25, 2016, http://www.al-monitor.com/pulse
/originals/2016/07/jordan-parliamentary-elections-boycott.html.

28. Author interview, Amman, August 2016.

29. Author interview, Amman, August 2016.

30. IEC, http://www.entikhabat.jo/ar.

31. IEC video, https://www.youtube.com/watch?v=GNPUHRanHso&feature
=youtu.be.

32. See, for example, their reports at http://www.hayatcenter.org/publi
cations/.

33. Hisham Bustani, "Himna Mustadamna: al-Intakhabat kaada li ta'ziz ihtikar al-
Sulta" (Sustainable dominance: the elections as a tool to strengthen the monopoly of power), *7iber*, August, 28, 2016, http://7iber.com/politics-economics
/monopolizing-power-through-elections/#.V9hx8_orKhc.

34. Anja Wehler-Schoek, "Parliamentary Elections in Jordan: A Competition of
Mixed Messages," *Friedrich Ebert Stiftung* (September 2016), http://library.fes
.de/pdf-files/iez/12783.pdf.

35. Ma'an list, Amman, District 3, http://maanlist.com/.

36. Curtis R. Ryan, "One Society of Muslim Brothers in Jordan or Two?" *Middle East Report Online*, March 5, 2015, http://merip.org/one-society-muslim-brothers-jordan-or-two.

37. Muhammad Abu Rumman, "ad-Din wa al-Intakhabat fi al-Urdun" (Religion and elections in Jordan), *al-Araby al-Jadid*, September 11, 2016, https://www.alaraby.co.uk/opinion/2016/9/10.

38. Author interview, Amman, August 2016.

7. Rebooting Reform

1. Rex Brynen, "Economic Crisis and Post-Rentier Democratization in the Arab World: The Case of Jordan," *Canadian Journal of Political Science* 25, no. 1 (1992): 69–97; Malik Mufti, "Elite Bargains and the Onset of Political Liberalization in Jordan," *Comparative Political Studies* 32, no. 1 (1999): 100–129; and Glenn E. Robinson, "Defensive Democratization in Jordan," *International Journal of Middle East Studies* 30, no. 3 (1998): 387–410.

2. Hani Hourani et al., *Dirasat fi al-Intakhabat al-Niyabiyya al-Urduniyya* (Studies in the 1997 representative [parliamentary] elections) (Amman: al-Urdun al-Jadid Research Center, 2002); Curtis R. Ryan and Jillian Schwedler, "Return to Democratization or New Hybrid Regime? The 2003 Elections in Jordan," *Middle East Policy* 11, no. 2 (2004): 138–51; and Curtis R. Ryan, "Elections and Parliamentary Democratization in Jordan," *Democratization* 5, no. 4 (1998): 194–214.

3. For a detailed analysis of Jordan's political and economic liberalization process and its transition from King Hussein to King Abdullah II, see Curtis R. Ryan, *Jordan in Transition: From Hussein to Abdullah* (Boulder, Colo.: Lynne Rienner, 2002).

4. Laurie A. Brand, "The Effects of the Peace Process on Political Liberalization in Jordan," *Journal of Palestine Studies* 28, no. 2 (1999): 52–67; and Jillian Schwedler, "Don't Blink: Jordan's Democratic Opening and Closing," *MERIP Press Information Note*, July 3, 2002, http://www.merip.org/mero/mero070302.

5. For detailed analyses of Jordanian policy and these two events, see Curtis R. Ryan, *Inter-Arab Alliances: Regime Security and Jordanian Foreign Policy* (Gainesville: University Press of Florida, 2009), chaps. 10 and 12.

6. Brand, "The Effects of the Peace Process"; and Schwedler, "Don't Blink."

7. For details and analysis, see Ryan, *Jordan in Transition*, 87–107.

8. Abul-Wahab Kayyali, "Reaping What We've Sown: The Economic Protests," *JO Magazine*, April 28, 2011. On the economic reform process, see Anne M. Peters and Pete W. Moore, "Beyond Boom and Bust: External Rents, Durable Authoritarianism, and Institutional Adaptation in the Hashemite

Kingdom of Jordan," *Studies in Comparative International Development* 44, no. 3 (2009): 256–85; and Sufian Alissa, *Rethinking Economic Reform in Jordan: Confronting Socioeconomic Realities*, Carnegie Papers no. 4 (Washington, D.C.: Carnegie Endowment for International Peace, July 2007).

9. Mustafa Hamarneh, "Political Truths: Interview," *Jordan Business* (March 2009): 58.

10. For a detailed discussion of this phenomenon in the context of the Arab world, see Curtis R. Ryan, "Security Dilemmas in Arab Politics," in Ryan, *Inter-Arab Alliances*, 23–42.

11. International Crisis Group, "The Challenge of Political Reform: Jordanian Democratisation and Regional Instability," *Middle East Briefing*, Amman/Brussels, October 8, 2003, 1.

12. International Crisis Group, "The Challenge of Political Reform," 2.

13. Jackson Diehl, "Jordan's Democracy Option," *Washington Post*, September 21, 2003.

14. Muasher's own discussion of the struggle for the National Agenda for reform is in Marwan Muasher, *The Arab Center: The Promise of Moderation* (New Haven, Conn.: Yale University Press, 2008). See specifically the discussion of the Arab reform question, 230–58.

15. Author interview, Amman, Jordan, May 2005.

16. Author interview, Amman, May 2005.

17. Author interview with Dr. Marwan Muasher. Washington, D.C., May 1, 2010.

18. For a discussion of resurgent ethnic identity politics in Jordan, see Curtis R. Ryan, " 'We Are All Jordan' . . . But Who Is We?," *Middle East Report Online*, July 13, 2010, http://www.merip.org/mero/mero071310.

19. Author interviews, Amman, June 2011 and June 2012.

20. Author interview, Amman, June 2011.

21. See the analysis by Ziad Abu Rish, who examines controversial 2016 amendments (discussed in chapter 8) in the context of Jordan's broader constitutional traditions. Ziad Abu Rish, "The Façade of Jordanian Reform: A Brief History of the Constitution," *Jadaliyya*, May 31, 2016, http://palestine.jadaliyya.com/pages/index/24563/the-facade-of-jordanian-reform_a-brief-history-of-.

22. Author interview, Amman, May 2012.

23. Author interview, Amman, June 2014.

24. See, for example, Daniel Brumberg, "The Trap of Liberalized Autocracy," *Journal of Democracy* 13, no. 4 (October 2002): 56–68; Thomas Carothers, "The End of the Transition Paradigm," *Journal of Democracy* 13, no. 2 (January 2002): 5–21; and Ryan and Schwedler, "Return to Democratization or New Hybrid Regime?"

25. Curtis R. Ryan, "The King's Speech," *Foreign Policy, Middle East Channel*, June 17, 2011, http://foreignpolicy.com/2011/06/17/the-kings-speech/.

26. Author interview, Amman, June 2011.

27. Ryan, "The King's Speech."

28. Marwan Muasher, "Jordan's Proposed Constitutional Amendments— A First Step in the Right Direction," Carnegie Endowment for International Peace, August 17, 2011, http://carnegieendowment.org/2011/08/17/jordan -s-proposed-constitutional-amendments-first-step-in-right-direction-pub -45366.

29. King Abdullah II Discussion Papers, http://www.kingabdullah.jo/index.php /en_US/pages/view/id/244.html.

30. King Abdullah II, Discussion Paper no. 5: "Goals, Achievements, and Conventions: Pillars for Deepening Our Democratic Transition," September 12, 2014, http://kingabdullah.jo/index.php/en_US/pages/view/id/254.html.

31. Author interview with Dr. Omar Razzaz, Amman, June 16, 2014.

32. Privatization Evaluation Committee, "Report: Privatization in Jordan: Evaluating the Past for the Sake of the Future," Amman, March 2014.

33. Author interview, Amman, June 2010.

34. Anne Marie Baylouny, "Militarizing Welfare: Neo-Liberalism and Jordanian Policy," *Middle East Journal* 62, no. 2 (Spring 2008): 277–303.

35. Author interview with Fayez Tarawneh, Amman, June 10, 2010.

36. Author interview, Amman, June 2010.

37. Osama al-Sharif, "Jordan's Reform Agenda on Hold," *al-Monitor*, October 28, 2013, http://www.al-monitor.com/pulse/originals/2013/10/jordan-focus -economic-security-reform-syrian-crisis.html

38. Sharif, "Jordan's Reform Agenda on Hold."

39. Author interviews, Amman, June 2015 and August 2016.

40. Constitution of the Hashemite Kingdom of Jordan, with amendments, https://www.iec.jo/sites/default/files/Jordan%20amended%20constitu tion%20%202016%20EN_0.pdf.

41. Rana Sweis, "Women's Rights at a Standstill in Jordan," *New York Times*, November 7, 2012, http://www.nytimes.com/2012/11/08/world/middleeast /womens-rights-at-a-standstill-in-jordan.html.

42. Rana Husseini, "In Historic Vote, House Abolishes Controversial Article 308," *Jordan Times*, August 1, 2017, http://www.jordantimes.com/news/local /historic-vote-house-abolishes-controversial-article-308.

43. Naseem Tarawneh, "Jordan's Internet Goes Dark," *Foreign Policy, Middle East Channel*, August 31, 2012, http://foreignpolicy.com/2012/08/31/jordans -internet-goes-dark/.

44. "Internet Blocking Begins in Jordan," *7iber*, June 2, 2013, http://www .7iber.com/2013/06/internet-blocking-begins-in-jordan/.

45. Author interview, Amman, June 2013.

46. Author interview, Amman, June 2013.

47. Author interview, Amman, June 2013.
48. Curtis R. Ryan, "Jordan's Web Blocking Controversy," *Foreign Policy, Middle East Channel*, June 20, 2013, http://foreignpolicy.com/2013/06/20 /jordans-website-blocking-controversy/.
49. Kirk H. Sowell, "Jordan's Quest for Decentralization," *Sada Journal*, Carnegie Endowment for International Peace, August 24, 2017, http://carnegieendow ment.org/sada/72905?utm_content=buffer46058&utm_medium=social&utm _source=twitter.com&utm_campaign=buffer.
50. Author interview, Amman, June 2015.
51. Author interview, Amman, June 2012.
52. Author interview, Amman, June 2011.
53. Author interview, Amman, June 2014.
54. Author interview, Amman, June 2011.
55. Marwan Muasher, *A Decade of Struggling Reform Efforts in Jordan: The Resilience of the Rentier System*, Carnegie Papers (Washington, D.C.: Carnegie Endowment for International Peace, May 2011), 23.

8. War, Refugees, and Regional Insecurity

1. Author interview, Amman, Jordan, June 2012.
2. Julian Barnes-Dacey, "The War Next Door: Syria and the Erosion of Stability in Lebanon, Jordan and Turkey," European Council on Foreign Relations (ECFR), *Policy Brief* no. 182 (July 2016).
3. On the international relations dynamics of the Syrian war and why it is reminiscent of the old "Arab Cold War," see Curtis R. Ryan, "The New Arab Cold War and the Struggle for Syria," *Middle East Report* 262 (Spring 2012): 28–31.
4. Curtis R. Ryan, "The Odd Couple: Ending the Jordanian-Syrian 'Cold War,'" *Middle East Journal* 60, no. 1 (2006): 33–56.
5. Edward W. Gnehm, "Jordan and the Current Unrest in Syria," United States Institute of Peace, *Peace Brief* 114, November 7, 2011.
6. These assessments are based on multiple interviews with Jordanian security and foreign policy officials in 2011, 2012, 2013, and 2014.
7. As the Jordanians predicted when they argued against a U.S. invasion of Iraq, political violence and terrorism followed the U.S. invasion and occupation and eventually spilled over into Jordan itself. Al-Qa'ida in Iraq emerged as a force (led for a time by a militant Jordanian national, Abu Musab al-Zarqawi) and eventually struck Jordan in what Jordanians consider to be "their 9/11." On November 9, 2005, suicide bombers struck three luxury hotels in Amman, killing more than sixty people.

8. Tony Karon, "Jordan Is Living Dangerously as Syria Burns," *Time*, January 16, 2013.

9. Gnehm, "Jordan and the Current Unrest in Syria."

10. Yezid Sayigh, "Jordan Reluctantly Takes Sides in Syria," al-Hayat via Carnegie Middle East Center, November 6, 2013.

11. Curtis R. Ryan, "A New Diplomatic Rift Between Jordan and Syria," *Middle East Report Online*, May 29, 2014, http://www.merip.org/new-diplomatic-rift-between-jordan-syria.

12. Dale Gavlak and Jamal Halabi, "Officials: Arms Shipments Rise to Syrian Rebels," *Associated Press*, March 27, 2013.

13. See, for example, the analyses by Nicolas Pelham, "Jordan's Syria Problem," *New York Review of Books Blog*, January 16, 2013; and Julian Borger and Nick Hopkins, "West Training Syrian Rebels in Jordan," *Guardian*, March 8, 2013.

14. Curtis R. Ryan, "Jordan's Security Dilemmas," *Foreign Policy, Middle East Channel*, May 1, 2013, http://foreignpolicy.com/2013/05/01/jordans-security-dilemmas/.

15. Author interviews, Amman, June 2014.

16. Author interviews, Amman, June 2014.

17. Author interviews, Amman, June 2015.

18. Yezid Sayigh, "Saudi-US Rift Pulls Jordan in Opposite Directions," *al-Monitor*, November 6, 2013, http://www.al-monitor.com/pulse/security/2013/11/jordan-torn-between-saudi-and-us.html.

19. Osama al-Sharif, "Jordan Sharpens Focus on IS as Gulf Confronts Iran," *al-Monitor*, April 1, 2015, http://www.al-monitor.com/pulse/originals/2015/04/jordan-yemen-saudi-iran-is-houthis-airstrike-fighting.html.

20. Osama al-Sharif, "Will Saudi Arabia Pressure Jordan to Join Ground Offensive in Syria?" *al-Monitor*, February 22, 2016, http://www.al-monitor.com/pulse/originals/2016/02/will-jordan-join-saudi-arabia-ground-invasion-syria.html.

21. Author interviews, Amman, June 2014 and June 2015.

22. Alexandra Francis, *Jordan's Refugee Crisis* (Washington D.C.: Carnegie Endowment for International Peace, 2015).

23. Musa Shteiwi, Jonathan Walsh, and Christina Klassen, *Coping with Crisis: A Review of the Response to Syrian Refugees in Jordan* (Amman: Center for Strategic Studies, 2014).

24. On these and many other points, I am indebted to Andrew Harper. Author interview with Andrew Harper, head of the UNHCR in Jordan, Khalda, Jordan, June 2015, and in Amman, August 2016.

25. Vicky Kelberer, "Seeking Shelter in Jordan's Cities: Housing Security and Urban Humanitarianism in the Syria Crisis," *Middle East Report Online*, November 5, 2015, http://www.merip.org/mero/mero110515.

26. Jordan's IMF austerity measures, and resultant riots were reminiscent of earlier such episodes in both 1989 and 1996. See Curtis R. Ryan, "Peace, Bread, and Riots: Jordan and the International Monetary Fund," *Middle East Policy* 6, no. 2 (Fall 1998): 54–66.

27. I am drawing here on an earlier online post that was, in effect, a dispatch from Za'atari: Curtis R. Ryan, "Refugee Need and Resilience in Zaatari," *Middle East Report Online*, June 22, 2014, http://www.merip.org/refugee-need -resilience-zaatari.

28. Denis Sullivan and Sarah Tobin, "Security and Resilience Among Syrian Refugees in Jordan," *Middle East Report Online*, October 14, 2014, http://merip .org/mero/mero101414.

29. This section draws on an earlier online piece, Curtis R. Ryan, "The Most Important Soccer Is Not Being Played in Brazil, but in Refugee Camps in Jordan," Monkey Cage Blog, *Washington Post*, June 20, 2014, http://www .washingtonpost.com/blogs/monkey-cage/wp/2014/06/20/the-most -important-soccer-is-not-being-played-in-brazil-but-in-refugee-camps-in -jordan/.

30. Author interview with Prince Ali bin al-Hussein, Amman, June 17, 2014.

31. Discussions with a Jordanian official from a northern governorate, June 2015.

32. See the more detailed analysis by Reva Dhingra, "Losing Syria's Youngest Generation: The Educational Crisis Facing Syrian Refugees in Jordan," *Middle East Report Online*, March 2, 2016, http://www.merip.org/mero /mero030216.

33. Discussions with Jordanian officials from the northern governorates, June 2015.

34. Merissa Khurma, "The Promise of Magdoos: A Sliver of Hope in the Syrian Refugee Crisis," *Harvard Kennedy School Review*, June 20, 2016, http://har vardkennedyschoolreview.com/the-promise-of-magdoos-a-sliver-of-hope -in-the-syrian-refugee-crisis/.

35. P. R. Kumaraswamy and Manjari Singh, "Population Pressure in Jordan and the Role of Syrian Refugees," *Migration and Development* 6, no. 3 (2016): 1–16.

36. Discussions with Jordanian officials from the northern governorates, June 2015.

37. Author interview with Daoud Kuttab. Amman, June 4, 2013.

38. Remarks of President Obama and His Majesty King Abdullah II of Jordan in Joint Press Conference, March 22, 2013, https://www.whitehouse .gov/the-press-office/2013/03/22/remarks-president-obama-and-his-majesty -king-abdullah-ii-jordan-joint-pr.

39. Doris Carrion, *Syrian Refugees in Jordan: Confronting Difficult Truths*, Middle East and North Africa Program, Chatham House, Royal Institute of International Affairs, September 2015, 7.

40. "Peace, Bread, and Work: Syrian Refugees in Jordan," *Economist*, May 7, 2016, http://www.economist.com/news/middle-east-and-africa/21698260-jobs-syrian-refugees-help-them-and-their-hosts-and-slow-their-exodus-peace.

41. Author interview, Amman, June 2015.

42. Svein Erik Stave and Solveig Hillesund, *Impact of Syrian Refugees on the Jordanian Labour Market* (Geneva and Beirut: International Labor Organization and FAFO, April 2015).

43. Sean Yom and Katrina Sammour, "Counterterrorism and Youth Radicalization in Jordan: Social and Political Dimensions," Combating Terrorism Center at West Point, *CTC Sentinal* 10, no. 4 (April 14, 2017): 25–30.

44. *Jordan Times*, October 20, 2014, http://jordantimes.com/there-is-no-grey-area-in-anti-terror-fight-king.

45. Remarks by H. M. King Abdullah II, 70th Plenary Session of the United Nations General Assembly, United Nations, New York, September 28, 2015.

46. Taylor Luck, "Four Imams Banned for Pro-Islamic State Sermons," *Jordan Times*, October 22, 2014, http://jordantimes.com/four-imams-banned-for-pro-islamic-state-friday-sermons.

47. Author interviews with Jordanian officials, Amman, June 2014.

48. David Schenker, "Preventing ISIS Inroads in Jordan," *Policy Watch* 2311, Washington Institute, September 3, 2014, http://www.washingtoninstitute.org/policy-analysis/view/preventing-isis-inroads-in-jordan.

49. "Lower House Endorses Constitutional Amendments," *Ammon News*, August 24, 2014, http://en.ammonnews.net/article.aspx?articleno=26439#.U_yvIU3lpdh.

50. Jillian Schwedler, "Jordan Drops the Pretense of Democratic Reform," *Middle East Report Online*, April 28, 2016, http://www.merip.org/jordan-drops-pretense-democratic-reform.

51. Osama al-Sharif, "Jordan's King Pushes to Expand Military, Intelligence Authority," *al-Monitor*, August 25, 2014, http://www.al-monitor.com/pulse/originals/2014/08/jordan-king-constitution-amendments.html.

52. Author interviews, Amman, August 2016.

53. Sufian Obeidat, "Jordan's 2016 Constitutional Amendments: A Return to Absolute Monarchy?" *Constitutionnet*, May 27, 2016, http://www.constitutionnet.org/news/jordans-2016-constitutional-amendments-return-absolute-monarchy. See also an earlier assessment of the reform process in Sufian Obeidat, "Jordan: A Flowerless Spring," *Arab Reform Initiative, Arab Reform Brief* 61 (August 2012), www.arab-reform.net/en/file/479/download?token=OQ2hnXZg.

54. Curtis R. Ryan, "Security Dilemmas and the Security State Question in Jordan," in *POMEPS Studies* 11: *The Arab Thermidor: The Resurgence of the Security*

State, February 27, 2017, 52–55, https://pomeps.org/wp-content/uploads
/2015/03/POMEPS_Studies_11_Thermidor_Web.pdf.

55. Taylor Luck, "50 Salafists Arrested," *Jordan Times*, August 27, 2014, http://
jordantimes.com/50-salafists-arrested.

56. On Maqdisi and Salafism in Jordan, see Joas Wagamakers, *A Quietist Jihadi:
The Ideology and Influence of Abu Muhammad al-Maqdisi* (Cambridge: Cambridge
University Press, 2012).

57. Author interviews, Amman, June 2015.

58. Osama al-Sharif, "Jordan's King Fends off Critics of ISIS War, Holds
Firm on al-Aqsa," *al-Monitor*, November 10, 2014, http://www.al-monitor
.com/pulse/originals/2014/11/jordan-king-internal-criticism-islamic-state
-al-aqsa.html.

59. The quotation is from an article by William Booth and Taylor Luck, who also
noted that "for those who adhere to the new guidelines, there are government
salaries of about $600 a month, religious workshops, travel assistance for pil-
grimages to Mecca, and weekly guidance. The ministry is providing suggested
topics for Friday sermons, available for download from the government's Facebook page." See Booth and Luck, "To Counter the Rise of Islamic State, Jordan Imposes Rules on Clerics," *Washington Post*, November 9, 2014, http://www
.washingtonpost.com/world/middle_east/to-counter-rise-of-the-islamic
-state-jordan-imposes-rules-on-muslim-clerics/2014/11/09/4d5fce22-5937
-11e4-bd61-346aee66ba29_story.html?wpmk=MK0000203.

60. Michael Robbins and Lawrence Rubin, "The Rise of Official Islam in Jordan," *Politics, Religion & Ideology* 14, no. 1 (2013).

61. Julian Pecquet, "Jordan's King Tells Congress 'Gloves Are off' in Fight Against
ISIS," *al-Monitor*, February 3, 2015, http://www.al-monitor.com/pulse/origi
nals/2015/02/jordan-pilot-islamic-state-congress-aid-package.html.

62. Suleiman al-Khalidi, "Jordanian King Vows 'Relentless' War on Islamic State's
Own Ground," *Reuters*, February 4, 2015, http://www.reuters.com/article/us
-mideast-crisis-killing-idUSKBN0L71XE20150204.

63. See, for example, the analysis by Tuqa Nusairat, "Jordan's Pilot and the
War on ISIS," *MenaSource* blog, Atlantic Council, February 3, 2015, http://
www.atlanticcouncil.org/blogs/menasource/jordan-s-pilot-and-the-war
-on-isis.

64. Ala' al-Rababa'h, "Public Outrage in Jordan at Murder of Pilot," Carnegie
Endowment for International Peace, February 4, 2015, http://carnegieen
dowment.org/syriaincrisis/?fa=58964.

65. See, for example, the poignant piece written by Alice Su, "It Wasn't Their
War," *Atlantic* (February 2015), http://www.theatlantic.com/international
/archive/2015/02/jordan-isis-pilot-response/385199/.

66. Peter Moore, "Jordan's Long War Economy," *Jadaliyya*, August 29, 2017, http://www.jadaliyya.com/pages/index/27078/jordan%E2%80%99s-long-war-economy.

67. Taylor Luck and William Booth, "Gunman in Jordan Kills 4, Including 2 Americans, at Police Training Site," *Washington Post*, November 9. 2015.

68. Rana Sweis, "Jordanian Sentenced to Life in Prison for Killing 3 U.S. Soldiers," *New York Times*, July 17, 2017, https://www.nytimes.com/2017/07/17/world/middleeast/jordan-killing-us-soldiers.html.

69. Sara Elizabeth Williams, "The Enemy Within: Jordan's Battle with Home-grown Terror," *Middle East Eye*, March 2, 2016, http://www.middleeasteye.net/news/enemy-within-jordans-battle-stop-home-grown-terrorism-481722991.

70. Williams, "The Enemy Within."

71. Kirk Sowell quoted in Williams, "The Enemy Within." See also his detailed analysis of these movements in Kirk H. Sowell, "Jordanian Salafism and the Jihad in Syria," Hudson Institute, March 12, 2015, http://hudson.org/research/11131-jordanian-salafism-and-the-jihad-in-syria.

72. Jeremy M. Sharp, "Jordan: Background and U.S. Relations" (Washington, D.C.: Congressional Research Service, January 25, 2017), 7.

73. Rana F. Sweis, "ISIS Is Said to Claim Responsibility for Deadly Attack in Jordan," *New York Times*, December 20, 2016.

74. David Schenker, "Terrorist Spillover in Jordan," *Cipher Brief*, Washington Institute for Near East Policy, June 23, 2016, http://www.washingtoninstitute.org/policy-analysis/view/terrorist-spillover-in-jordan.

75. Sara Elizabeth Williams, "Analysis: Jordan, the Island of Stability Crumbling at Its Edges," *Middle East Eye*, June 27, 2016, http://www.middleeasteye.net/news/analysis-jordan-island-stability-crumbling-its-edges-2107772653.

76. Author interview, Amman, June 2014.

77. Author interview, Amman, June 2014.

78. Osama al-Sharif, "Jordan's Reform Agenda on Hold," *al-Monitor*, October 28, 2013, http://www.al-monitor.com/pulse/originals/2013/10/jordan-focus-economic-security-reform-syrian-crisis.html.

79. Ziad Abu Rish, "Doubling Down: Jordan Six Years Into the Arab Uprisings," *Jadaliyya*, February 16, 2017, http://www.jadaliyya.com/pages/index/25886/doubling-down_jordan-six-years-into-the-arab-upris.

80. Hassan A. Barari, "The Limits of Political Reform in Jordan: The Role of External Actors," Friedrich Ebert Shiftung, International Policy Analysis (December 2013), http://library.fes.de/pdf-files/iez/10455-20140108.pdf.

9. Jordanian Politics Beyond the Arab Uprisings

1. Steven Heydemann, "Upgrading Authoritarianism in the Arab World," Brookings Institution, Saban Center Analysis Paper no. 13 (2007); and Steven Heydemann and Renauld Leenders, "Authoritarian Learning and Authoritarian Resilience: Regime Responses to the Arab Awakening," *Globalizations* 8, no. 5 (2011): 647–53.
2. Author interview, Amman, Jordan, June 2013.
3. Author interview, Amman, June 2011.
4. Author interview, Amman, June 2015.
5. Author interview, Amman, June 2015.

Bibliography

Ababneh, Sarah. "Troubling the Political: Women and the Jordanian Day-Waged Labor Movement." *International Journal of Middle East Studies* 48 (2016): 87–112.

Abdalat, Muhammad Al-. *Kharita al-Ahzab al-Siyasiyya al-Urduniyya* (Map of Jordanian political parties). Amman: Dar al-Ubra, 1992.

Abu Jaber, Kamel, and Schirin H. Fathi. "The 1989 Jordanian Parliamentary Elections." *Orient* 31, no. 1 (1990): 67–86.

Abu Khusa, Amad. *al-Dimuqratiyya wa al-Ahzab al-Siyasiyya al-Urduniyya* (Democracy and Jordanian political parties). Amman: Middle East Publishing Company, 1991.

Abu Odeh, Adnan. *Jordanians, Palestinians, and the Hashemite Kingdom in the Middle East Peace Process.* Washington, D.C.: United States Institute of Peace, 1999.

Abu Rish, Ziad. "The Façade of Jordanian Reform: A Brief History of the Constitution." *Jadaliyya*, May 31, 2016. http://palestine.jadaliyya.com/pages/index /24563/the-facade-of-jordanian-reform_a-brief-history-of-.

Abu Rumman, Muhammad. *"ad-Din wa al-Intakhabat fi al-Urdun"* (Religion and elections in Jordan). *al-Araby al-Jadid*, September 11, 2016. https://www.alaraby .co.uk/opinion/2016/9/10.

———. "Jordan's Parliamentary Elections and Islamist Boycott." *Arab Reform Bulletin*, October 20, 2010.

Alissa, Sufian. *Rethinking Economic Reform in Jordan: Confronting Socioeconomic Realities.* Carnegie Papers no. 4. Washington, D.C.: Carnegie Endowment for International Peace, 2007.

Alon, Yoav. *The Making of Jordan: Tribes, Colonialism, and the Modern State.* London: I. B. Tauris, 2007.

———. *The Shaykh of Shaykhs: Mithqal al-Fayiz and Tribal Leadership in Modern Jordan.* Stanford, Calif.: Stanford University Press, 2016.

Anderson, Betty S. *Nationalist Voices in Jordan: The Street and the State.* Austin: University of Texas Press, 2005.

———. "The Status of 'Democracy' in Jordan." *Critique* 10 (1997): 55–76.

Anderson, Lisa. "Absolutism and the Resilience of Monarchy in the Middle East." *Political Science Quarterly* 106, no. 1 (1991): 1–15.

———. "Searching Where the Light Shines: Studying Democratization in the Middle East." *Annual Review of Political Science* 9 (2006): 189–214.

Andoni, Lamis. "Jordan Is Not Palestine." *Al-Jazeera,* July 4, 2010. http://english .aljazeera.net/news/2010/07/2010748131864654.html.

———. "Jordanians Demand Change." *Al-Jazeera,* February 21, 2010. http://www .aljazeera.com/indepth/opinion/2011/02/2011220105658153939.html.

Antoun, Richard. "Civil Society, Tribal Process, and Change in Jordan." *International Journal of Middle East Studies* 32 (2000): 441–63.

Bani Rashid, Zaki. "The Jordanian Spring Has Begun." *Guardian,* October 19, 2012.

Bank, André. "Rents, Cooptation, and Economizing Discourse: Three Dimensions of Political Rule in Jordan, Morocco, and Syria." *Journal of Mediterranean Studies* 14 (2004): 155–79.

Bank, André, and Oliver Schlumberger. "Jordan: Between Regime Survival and Economic Reform." In *Arab Elites: Negotiating the Politics of Change,* edited by Volker Perthes. Boulder: Lynne Rienner, 2004.

Barakat, Sultan, and Andrew Leber. "Fortress Jordan: Putting the Money to Work." *Brookings Doha Center Policy Briefing* (February 2015).

Barari, Hassan A. "Four Decades After Black September: A Jordanian Perspective." *Civil Wars* 10, no. 3 (2008): 231–43.

———. *Jordan and Israel: Ten Years Later.* Amman: Center for Strategic Studies, University of Jordan, 2004.

———. "The Limits of Political Reform in Jordan: The Role of External Actors." Friedrich Ebert Shiftung, International Policy Analysis, December 2013. http:// library.fes.de/pdf-files/iez/10455-20140108.pdf.

———. "The Persistence of Autocracy: Jordan, Morocco and the Gulf." *Middle East Critique* 24, no. 1 (2015): 99–111.

Barnes-Dacey, Julian. "Jordanian Tremors: Elusive Consensus, Deepening Discontent." European Council on Foreign Relations, *Policy Memo* no. 68, November 2012.

———. "The War Next Door: Syria and the Erosion of Stability in Lebanon, Jordan and Turkey." European Council on Foreign Relations (ECFR) *Policy Brief* no. 182, July 2016.

Bayat, Asef. *Life as Politics: How Ordinary People Change the Middle East.* Stanford, Calif.: Stanford University Press, 2010.

Baylouny, Anne Marie. "Militarizing Welfare: Neo-Liberalism and Jordanian Policy." *Middle East Journal* 62, no. 2 (Spring 2008): 277–303.

Beck, Martin. "Jordan and the 'Arab Spring:' No Challenge, No Change?" *Middle East Critique* 24, no. 1 (2015): 83–97.

Bellin, Eva. "The Robustness of Authoritarianism in the Middle East." *Comparative Politics* 36, no. 2 (2004): 139–57.

Bouziane, Malika. "The State from Below: Local Governance Practices in Jordan." *Journal of Economic and Social Research* 12, no. 1 (2010): 33–61.

Bouziane, Malika, and Katharina Lenner, "Protests in Jordan: Rumblings in the Kingdom of Dialogue." In *Protests, Revolutions, and Transformations—The Arab World in Upheaval.* Working Paper no. 1. Center for Middle Eastern & North African Studies, Freie Universitat Berlin, July 2011, 148–65.

Brand, Laurie A. "Economic and Political Liberalization in a Rentier Economy: The Case of the Hashemite Kingdom of Jordan." In *Privatization and Liberalization in the Middle East,* edited by Iliya Harik and Denis J. Sullivan. Bloomington: Indiana University Press, 1992.

——. "The Effects of the Peace Process on Political Liberalization in Jordan." *Journal of Palestine Studies* 28, no. 2 (1999): 52–67.

——. "In the Beginning Was the State . . .: The Quest for Civil Society in Jordan." In *Civil Society in the Middle East,* edited by August Richard Norton. Vol. 1. Leiden: E. J. Brill, 1995.

——. *Jordan's Inter-Arab Relations: The Political Economy of Alliance-Making.* New York: Columbia University Press, 1994.

——. "Palestinians and Jordanians: A Crisis of Identity." *Journal of Palestine Studies* 24, no. 4 (1995): 46–61.

Brand, Laurie A., Rym Kaki, and Joshua Stacher. "First Ladies as Focal Points for Discontent." *Foreign Policy, Middle East Channel,* February 16, 2011. http://mid east.foreignpolicy.com/posts/2011/02/16/first_ladies_as_focal_points_for _discontent.

Browers, Michaelle. *Political Ideology in the Arab World: Accommodation and Transformation.* Cambridge: Cambridge University Press, 1999.

Brownlee, Jason. ". . . And Yet They Persist: Explaining Survival and Transition in Neopatrimonial Regimes." *Studies in Comparative International Development* 37, no. 3 (2002): 35–63.

——. *Democracy Prevention: The Politics of the U.S.-Egyptian Alliance.* Cambridge: Cambridge University Press, 2012.

——. "Low Tide After the Third Wave: Exploring Politics Under Authoritarianism." *Comparative Politics* 34, no. 4 (2002): 477–99.

Brownlee, Jason, Tarek E. Masoud, and Andrew Reynolds, *The Arab Spring: Pathways of Repression and Reform*. Oxford: Oxford University Press, 2015.

Brumberg, Daniel. "The Trap of Liberalized Autocracy." *Journal of Democracy* 13, no. 4, (2002): 56–68.

Brynen, Rex. "Economic Crisis and Post-rentier Democratization in the Arab World." *Canadian Journal of Political Science* 25, no. 1 (1992): 69–97.

——. "The Politics of Monarchical Liberalism: Jordan." In *Political Liberalization and Democratization in the Arab World*, vol. 2: *Comparative Experiences*, edited by Rex Brynen, Bahgat Korany, and Paul Noble. Boulder, Colo.: Lynne Rienner, 1998.

Brynen, Rex, Bahgat Korany, and Paul Noble. "Introduction: Theoretical Perspectives on Arab Liberalization and Democratization." In *Political Liberalization and Democratization in the Arab World*, vol. 1, edited by Rex Brynen, Bahgat Korany, and Paul Noble. Boulder, Colo.: Lynne Rienner, 1995.

Brynen, Rex, Pete Moore, Bassel F. Salloukh, and Joelle Zahar. *Beyond the Arab Spring: Authoritarianism and Democratization in the Arab World*. Boulder, Colo.: Lynne Rienner, 2012.

Bustani, Hisham. "The Alternative Opposition in Jordan and the Failure to Understand the Lessons of Tunisian and Egyptian Revolutions." *Jadaliyya*, March 20, 2011. http://www.jadaliyya.com/pages/index/959.

——. "Himna Mustadamna. al-Intakhabat kaada li ta'ziz ihtikar al-Sulta" (Sustainable dominance: the elections as a tool to strengthen the monopoly of power). *7iber*, August 28, 2016. http://7iber.com/politics-economics/monop olizing-power-through-elections/#.V9hx8_orKhc.

——. "Jordan: A Failed Uprising and a Regime in Renewal." *Your Middle East*, May 6, 2013.

——. "Jordan's New Opposition and the Traps of Identity and Ambiguity." *Jadaliyya*, April 20, 2011. http://www.jadaliyya.com/pages/index/1303.

Carothers, Thomas. "The End of the Transition Paradigm." *Journal of Democracy* 13, no. 2 (2002): 5–21.

Carrion, Doris. *Syrian Refugees in Jordan: Confronting Difficult Truths*. Middle East and North Africa Program. Chatham House, Royal Institute of International Affairs, September 2015.

Cavatorta, Francesco. "Divided They Stand, Divided They Fail: Opposition Politics in Morocco." *Democratization* 16, no. 2 (2009): 137–56.

——. "More than Repression; Strategies of Regime Survival: The Significance of Divide et Impera in Morocco." *Journal of Contemporary African Studies* 25, no. 2 (2007): 187–203.

Chalcraft, John. *Popular Politics in the Making of the Modern Middle East*. Cambridge: Cambridge University Press, 2016.

Chatelus, Michel. "Rentier or Producer Economy in the Middle East? The Jorda-nian Response." In *The Economic Development of Jordan*, edited by Bichara Khader and Adnan Badran. London: Croom Helm, 1987.

Christophersen, Mona. *Protest and Reform in Jordan: Popular Demand and Govern-ment Response.* Oslo: Fafo Report, 2013.

Clark, Janine A. "The Conditions of Islamist Moderation: Unpacking Cross-Ideological Cooperation in Jordan." *International Journal of Middle East Studies* 38, no. 4 (2006): 539–60.

——. "Threats, Structures and Resources: Cross-Ideological Coalition Building in Jordan." *Comparative Politics* 43, no. 3 (2010): 101–20.

Cohen, Amnon. *Political Parties in the West Bank Under the Jordanian Regime, 1949–1967.* Ithaca, N.Y.: Cornell University Press, 1982.

David, Assaf. "The Revolt of Jordan's Military Veterans." *Foreign Policy, Middle East Channel,* June 16, 2010. http://mideast.foreignpolicy.com/articles/2010/06/15/the_revolt_of_jordans_military_veterans.

Day, Arthur. *East Bank/West Bank: Jordan and the Prospects for Peace.* New York: Council on Foreign Relations, 1986.

Dhingra, Reva. "Losing Syria's Youngest Generation: The Educational Crisis Fac-ing Syrian Refugees in Jordan." *Middle East Report Online,* March 2, 2016. http://www.merip.org/mero/mero030216.

Diamond, Larry. "Hybrid Regimes." *Journal of Democracy* 13, no. 2 (2002): 21–35.

Diehl, Jackson. "Jordan's Democracy Option." *Washington Post,* September 21, 2003.

Dougherty, Pamela. "The Pain of Adjustment: Kerak's Bread Riots as a Response to Jordan's Continuing Economic Restructuring Programme: A General Over-view." *Jordanies* 2 (1996): 95–99.

El-Anis, Imad. *Jordan and the United States: The Political Economy of Trade and Eco-nomic Reform in the Middle East.* London: I. B. Tauris, 2011.

Fathi, Schirin H. *Jordan—An Invented Nation? Tribe-State Dynamics and the Forma-tion of National Identity.* Hamburg: Deutsches Orient-Institut, 1994.

Feiler, Gil. "Jordan's Economy, 1970–90: The Primary of Exogenous Factors." In *Jordan in the Middle East: The Making of a Pivotal State,* edited by Joseph Nevo and Ilan Pappé. London: Frank Cass, 1994.

Fisk, Robert. "Why Jordan Is Occupied by Palestinians." *Independent,* July 22, 2010.

Fox, David, and Katrina Sammour. *Disquiet on the Jordanian Front.* Carnegie Endow-ment for International Peace, September 27, 2012.

Francis, Alexandra. *Jordan's Refugee Crisis.* Washington D.C.: Carnegie Endow-ment for International Peace, 2015.

Gandhi, Jennifer, and Ellen Lust. "Elections Under Authoritarianism." *Annual Review of Political Science* 12, no. 1 (2009): 403–22.

Gandolfo, Luisa. *Palestinians in Jordan: The Politics of Identity*. London: I. B. Tauris, 2012.

Gause, F. Gregory, III. "Kings for All Seasons: How the Middle East Monarchies Survived the Arab Spring." Brookings Doha Center Analysis Paper no. 8 (2013).

——. "Why Middle East Studies Missed the Arab Spring: The Myth of Authoritarian Stability." *Foreign Affairs* 90, no. 4 (July/August 2011): 81–90.

Gavlak, Dale, and Jamal Halabi. "Officials: Arms Shipments Rise to Syrian Rebels." *Associated Press*, March 27, 2013.

George, Alan. *Jordan: Living in the Crossfire*. London: Zed Books, 2005.

Goldberg, Jeffrey. "Monarch in the Middle: the Modern King in the Arab Spring." *Atlantic*, March 18, 2013.

Gnehm, Edward W. "Jordan and the Current Unrest in Syria." United States Institute of Peace, *Peace Brief* 114, November 7, 2011.

Greenwood, Scott. "Jordan's 'New Bargain:' The Political Economy of Regime Security." *Middle East Journal* 57 (2003): 248–68.

Hamarneh, Mustafa. "Political Truths: Interview." *Jordan Business* (March 2009): 58.

Hamarneh, Mustafa, Rosemary Hollis, and Khalil Shikaki. *Jordanian-Palestinian Relations: Where To? Four Scenarios for the Future*. London: Royal Institute of International Affairs, 1997.

Hamid, Shadi, and Courtney Freer. "How Stable Is Jordan? King Abdullah II's Half-hearted Reforms and the Challenge of the Arab Spring." *Brookings Doha Center Policy Briefing* (November 2011).

Hammad, Khalil. "The Role of Foreign Aid in the Jordanian Economy, 1959–1983." In *The Economic Development of Jordan*, edited by Bichara Khader and Adnan Badran. London: Croom Helm, 1987.

Hanieh, Adam. *Lineages of Revolt: Issues of Contemporary Capitalism in the Middle East*. Chicago: Haymarket Books, 2013.

Harrigan, Jane, Hamed al-Said, and Chengang Wang. "The IMF and the World Bank in Jordan: A Case of Over Optimism and Elusive Growth." *Review of International Organizations* 1, no. 3 (2006): 263–92.

Harris, Marty. Report 957 "Jordan's Youth After the Arab Spring." Lowy Institute for International Policy (February 2015).

Helfont, Samuel, and Tally Helfont. "Jordan Between the Arab Spring and the Gulf Cooperation Council." *Orbis* 56, no. 1 (2012).

——. "Jordan's Protests: Arab Spring Lite?" Foreign Policy Research Institute (July 2011).

Herb, Michael. *All in the Family: Absolutism, Revolution, and Democracy in the Middle Eastern Monarchies*. Albany, N.Y.: SUNY Press, 1999.

Heydemann, Steven. "Upgrading Authoritarianism in the Arab World." Brookings Institution, Saban Center Analysis Paper no. 13 (2007).

Heydemann, Steven, and Renauld Leenders. "Authoritarian Learning and Authoritarian Resilience: Regime Responses to the Arab Awakening." *Globalizations*
8, no. 5 (2011): 647–53.

Hinnebusch, Raymond. "Authoritarian Persistence, Democratization Theory and
the Middle East: An Overview and a Critique," *Democratization* 13, no. 3 (2006):
373–95.

Homoud, A. T. "Reform Gets a Heavyweight." *JO Magazine*, July 3, 2011.

Hourani, Hani, et al. *Dirasat fi al-Intakhabat al-Niyabiyya al-Urduniyya* (Studies in
the 1997 representative [parliamentary] elections). Amman: al-Urdun al-Jadid
Research Center, 2002.

Human Rights Watch. "Jordan: End Trials of Protesters for 'Undermining
Regime,'" October 29, 2013.

International Crisis Group. "The Challenge of Political Reform: Jordanian
Democratisation and Regional Instability." *Middle East Briefing*, Amman/
Brussels, October 8, 2003.

——. "Popular Protest in North Africa and the Middle East (IX): Dallying with
Reform in a Divided Jordan." *ICJ Middle East/North Africa Report* no. 118 (March
2012).

"Internet Blocking Begins in Jordan." *7iber*, June 2, 2013. http://www.7iber.com
/2013/06/internet-blocking-begins-in-jordan/.

Iyad, R. K. *al-Tayarat al-Siyasiyya fi al-Urdun wa Nas al-Mithaq al-Watani al-Urduni*
(Political tendencies in Jordan and text of the Jordanian National Charter).
Amman: Al-Matba'a al-Wataniyya, 1991.

Joffé, George, ed. *Jordan in Transition*. London: Hurst, 2002.

Kamrava, Mehran. "The Arab Spring and the Saudi-led Counter-revolution."
Orbis 56, no. 1 (2012): 96–104.

Kanaan, Taher. "Relative Roles of the Public and Private Sectors." In *The Jordanian Economy*, edited by Tejinder Minhas, Kanaan, Said Mammamy, and Ali
Kassay. Amman: Steering Committee and Allied Accountants, 1995.

Karmel, Ezra. "How Revolutionary Was Jordan's Hirak?" Identity Center.
Amman, Jordan. June 2014.

Karon, Tony. "Jordan Is Living Dangerously as Syria Burns." *Time*, January 16,
2013.

Kayyali, Abdul-Wahab. "Reaping What We've Sown: The Economic Protests."
JO Magazine, April 28, 2011.

Kelberer, Vicky. "Seeking Shelter in Jordan's Cities: Housing Security and Urban
Humanitarianism in the Syria Crisis," *Middle East Report Online*, November 5,
2015. http://www.merip.org/mero/mero110515.

Khalidi, Suleiman al-. "Divisions, Fear of Turmoil Dampen Jordanian Dissent."
Reuters, January 24, 2014. http://www.reuters.com/article/2014/01/24/us
-jordan-stability-idUSBREA0N0AK20140124.

———. "Jordanian King Vows 'Relentless' War on Islamic State's Own Ground." *Reuters*, February 4, 2015. http://www.reuters.com/article/us-mideast-crisis -killing-idUSKBN0L71XE20150204.

Khatib, Lina, and Ellen Lust, eds. *Taking to the Streets: The Transformation of Arab Activism*. Baltimore: Johns Hopkins University Press, 2014.

Khoury, Nabeel A. "The National Consultative Council of Jordan: A Study in Legislative Development." *International Journal of Middle East Studies* 13, no. 4 (1981): 427–39.

Khurma, Merissa. "The Promise of Magdoos: A Sliver of Hope in the Syrian Refugee Crisis." *Harvard Kennedy School Review*, June 20, 2016. http://harvard kennedyschoolreview.com/the-promise-of-magdoos-a-sliver-of-hope-in-the -syrian-refugee-crisis/.

Kilani, Sa'eda. "Black Year for Democracy in Jordan: The 1998 Press and Publication Law." Working Paper of the Danish Centre for Human Rights/ Euro-Mediterranean Human Rights Network, 1998.

King Abdullah II. Discussion Papers. http://www.kingabdullah.jo/index.php/en _US/pages/view/id/244.html.

———. Discussion Paper No. 4: "Toward Democratic Empowerment and 'Active Citizenship,'" June 2, 2013. http://www.kingabdullah.jo/index.php/en_US /pages/view/id/253.html.

———. Discussion Paper No. 5: "Goals, Achievements, and Conventions: Pillars for Deepening Our Democratic Transition," September 12, 2014. http://king abdullah.jo/index.php/en_US/pages/view/id/254.html/.

———. *Our Last Best Chance: The Pursuit of Peace in a Time of Peril*. New York: Viking, 2011.

———. 70th Plenary Session of the United Nations General Assembly. United Nations, New York. September 28, 2015.

Koprulu, Nur. "Consolidated Monarchies in the Post-Arab Spring Era." *Israel Affairs* 20, no. 3 (2014): 318–27.

Kumaraswamy, P. R., and Manjari Singh, "Population Pressure in Jordan and the Role of Syrian Refugees," *Migration and Development* 6, no. 3 (2016): 1–16.

Larzillière, Pénélope. *Activism in Jordan*. London: Zed Books, 2016.

Layne, Linda L. *Home and Homeland: The Dialogics of Tribal and National Identities in Jordan*. Princeton, N.J.: Princeton University Press, 1994.

Lucas, Russell E. *Institutions and the Politics of Survival in Jordan: Domestic Responses to External Challenges, 1988–2001*. Albany: State University of New York Press, 2005.

———. "Monarchical Authoritarianism: Survival and Political Liberalization in a Middle Eastern Regime Type." *International Journal of Middle East Studies* 36, no. 1 (2004): 103–19.

Luck, Taylor. "Despite Differences, Youth Movements Still Depend on Traditional Parties to Materialise." *Jordan Times*, July 29, 2011. http://www.jordantimes.com/index.php?news=39944.

——. "50 Salafists Arrested." *Jordan Times*, August 27, 2014. http://jordantimes.com/50-salafists-arrested.

——. "Four Imams Banned for pro-Islamic State Sermons." *Jordan Times*, October 22, 2014. http://jordantimes.com/four-imams-banned-for-pro-islamic-state-friday-sermons.

——. "Southern Protests Continue." *Jordan Times*, July 8, 2011.

Luck, Taylor, and William Booth. "Gunman in Jordan Kills 4, Including 2 Americans, at Police Training Site." *Washington Post*, November 9, 2015.

Lust, Ellen. "Elections Under Authoritarianism: Preliminary Lessons from Jordan." *Democratization* 13, no. 3 (2006): 456–71.

Lust-Okar, Ellen. "The Decline of Jordanian Political Parties: Myth or Reality." *International Journal of Middle East Studies* 33, no. 4 (2001): 545–69.

——. "Divided They Rule: The Management and Manipulation of Political Opposition." *Comparative Politics* 36, no. 2 (2004): 159–79.

——. *Structuring Conflict in the Arab World: Incumbents, Opponents, and Institutions.* Cambridge: Cambridge University Press, 2005.

Lynch, Marc. *The Arab Uprising: The Unfinished Revolutions of the New Middle East.* New York: Public Affairs, 2012.

——, ed. *The Arab Uprisings Explained: New Contentious Politics in the Middle East.* New York: Columbia University Press, 2014.

——. *State Interests and Public Spheres: The International Politics of Jordan's Identity.* New York: Columbia University Press, 1999.

——. *Voices of the New Arab Public: Iraq, al-Jazeera, and Middle East Politics Today.* New York: Columbia University Press, 2006.

Madfai, Madiha Rashid al-. *Jordan, The United States and the Middle East Peace Process.* New York: Cambridge University Press, 1993.

Magid, Aaron. "Why Many Jordanians Have Little Stomach for Upcoming Elections." *Al-Monitor*, July 25, 2016. http://www.al-monitor.com/pulse/originals/2016/07/jordan-parliamentary-elections-boycott.html.

Marar, Marianne. "Dual/Duel Identities: Jordanian Perceptions of Academic Equity." *Intercultural Education* 20, no. 4 (2009): 371–78.

——. "I Know There Is No Justice: Palestinian Perceptions of Higher Education in Jordan." *Intercultural Education* 22, no. 2 (2011): 177–90.

Massad, Joseph A. *Colonial Effects: The Making of National Identity in Jordan.* New York: Columbia University Press, 2001.

Milton-Edwards, Beverly. "Façade Democracy and Jordan." *British Journal of Middle Eastern Studies* 20, no. 2 (1993): 191–203.

Milton-Edwards, Beverly, and Peter Hinchcliffe. *Jordan: A Hashemite Legacy*. London: Routledge, 2001.

Momani, Bessma. *Arab Dawn: Arab Youth and the Demographic Dividend They Will Bring*. Toronto: University of Toronto Press, 2015.

Montague, James. "Football's Greatest Rivalries: al-Faisaly v al-Wehdat." *World Soccer*, December 26, 2015. http://www.worldsoccer.com/features/footballs-greatest-rivalries-al-faisaly-v-al-wehdat-366655.

Moore, Pete. "Before and After Uprising: Political Economies of the 2011 Uprisings." *Taiwan Journal of Democracy* 10, no. 1 (July 2014): 63–77.

——. "The Bread Revolutions of 2011: Teaching Political Economies of the Middle East." *PS: Political Science and Politics* 46, no. 2 (April 2013): 225–29.

——. *Doing Business in the Middle East: Politics and Economic Crisis in Jordan and Kuwait*. Cambridge: Cambridge University Press, 2004.

——. "Fiscal Politics of Enduring Authoritarianism." In *The Arab Thermidor: The Resurgence of the Security State*. Project on Middle East Political Science (December 2014).

——. "Jordan's Long War Economy." *Jadaliyya*, August 29, 2017. http://www.jadaliyya.com/pages/index/27078/jordan%E2%80%99s-long-war-economy.

Muasher, Marwan. *The Arab Center: The Promise of Moderation*. New Haven, Conn.: Yale University Press, 2008.

——. *A Decade of Struggling Reform Efforts in Jordan: The Resilience of the Rentier System*. Washington, D.C.: Carnegie Endowment for International Peace, 2011.

——. "Jordan's Proposed Constitutional Amendments—a First Step in the Right Direction." Carnegie Endowment for International Peace, August 17, 2011. http://carnegieendowment.org/2011/08/17/jordan-s-proposed-constitutional-amendments-first-step-in-right-direction-pub-45366.

——. *The Second Arab Awakening: And the Battle for Pluralism*. New Haven, Conn.: Yale University Press, 2014.

Mufti, Malik. "Elite Bargains and the Onset of Political Liberalization in Jordan." *Comparative Political Studies* 32, no. 1 (1999): 100–129.

——. "A King's Art: Dynastic Ambition and State Interest in Hussein's Jordan." *Diplomacy and Statecraft* 13, no. 3 (2002): 1–22.

Nasser, Riad. 2004. "Exclusion and the Making of Jordanian National Identity: An Analysis of School Textbooks." *Nationalism and Ethnic Politics* 10, no. 2 (2004): 221–49.

National Democratic Institute. "In Jordan, Coalition Unites for Electoral Reform," March 3, 2010. http://www.ndi.org/print/16087.

Nusairat, Tuqa. "Jordan's Pilot and the War on ISIS." *MenaSource* blog, Atlantic Council, February 3, 2015. http://www.atlanticcouncil.org/blogs/menasource/jordan-s-pilot-and-the-war-on-isis.

Obeidat, Sufian. "Jordan: A Flowerless Spring." *Arab Reform Initiative, Arab Reform Brief* 61 (August 2012). www.arab-reform.net/en/file/479/download?token =OQ2hnXZg.

——. "Jordan's 2016 Constitutional Amendments: A Return to Absolute Monarchy?" *Constitutionnet*, May 27, 2016. http://www.constitutionnet.org/news /jordans-2016-constitutional-amendments-return-absolute-monarchy.

O'Donnell, Guillermo, Phillipe Schmitter, and Lawrence Whitehead. *Transitions from Authoritarian Rule.* Baltimore: Johns Hopkins University Press, 1986.

Omari, Raed. "New Electoral Law Sheds One Vote System." *Jordan Times*, September 1, 2015. http://www.jordantimes.com/news/local/new-elections-bill -sheds-one-vote-system.

Oudat, Mohammed Ali Al, and Ayman Alshboul. "Jordan First: Tribalism, Nationalism and Legitimacy of Power in Jordan." *Intellectual Discourse* 18, no. 1 (2010): 65–96.

Parker, Ned. "Jordan Democracy Activists Enjoy Camaraderie, Freedom to Protest." *Los Angeles Times*, January 24, 2013. http://articles.latimes.com/2013/jan /24/world/la-fg-jordan-herak-20130125.

Pecquet, Julian. "Jordan's King Tells Congress 'Gloves Are Off' in Fight Against ISIS." *al-Monitor*, February 3, 2015. http://www.al-monitor.com/pulse/origi nals/2015/02/jordan-pilot-islamic-state-congress-aid-package.html.

Pelham, Nicolas. "Jordan Starts to Shake." *New York Review of Books*, December 8, 2011.

——. "Jordan's Balancing Act." *Middle East Report Online*, February 22, 2011. http:// www.merip.org/mero/mero022211.

——. "Jordan's Syria Problem." *New York Review of Books*, January 16, 2013.

Peters, Ann Mariel, and Pete W. Moore. "Beyond Boom and Bust: External Rents, Durable Authoritarianism, and Institutional Adaptation in the Hashemite Kingdom of Jordan." *Studies in Comparative International Development* 44, no. 3 (2009): 256–85.

Pfeifer, Karen. "How Tunisia, Morocco, Jordan, and even Egypt Became IMF 'Success Stories' in the 1990s." *Middle East Report* 210 (1999): 23–27.

Pillai, Vel. "External Economic Dependence and Fiscal Policy Imbalances in Developing Countries: A Case Study of Jordan." *Journal of Development Studies* 19 (1982): 5–18.

Piro, Timothy J. *The Political Economy of Market Reform in Jordan.* Lanham, Md.: Rowman & Littlefield, 1998.

Posusney, Marsha Pripstein, and Michele Penner Angrist, eds. *Authoritarianism in the Middle East: Regimes and Resistance.* Boulder, Colo.: Lynne Rienner, 2005.

Project on Middle East Political Science (POMEPS). *The Arab Monarchy Debate.* POMEPS Briefings no. 16, 2012.

——. *Jordan, Forever on the Brink.* POMEPS Briefings no. 11, 2012.

Quds Center for Political Studies, al-. *al-Dawla wa al-Ikhwan* (The state and the Brotherhood) *1999–2008*. Amman: al-Quds Center for Political Studies, 2008.

——. *al-Dimuqratiyya fi al-Hayat al-Dakhiliyya li al-Ahzab al-Siyasiyya al-'Arabiyya* (Democracy in the practice of Arab political parties). Amman: al-Quds Center for Political Studies, 2010.

——. *al-Din wa al-Dawla: al-Urdun* (Religion and the state: Jordan). Amman: al-Quds Center for Political Studies, 2010.

——. *al-Qu'anin al-Nazimat li al-'Amal al-Hizbi fi al-Urdun* (Revisiting political party legislation in Jordan). Amman: al-Quds Center for Political Studies, 2010.

Rababa'h, Ala' al-. "Public Outrage in Jordan at Murder of Pilot." Carnegie Endowment for International Peace, February 4, 2015. http://carnegieendow ment.org/syriaincrisis/?fa=58964

Rath, Katherine. "The Process of Democratization in Jordan." *Middle Eastern Studies* 30, no. 3 (1994): 530–57.

Reed, Stanley. "Jordan and the Gulf Crisis." *Foreign Affairs* 69, no. 5 (1991): 21–35.

Reiter, Yitzhak. "Higher Education and Sociopolitical Transformation in Jordan." *British Journal of Middle East Studies* 29, no. 2 (2002): 137–64.

——. "The Palestinian-Transjordanian Rift: Economic Might and Political Power in Jordan." *Middle East Journal* 58, no. 1 (2004): 72–92.

Riedel, Tim H. "The 1993 Parliamentary Elections in Jordan." *Orient* 35, no. 1 (1994): 51–63.

Rintawi, Oraib al-. "Coalition Presses for Electoral Reform in Jordan." *Arab Reform Bulletin*, April 14, 2010.

Robbins, Michael, and Lawrence Rubin. "The Rise of Official Islam in Jordan." *Politics, Religion & Ideology* 14, no. 1 (2013).

Robins, Philip. *A History of Jordan*. Cambridge: Cambridge University Press, 2004.

Robinson, Glenn E. "Defensive Democratization in Jordan." *International Journal of Middle East Studies* 30, no. 3 (1998): 387–410.

Ryan, Curtis R. "The Armed Forces and the Arab Uprisings: The Case of Jordan." *Middle East Law and Governance* 4 (2012): 153–67.

——. "Déjà Vu All Over Again? Jordan's 2010 Elections." *Foreign Policy, Middle East Channel*, November 15, 2010. http://mideast.foreignpolicy.com/posts/2010/11/15 /jordanians_go_to_the_polls.

——. "Elections and Parliamentary Democratization in Jordan." *Democratization* 5, no. 4 (1998): 194–214.

——. "Elections, Parliament, and a 'New' Prime Minister in Jordan." *Foreign Policy, Middle East Channel*, March 11, 2013. http://foreignpolicy.com/2013/03/11 /elections-parliament-and-a-new-prime-minister-in-jordan/.

———. "Governance, Reform, and Resurgent Ethnic Identity Politics in Jordan." In *Governance and Politics in the Middle East*, edited by Abbas Khadim, 342–56. London: Routledge, 2013.

———. "Identity Politics, Reform, and Protest in Jordan." *Studies in Ethnicity and Nationalism* 11, no. 3 (2011): 564–78.

———. "The Implications of Jordan's New Electoral Law." *Foreign Policy, Middle East Channel*, April 12, 2012. http://foreignpolicy.com/2012/04/13/the-implications -of-jordans-new-electoral-law/.

———. *Inter-Arab Alliances: Regime Security and Jordanian Foreign Policy*. Gainesville: University Press of Florida, 2009.

———. "Islamist Political Activism in Jordan: Moderation, Militancy, and Democracy." *Middle East Review of International Affairs* 12, no. 2 (2008): 1–13.

———. "Jordan and the Arab Spring." In *The Arab Spring: Change and Resistance in the Middle East*, edited by Michael L. Haas and David W. Lesch, 116–30. Boulder, Colo.: Westview Press, 2013.

———. "Jordanian Foreign Policy and the Arab Spring." *Middle East Policy* 21, no. 1 (2014): 144–53.

———. "Jordan in the Crossfire of Middle East Conflicts." *Orient: German Journal for Politics, Economics, and Culture of the Middle East* 56, no. 4 (2015): 32–49.

———. *Jordan in Transition: From Hussein to Abdullah*. Boulder, Colo.: Lynne Rienner, 2002.

———. "Jordan's High Stakes Electoral Reform." *Foreign Policy, Middle East Channel*, June 29, 2012. http://foreignpolicy.com/2012/06/29/jordans-high-stakes-elec toral-reform/.

———. "Jordan's New Electoral Law: Reform, Reaction, or Status Quo?" *Foreign Policy, Middle East Channel*, May 24, 2010. http://mideast.foreignpolicy.com /posts/2010/05/24/jordan_s_new_electoral_law_reform_reaction_or_status _quo.

———. "Jordan's Security Dilemmas." *Foreign Policy, Middle East Channel*, May 7, 2013. http://mideastafrica.foreignpolicy.com/posts/2013/05/01/jordans_security _dilemmas#sthash.92FfWeWZ.dpbs.

———. "Jordan's Unfinished Journey: Parliamentary Elections and the State of Reform." POMED: Project on Middle East Democracy, Policy Brief (March 2013).

———. "Jordan's Web Blocking Controversy." *Foreign Policy, Middle East Channel*, June 20, 2013. http://foreignpolicy.com/2013/06/20/jordans-website-block ing-controversy/.

———. "The King's Speech." *Foreign Policy, Middle East Channel*, June 17, 2011. http:// foreignpolicy.com/2011/06/17/the-kings-speech/.

———. "The Most Important Soccer Is Not Being Played in Brazil, but in Refugee Camps in Jordan." Monkey Cage Blog, *Washington Post*, June 20, 2014. http://

www.washingtonpost.com/blogs/monkey-cage/wp/2014/06/20/the-most
-important-soccer-is-not-being-played-in-brazil-but-in-refugee-camps-in
-jordan/.

——. "The New Arab Cold War and the Struggle for Syria." *Middle East Report*
262 (Spring 2012): 28–31.

——. "A New Diplomatic Rift Between Jordan and Syria." *Middle East Report
Online*, May 29, 2014. http://www.merip.org/new-diplomatic-rift-between
-jordan-syria.

——. "Not Running on Empty: Democratic Activism Against Israeli Gas in Jordan." *Middle East Report Online*, April 16, 2015. http://www.merip.org/not
-running-empty-democratic-activism-against-israeli-gas-jordan.

——. "Oasis or Mirage? Jordan's Unlikely Stability in a Changing Middle East."
World Politics Review, January 15, 2015.

——. "The Odd Couple: Ending the Jordanian-Syrian 'Cold War.'" *Middle East
Journal* 60, no. 1 (2006): 33–56.

——. "One Society of Muslim Brothers in Jordan or Two?" *Middle East Report
Online*, March 5, 2015. http://merip.org/one-society-muslim-brothers-jordan
-or-two.

——. "Political Opposition and Reform Coalitions in Jordan." *British Journal of
Middle East Studies* 38, no. 3 (2011): 367–90.

——. "Political Strategies and Regime Survival: The Case of Egypt." *Journal of
Third World Studies* 18, no. 2 (2001): 25–46.

——. "Refugee Need and Resilience in Zaatari." *Middle East Report Online*, June
22, 2014. http://www.merip.org/refugee-need-resilience-zaatari.

——. "Regional Responses to the Rise of ISIS." *Middle East Report* 276 (2015):
18–23.

——. "Reviving Activism in Jordan." *Middle East Report* 46 (2016).

——. "Security Dilemmas and the Security State Question in Jordan." *POMEPS
Studies* 11: *The Arab Thermidor: The Resurgence of the Security State*, February 27,
2015: 52–55.

——. "'We Are All Jordan' . . . but Who Is We?" *Middle East Report Online*, July 13,
2010. http://www.merip.org/mero/mero071310.

——. "What's (Maybe) New in Jordan." *Foreign Policy, Middle East Channel*,
October 11, 2012. http://foreignpolicy.com/2012/10/11/whats-maybe-new
-in-jordan/.

——. "What to Expect from Jordan's Elections." *Foreign Policy, Middle East Channel*, January 18, 2013. http://foreignpolicy.com/2013/01/18/what-to-expect
-from-jordans-elections/.

Ryan, Curtis R., and Jillian Schwedler. "Return to Democratization or New
Hybrid Regime? The 2003 Elections in Jordan." *Middle East Policy* 11, no. 2
(2004): 138–51.

Salibi, Kamal. *The Modern History of Jordan.* London: I. B. Tauris, 1993.

Salloukh, Bassel F. "State Strength, Permeability, and Foreign Policy Behavior: Jordan in Theoretical Perspective." *Arab Studies Quarterly* 18, no. 2 (1996): 39–65.

Samadi, Tamer al-. "Jordan Steps Up Campaign Against Opposition Groups." *al-Monitor,* October 22, 2013.

Satloff, Robert, and David Schenker. "Political Instability in Jordan." Contingency Planning Memorandum no. 19, Council on Foreign Relations, October 2013. http://www.cfr.org/jordan/political-instability-jordan/p30698.

Sawalha, F. "Opposites Attract on Petition to Declare War on Iraq 'Illegal.'" *Jordan Times,* April 1, 2003.

Sayigh, Yezid. "Jordan Reluctantly Takes Sides in Syria." *al-Hayat* via Carnegie Middle East Center, November 6, 2013.

——. "Saudi-US Rift Pulls Jordan in Opposite Directions." *al-Monitor,* November 6, 2013. http://www.al-monitor.com/pulse/security/2013/11/jordan-torn-between-saudi-and-us.html.

Scham, Paul L., and Russell E. Lucas. "'Normalization' and 'Anti-Normalization' in Jordan: The Public Debate." *Israel Affairs* 9, no. 3 (2003): 141–64.

Schenker, David. "Preventing ISIS Inroads in Jordan." *Policy Watch* 2311, Washington Institute, September 3, 2014. http://www.washingtoninstitute.org/policy-analysis/view/preventing-isis-inroads-in-jordan.

——. "Terrorist Spillover in Jordan," *Cipher Brief,* Washington Institute for Near East Policy, June 23, 2016. http://www.washingtoninstitute.org/policy-analysis/view/terrorist-spillover-in-jordan.

Schwedler, Jillian. "Don't Blink: Jordan's Democratic Opening and Closing." *MERIP Press Information Note,* July 3, 2002. http://www.merip.org/mero/mero070302.

——. "Cop Rock: Protest, Identity, and Dancing Riot Police in Jordan." *Social Movement Studies* 4, no. 2 (2005): 155–75.

——. *Faith in Moderation: Islamist Parties in Jordan and Yemen.* Cambridge: Cambridge University Press, 2006.

——. "Jordan Drops the Pretense of Democratic Reform." *Middle East Report Online,* April 28, 2016. http://www.merip.org/jordan-drops-pretense-democratic-reform.

——. "Jordan's Islamists Lose Faith in Moderation." *Foreign Policy, Middle East Channel,* June 30, 2010.

——. "Jordan's Risky Business as Usual." *Middle East Report Online,* June 30, 2010. http://www.merip.org/mero/mero063010.

——. "More than a Mob: The Dynamics of Political Demonstrations in Jordan." *Middle East Report* 226 (2003): 18–23.

——. "The Political Geography of Protest in Neoliberal Jordan." *Middle East Critique* 21, no. 3 (2012): 259–70.

——. "Spatial Dynamics of the Arab Uprisings." *PS: Political Science & Politics* 46, no. 2, (2013): 230–34.

Schwedler, Jillian, and Janine A. Clark. "Islamist-Leftist Cooperation in the Arab World." *ISIM Review* 18 (2006): 10–11.

Seeberg, Peter. "European Neighborhood Policy, Post-normativity and Legitimacy. EU Policies Towards Jordan, Lebanon, and Syria." Working Paper no. 14, Centre for Contemporary Middle East Studies (November 2008).

Sharif, Osama al-. "Jordan Sharpens Focus on IS as Gulf Confronts Iran." *al-Monitor*, April 1, 2015. http://www.al-monitor.com/pulse/originals/2015/04/jordan-yemen-saudi-iran-is-houthis-airstrike-fighting.html.

——. "Jordan's King Fends off Critics of ISIS War, Holds Firm on al-Aqsa." *al-Monitor*, November 10, 2014. http://www.al-monitor.com/pulse/originals/2014/11/jordan-king-internal-criticism-islamic-sta te-al-aqsa.html.

——. "Jordan's King Pushes to Expand Military, Intelligence Authority." *al-Monitor*, August 25, 2014. http://www.al-monitor.com/pulse/originals/2014/08/jordan-king-constitution-amendments.html.

——. "Jordan's Reform Agenda on Hold." *al-Monitor*, October 28, 2013. http://www.al-monitor.com/pulse/originals/2013/10/jordan-focus-economic-security-reform-syrian-crisis.html.

——. "Will Saudi Arabia Pressure Jordan to Join Ground Offensive in Syria?" *al-Monitor*, February 22, 2016. http://www.al-monitor.com/pulse/originals/2016/02/will-jordan-join-saudi-arabia-ground-invasion-syria.html.

Sharp, Jeremy M. "Jordan: Background and U.S. Relations." Washington, D.C.: Congressional Research Service, January 25, 2017.

Shryock, Andrew. "Dynastic Modernism and Its Contradictions: Testing the Limits of Pluralism, Tribalism, and King Hussein's Example in Hashemite Jordan." *Arab Studies Quarterly* 22, no. 3 (2000): 57–79.

——. *Nationalism and the Genealogical Imagination: Oral History and Textual Authority in Tribal Jordan.* Berkeley: University of California Press, 1997.

Shteiwi, Musa, Jonathan Walsh, and Christina Klassen, *Coping with Crisis: A Review of the Response to Syrian Refugees in Jordan.* Amman: Center for Strategic Studies, 2014.

Sowell, Kirk H. "Jordanian Salafism and the Jihad in Syria." Hudson Institute, March 12, 2015. http://www.hudson.org/research/11131-jordanian-salafism-and-the-jihad-in-syria.

Stacher, Joshua. *Adaptable Autocrats: Regime Power in Egypt and Syria.* Stanford, Calif.: Stanford University Press, 2012.

Staton, Bethan. "Jordan's Women fight for Political Representation." *Al-Jazeera*, March 8, 2016. http://www.aljazeera.com/news/2016/03/jordan-women-fight-political-representation-160306101829565.html.

Stave, Svein Erik, and Solveig Hillesund. *Impact of Syrian Refugees on the Jordanian Labour Market*. Geneva and Beirut: International Labor Organization and FAFO, April 2015.

Su, Alice. "It Wasn't Their War." *Atlantic* (February 2015). http://www .theatlantic.com/international/archive/2015/02/jordan-isis-pilot-response /385199/.

Sullivan, Denis, and Sarah Tobin, "Security and Resilience Among Syrian Refugees in Jordan." *Middle East Report Online*, October 14, 2014. http://merip.org /mero/mero101414.

Susser, Asher. *Jordan: Case Study of a Pivotal State*. Washington, D.C.: Washington Institute for Near East Policy, 2000.

——. "Jordan: Preserving Domestic Order in a Setting of Regional Turmoil." *Middle East Brief* 27 (March 2008).

——. "The Palestinians in Jordan: Demographic Majority, Political Minority." In *Minorities and the State in the Arab World*, edited by Ofra Bengio and Gabriel Ben-Dor. Boulder, Colo.: Lynne Rienner, 1999.

Sways, Suleiman. "Kharita al-Ahzab al-Siyasiyya fi al-Urdun" (A map of political parties in Jordan). *al-Urdun al-Jadid* (1990): 122–41.

Tarawneh, Naseem. "Jordan's Internet Goes Dark." *Foreign Policy, Middle East Channel*, August 31, 2012. http://foreignpolicy.com/2012/08/31/jordans -internet-goes-dark/.

——. "Jordan's Tribal Myth." *Black Iris* (blog), February 18, 2014. http://black-iris .com/2014/02/18/on-jordans-tribal-myth/.

——. "The Quick Death of Shabab March 24 and What It Means for Jordan." *Black Iris* (blog), March 26, 2011. http://www.black-iris.com/2011/03/26/the -quick-death-of-shabab-march-24-and-what-it-means-for-jordan/.

——. "Troubling Tribalism." *Jordan Business* (June 2010): 69.

Tell, Nawaf. "Jordanian Security Sector Governance Between Theory and Practice." Working Paper no. 145, Geneva Centre for the Democratic Control of Armed Forces, 2004.

Tell, Tariq. "Early Spring in Jordan: Revolt of the Military Veterans." Carnegie Middle East Center, November 4, 2015.

——. *The Social and Economic Origins of Monarchy in Jordan*. New York: Palgrave Macmillan, 2013.

Terrill, W. Andrew. "Saddam's Closest Ally: Jordan and the Gulf War." *Journal of South Asian and Middle Eastern Studies* 9, no. 2 (1985): 43–54.

Tobin, Sarah. "Jordan's Arab Spring: The Middle Class and Anti-Revolution." *Middle East Policy* 19, no. 1 (Spring 2012): 96–109.

Tripp, Charles. *The Power and the People: Paths to Resistance in the Middle East*. Cambridge: Cambridge University Press, 2013.

Valbjorn, Morten. "Reflections on Self-Reflections: On Framing the Analytical Implications of the Arab Uprisings for the Study of Arab Politics." *Democratization* 22, no. 2 (2015): 218–38.

Volpi, Frederic. "Pseudo-democracy in the Muslim World," *Third World Quarterly* 25, no. 6 (2004): 1061–78.

Wagamakers, Joas. *A Quietist Jihadi: The Ideology and Influence of Abu Muhammad al-Maqdisi*. Cambridge: Cambridge University Press, 2012.

——. *Salafism in Jordan: Political Islam in a Quietist Community*. Cambridge: Cambridge University Press, 2016.

Warrick, Joby, and Taylor Luck. "Jordan Calm for Now, but New Storms Loom." *Washington Post*, November 21, 2012.

Wedeen, Lisa. *Ambiguities of Domination: Politics, Rhetoric, and Symbols in Contemporary Syria*. Chicago: University of Chicago Press, 1999.

Wehler-Schoek, Anja. "Parliamentary Elections in Jordan: A Competition of Mixed Messages." Friedrich Ebert Stiftung (September 2016). http://library.fes.de/pdf-files/iez/12783.pdf.

Wiktorowicz, Quintan. "Civil Society as Social Control." *Comparative Politics* 33, no. 1 (2000): 43–61.

——. "The Limits of Democracy in the Middle East: The Case of Jordan." *Middle East Journal* 53 (4): 606–20.

——. *The Management of Islamic Activism: Salafis, the Muslim Brotherhood, and State Power in Jordan*. Albany: State University of New York Press, 2000.

Williams, Sara Elizabeth. "Analysis: Jordan, the Island of Stability Crumbling at Its Edges." *Middle East Eye*, June 27, 2016. http://www.middleeasteye.net/news/analysis-jordan-island-stability-crumbling-its-edges-2107772653.

——. "The Enemy Within: Jordan's Battle with Homegrown Terror." *Middle East Eye*, March 2, 2016. http://www.middleeasteye.net/news/enemy-within-jordans-battle-stop-home-grown-terrorism-481722991.

Wilson, Mary C. "Jordan: Bread, Freedom, or Both?" *Current History* (February 1994): 87–90.

——. *King Abdullah, Britain, and the Making of Jordan*. Cambridge: Cambridge University Press, 1987.

Yaghi, Mohammed, and Janine A. Clark, "Jordan: Evolving Activism in a Divided Society." In *Taking to the Streets: The Transformation of Arab Activism*, edited by Lina Khatib and Ellen Lust, 236–67. Baltimore: Johns Hopkins University Press, 2014.

Yefet, Bosmat. *The Politics of Human Rights in Egypt and Jordan*. Boulder: Lynne Rienner, 2015.

Yesilyurt, Nuri. "Jordan and the Arab Spring: Challenges and Opportunities." *Perceptions* 19, no. 4 (Winter 2014): 169–94.

Yom, Sean L. *From Resilience to Revolution: How Foreign Interventions Destabilize the Middle East.* New York: Columbia University Press, 2015.

——. "Jordan: The Ruse of Reform." *Journal of Democracy* 24, no. 3 (July 2013): 127–39.

——. "Jordan's Stubborn Regime Hangs in the Balance." *Foreign Policy, Middle East Channel*, March 13, 2011. http://mideast.foreignpolicy.com/posts/2011/03/31/jordans_stubborn_regime_hangs_in_the_balance.

——. "The New Landscape of Jordanian Politics: Social Opposition, Fiscal Crisis, and the Arab Spring." *British Journal of Middle Eastern Studies* 42, no. 3 (2015): 284–300.

——. "Tribal Politics in Contemporary Jordan: The Case of the Hirak Movement." *Middle East Journal* 68, no. 2 (2014): 229–47.

Yom, Sean L., and Wael al-Khatib. "Jordan's New Politics of Tribal Dissent." *Foreign Policy, Middle East Channel*, August 7, 2012. http://foreignpolicy.com/2012/08/07/jordans-new-politics-of-tribal-dissent/.

Yom, Sean, and Katrina Sammour. "Counterterrorism and Youth Radicalization in Jordan: Social and Political Dimensions." Combating Terrorism Center at West Point, *CTC Sentinal* 10, no. 4 (April 14, 2017): 25–30.

Index

Hamarneh, Mustafa, 141, 168

Hamas, 48, 49; Israeli wars with, 2, 83, 178; and Muslim Brotherhood, 47, 74

Harper, Andrew, 198

Hashed Party (People's Democratic Party), 46, 120

Hashemite family, 93, 106

Hashemite monarchy and regime: cosmetic changes by, 87, 99, 143, 158, 172, 213; divide-and-rule strategy of, 45, 52, 66–67, 98, 99, 111, 219; as hybrid regime, 15, 158, 220; Jordanians' support for monarchy, 21, 143, 220–21; lèse-majesté laws, 27, 77–78; and monarchical succession, 221; and national identity, 93, 96–99, 107–9; oppositionists and activists' view of, 50, 52, 71–72, 107–8, 113; and political reform, 143, 145, 146–51, 158–62, 171–72, 218; regional security as concern of, 176–87; responses to Arab Spring by, 21, 36–41; "soft security" used by, 10–11, 32, 77–78, 152, 215, 217, 218; strategies of, 8, 10–11, 61, 77, 78, 98, 110–11, 157, 218, 219; as survivor, 221; symbolism of, 154–55. See also Abdullah II; Hussein, King

Hattar, Nahed, 69, 210–11

Hayat Center, al, 139

Heydemann, Steven, 8

Hiber (7iber), 80–81

Higher Committee for the Coordination of National Opposition Parties (HCCNOP), 53, 54, 55, 57

Hirak, 66–76, 79, 84, 88; and Arab Spring protests, 29, 31, 66–67, 73; crackdown on, 77–78; diversity of, 69, 70; and East Jordanians, 69, 71, 90; and identity politics, 29, 69, 90–91, 109–11; and Jordanian monarchy, 71–72; as new generation of activists, 69–71; and regional politics, 78; rise of, 65, 68–69; as "southern movement," 60, 66; as term, 66, 68, 76–77. *See also* grassroots activism

Hizbullah, 48, 178, 186

Hroub, Rula, 141

Hussein, King, 25, 160, 180, 221; and Black September, 94; and identity politics, 67, 99; and Israel peace treaty, 147, 148; neoliberal agenda of, 67–68, 146

Hussein, Prince, 220

Huwaytat, 68, 208

identity politics: as Achilles' heel in Jordan, 91, 113, 151; and Arab Spring protests, 104–5, 109–11; continuity and change in, 111–13; and electoral laws, 59, 100–101, 168; and ethnic division of labor, 67–68, 90, 94–95, 102; and ethnic stereotypes, 103–4; external events impacting, 99–101, 153, 179; and Hashemite monarchy, 96–99, 107–9, 220; and Hirak, 29, 69, 90–91, 109–11; and Islamist divisions, 74–75; and Jordanian national identity, 91–96; nationalist and nativist views on, 31, 101–4, 195; and neoliberalism, 60, 163–64; and opposition manifestos, 31, 107–9; and refugee crisis, 100, 196, 198

Independent Electoral Commission (IEC), 127, 128–29, 133, 139, 160, 161

intelligence service. *See* Mukhabarat

International Crisis Group (ICG), 37, 150–51

149, 181, 200; and ISIS, 199–211; Israel peace treaty with, 50, 147–48, 230–31n26; labor activism and laws in, 65–66, 69, 198; mass media in, 33, 58, 212; movement against Israeli gas in, 82–83, 85–86; nationalism and nativism in, 31, 101–4, 106, 195; neoliberal and austerity policies in, 24–25, 34, 59–60, 65–66, 72, 81–82, 101, 136, 147, 149, 157, 162–64, 166; Palestinian Jordanians in, 24, 31, 59, 67, 71, 90–92, 94–96, 98–99, 102–5, 108; and refugee crisis, 187–99; resource deficiency of, 14, 82–83, 85, 163; riots of 1989 in, 24–25, 34, 67, 146–47; security dilemmas of, 12, 150, 184, 212; short-lived governments in, 37–41; and Syrian civil war, 179–87; terrorist attacks in, 38, 49, 200, 206, 207–8, 244n7; tribal and clan lineages in, 31, 68, 106; U.S. military support to, 183, 207, 208; U.S. relations with, 147–48, 149, 164, 195; vulnerability of, 11, 13, 14, 77, 85, 165, 175–76, 211, 222. *See also* Arab Spring; electoral laws and systems; grassroots activism; Hashemite monarchy and regime; identity politics

Jordan Compact, 197

Jordan First, 99, 111

Jordanian Campaign for Change (Jayeen), 56–57, 88

Jordanian Communist Party (JCP), 46

Jordanian-Israeli peace treaty (1994), 50, 147–48, 230–31n26

Jordanian Muslim Brotherhood Society, 75

Jordanian National Commission for Women (JNCW), 138

Jordanian Popular Movement, 65

Jordanian Social Movement, 69

Jordanian Women's Union, 63

Jordanian Youth Movement, 65

Jordan International Police Training Center (JIPTC), 208

Jordan Press Association (JPA), 168–69

Judeh, Nasser, 189, 206

judiciary, 79, 161–62

Kabariti, 'Abd al-Karim al-, 167

Karbuli, Ziyad, 206

Karon, Tony, 181–82

Kassasbeh, Muath al-, 205–7

Kerak, 33, 73, 120, 210; Arab Spring protests in, 26, 60, 66, 104–5

Kerak Popular Youth Movement, 60, 70, 232n54

Kerry, John, 206

Khasawneh, 'Awn al-, 123, 166, 167; government of, 38–40

Khatib, Lina, 10

Khatib, 'Abd al-Ilah al-, 128

King Abdullah Special Operations Training Centre (KASOTC), 208

Kuttab, Daoud, 169, 195

Kuwait, 148, 200

labor activism, 65–66, 69

labor laws, 198

lèse-majesté laws, 27, 77–78

Libya, 4, 7, 19, 128, 181, 204

Luck, Taylor, 62, 248n59

Lust, Ellen, 10, 52

Lynch, Marc, 9, 10

Ma'an, 60, 73, 209; Arab Spring protests in, 26, 66, 104–5; pro-ISIS rallies in, 199, 201; violence and unrest in, 118, 151, 170

youth movements, 60, 70, 232n48; and traditional opposition, 61–62, 63–64, 88. *See also* Hirak

Za'atari refugee camp, 189, 190–93
Zamzam reform movement, 74–75, 140, 142

Zarqa, 61, 73, 190, 199, 209; elections in, 118, 120, 170; Palestinian population in, 59, 105; political representation for, 137, 230n20
Zarqawi, Abu Musab al-, 180, 200, 209, 244n7
Zayd Bin Raad, Prince, 195

GPSR Authorized Representative: Easy Access System Europe, Mustamäe tee 50, 10621 Tallinn, Estonia, gpsr.requests@easproject.com

www.ingramcontent.com/pod-product-compliance
Lightning Source LLC
Chambersburg PA
CBHW021853020426
42334CB00013B/311